POSTFEMINISM

Cultural Texts and Theories

Stéphanie Genz and Benjamin A. Brabon

EDINBURGH UNIVERSITY PRESS

© Stéphanie Genz and Benjamin A. Brabon, 2009

Edinburgh University Press Ltd
22 George Square, Edinburgh

Reprinted 2010, 2012

www.euppublishing.com

Typeset in 11/13 pt Monotype Bembo
by Servis Filmsetting Ltd, Stockport, Cheshire, and
printed and bound in Great Britain by
CPI Antony Rowe, Chippenham and Eastbourne

A CIP record for this book is available from the British Library

ISBN 978 0 7486 3579 5 (hardback)
ISBN 978 0 7486 3580 1 (paperback)

The right of Stéphanie Genz and Benjamin A. Brabon
to be identified as authors of this work
has been asserted in accordance with
the Copyright, Designs and Patents Act 1988.

POSTFEMINISM

Contents

Acknowledgements

We would like to thank Alistair McCleery for his encouragement in the early stages of this project and for suggesting Edinburgh University Press. Also, we want to express our gratitude to Edge Hill University for their backing and to Jackie Jones at EUP for her belief in this book and unfailing patience. As always, we are grateful to our families for their support.

Introduction: Postfeminist Contexts

Postfeminism is a concept fraught with contradictions. Loathed by some and celebrated by others, it emerged in the late twentieth century in a number of cultural, academic and political contexts, from popular journalism and media to feminist analyses, postmodern theories and neo-liberal rhetoric. Critics have claimed and appropriated the term for a variety of definitions, ranging from a conservative backlash, Girl Power, third wave feminism and postmodern/poststructuralist feminism. In popular culture, it has often been associated with female characters like the Spice Girls and Helen Fielding's chick heroine Bridget Jones, who has been embraced/criticised as the poster child of postfeminism. In academic writings, it sits alongside other 'post-' discourses – including postmodernism and postcolonialism – and here, it refers to a shift in the understanding and construction of identity and gender categories (like 'Woman', 'Man' and 'Feminist'). Likewise, in social and political investigations, postfeminism has been read as indicative of a 'post-traditional' era characterised by dramatic changes in basic social relationships, role stereotyping and conceptions of agency (Gauntlett; Mann). While commentators have found fault with postfeminism's interpretative potential and flexibility – Coppock and Gamble, for example, deplore the fact that 'postfeminism remains a product of assumption' and 'exactly what it constitutes . . . is a matter for frequently impassioned debate' (Coppock et al. 4; Gamble 43) – they also have acknowledged its significance and impact. As Rosalind Gill writes, '[t]here is, as yet, no parallel for postfeminism' (*Gender and the Media* 250).

This book endeavours to take stock of the postfeminist phenomenon, which has confounded and split contemporary critics with its contradictory meanings and pluralistic outlook. It provides an overview of postfeminism's underpinnings and critical contexts, different perceptions of and theories related to it and popular media representations that have been characterised as 'postfeminist'. Rather than implementing a single frame of definition, we discuss diverse manifestations of postfeminism in order to highlight the term's multiplicity and draw connections between these postfeminist expressions. In this introduction, we contextualise postfeminism by considering its position within feminist histories and its emergence in popular culture, academia and politics. We outline the differences and similarities between these postfeminist contexts in order to present a bigger picture of the cultural landscape and historical moment that can be described as postfeminist. From here, we examine a range of theories and texts that have appeared in postfeminist contexts and we analyse a number of case studies, from popular icons like David Beckham and Lara Croft to the underground punk movement Riot Grrrl and the controversial American women's rights activist Periel Aschenbrand. The chapters are dedicated to specific postfeminist strands — including new traditionalism, do-me feminism, cyberfeminism and micro-politics — and they follow the structure of the introduction in the way that they progress from popularised conceptions of postfeminism to more theoretical and political notions. Importantly, however, we do not want to impose a value judgement and hierarchical structure that privileges one version/location of postfeminism over another — indeed, as we will see, in some critical evaluations this involves a denigration of popular postfeminism in comparison to (supposedly) more complex academic/political ideas. It is a founding premise of this book that all articulations of or movements associated with postfeminism are valid and they inform one another. In this sense, we argue against a polarised understanding of postfeminism that separates its theories, texts and contexts into disparate and disconnected postfeminist versions and locations. The contextualising approach that we adopt allows us to explore the different uses and ramifications of postfeminism, making explicit how its various contexts, texts and theories are linked. Perplexing and troubling for some, postfeminism is also a compelling and provocative feature of contemporary culture, society, academia and politics that demands our critical attention and scrutiny.

POST-ING FEMINISM

Before we go on to examine the intricacies and contents of postfeminism, it is essential that we address the semantic confusion surrounding a 'post-ing' of feminism. While the prefix 'post' has long been the subject of academic and theoretical analyses (in particular in its expression as postmodernism, poststructuralism and postcolonialism), it has achieved particular notoriety and ferocity ever since it attached itself to the social and political phenomenon that is feminism. The disagreements over and multiplicity of postfeminism's meaning(s) are to a large extent due to indefiniteness and precariousness of the 'post' prefix, whose connotations may be complex if not contradictory.[1] Proponents and detractors of postfeminism have deliberated over the uses of the prefix and vied for their respective take on how a 'post-ing' of feminism can be effected and understood. What these debates centre on is exactly what this prefixation accomplishes (if anything), what happens to feminist perspectives and goals in the process and what the strange hybrid of 'post-feminism' entails. We choose to omit the hyphen in our spelling of postfeminism in order to avoid any predetermined readings of the term that imply a semantic rift between feminism and postfeminism, instantly casting the latter as a negation and sabotage of the former. Also, by forgoing the hyphen, we seek to credit and endow postfeminism with a certain cultural independence that acknowledges its existence as a conceptual entity in its own right.

Regardless of our spelling, it is not so much the hyphen as the prefix itself that has been the focus of critical investigations. As Misha Kavka observes, the question that has haunted – or enlivened, depending on your point of view – the discussions can be summarised as 'how can we make sense of the "post" in "postfeminism"' (31). Even though the structure of postfeminism seems to invoke a narrative of progression insisting on a time 'after' feminism, the directionality and meaning of the 'post' prefix are far from settled. 'Post' can be employed to point to a complete rupture, for, as Amelia Jones declares, 'what is post but the signification of a kind of termination – a temporal designation of whatever it prefaces as ended, done with, obsolete' (8). In this prescriptive sense, postfeminism acquires deadly and even murderous connotations as it proclaims the passing of feminism – feminism as 'homeless and groundless', 'gone, departed, dead' (Hawkesworth 969). For example, this is the case in the numerous obituaries for feminism that have appeared in some political and media quarters, announcing if not the death then at least the redundancy of feminism.[2] In this context, postfeminism signals the 'pastness' of feminism – or, at any rate the end of a particular stage in feminist histories – and a generational shift in understanding the relationships between men and women and, for that matter, between women themselves. As we will see, postfeminism is often evoked by a generation of younger feminists as indicative of the fact that 'we are no longer in a second wave of feminism' (Gillis and Munford, 'Harvesting' 2). This awareness of feminist change has resulted in a number of bitter ownership battles and wrangling, often cast in familial terms as mother–daughter conflicts.

Diametrically opposed to the view of 'post' as 'anti' or 'after' is the idea that the prefix denotes a genealogy that entails revision or strong family resemblance. This approach is favoured by advocates of another 'post' derivative – postmodernism – and here, the prefix is understood as part of a process of ongoing transformation. As Best and Kellner write in their analysis of postmodern theory, the 'post' signifies 'a dependence on, a continuity with, that which follows' (29). In this sense, the 'post-ing' of feminism does not necessarily imply its rejection and eradication but means that feminism remains in the postfeminist frame. A third, and perhaps more problematical, interpretation locates the 'post' in a precarious middle ground typified by a contradictory dependence on and independence from the term that follows it. This is the viewpoint taken by Linda Hutcheon, who detects a paradox at the heart of the 'post' whereby 'it marks neither a simple and radical break . . . nor a straightforward continuity . . . it is both and neither' (*A Poetics of Postmodernism* 17). As Sarah Gamble puts it, 'the prefix "post" does not necessarily always direct us back the way we've come' (44). Instead, its trajectory is bewilderingly uncertain, making it impossible and even redundant to offer a single definition of any 'post' expression, as this reductive strategy narrows the critical potential, the instructive ambiguity and contradictoriness of the prefix.

Adding to this interpretative struggle is the fact that the root of post-feminism, feminism itself, has never had a universally accepted agenda and meaning against which one could measure the benefits and/or failings of its post- offshoot. As Geraldine Harris emphasises, feminism has never had 'a single, clearly defined, common ideology' or been constituted around 'a political party or a central organization or leaders or an agreed policy or manifesto, or even been based upon an agreed principle of collective action' (9). At best, feminism can be said to have a number of working definitions that are always relative to particular contexts, specific issues and personal practices. It exists on both local and abstract levels, dealing with specific issues and consisting of diverse individuals while promoting a universal politics of equality for women. Feminists are simultaneously united by their investment in a general concept of justice and fractured by the multiple goals and personal practices that delineate the particular conception of justice to which they aspire. In this way, the assumption that there is – or was – a monolith easily (and continuously) identifiable as 'feminism' belies its competing understandings, its different social and political programmes sharply separated by issues of race, sexuality, class and other systems of social differentiation. Thus, we cannot simply 'hark back' to a past when feminism supposedly had a stable signification and unity, a mythical time prior to 'the introduction of a particular vigorous and invasive weed [postfeminism] into the otherwise healthy garden of feminism' (Elam 55).

From this perspective, the attempt to fix *the* meaning of postfeminism looks futile and even misguided, as each articulation is by itself a definitional act that (re)constructs the meaning of feminism and its own relation to it. There is no *original* or *authentic* postfeminism that holds the key to its definition. Nor is there a secure and unified origin from which this genuine postfeminism could be fashioned. Instead, we understand postfeminism in terms of a network of possible relations that allows for a variety of permutations and readings. In particular, we argue that post-feminism is context-specific and has to be assessed dynamically in the relationships and tensions between its various manifestations and contexts. Postfeminism exists both as a journalistic buzzword and as a theoretical stance, as well as a more generalised late twentieth- and early twenty-first-century 'atmosphere' and 'aura' – what Gill calls 'a postfeminist sensibility' (*Gender and the Media* 254) – that is characterised by a range of contradictions and entanglements within the social, cultural, political, academic and discursive fields (Mazza 17). Rather than being tied to a specific contextual and epistemological framework, postfeminism emerges in the intersections and hybridisation of mainstream media, consumer culture, neo-liberal politics, postmodern theory and, significantly, feminism. Due to its inherently 'impure' status and multiple origins, postfeminism has often been criticised for its disloyalty and bastardisation, for 'feeding upon its hosts' (Dentith 188). It has been denounced – particularly by feminist critics – as a contaminating presence, a parasite charged with infiltration and appropriation. Commentators have often applied a generational logic to discard postfeminism as a corruption and 'failed reproduction of feminist consciousness', condemning a generation of younger feminists for 'forget-ting their feminist legacies, and in effect not allowing feminist political consciousness to be passed on' (Adkins 429–30).

A particular point of contention has been postfeminism's commercial appeal and its consumerist implications, which are viewed by many as a 'selling out' of feminist principles and their co-option as a marketing device. As we will discuss, these ideas and accusations have resurfaced for the most part in examinations of popular postfeminist strands – like Girl Power and chick lit – that combine an emphasis on feminine fun and female friendship with a celebration of (mostly pink-coloured) commodities and the creation of a market demographic of 'Girlies' and 'chicks'. The end result of this main-streaming and commoditisation – it is feared – is a 'free market feminism' that works 'through capitalism' and is 'based on competitive choices in spite of social conditions being stacked against women as a whole' (Whelehan, *Feminist Bestseller* 155). In the most denunciatory accounts, this leads to a perception of postfeminism as a retrogressive, anti-feminist backlash that retracts and invalidates the gains and social transformations brought on by or through the feminist movement.

While we do not wish to deny the importance and relevance of such critiques, we want to counter the assumption of causality that underlies many of these investigations and forces postfeminism into a fixed and delimited structure of analysis and definition. The understanding of postfeminism as an unfaithful reproduction of feminism – or worse, 'a ritualistic denunciation' that renders feminism 'out of date' (McRobbie, 'Post-Feminism and Popular Culture' 258) – is problematic for a number of reasons: it presupposes a distinction between a more 'authentic' and unadulterated feminism on the one hand and a suspect, usually commercialised postfeminism on the other; it adopts a one-dimensional reading of the 'post' – and by implication the 'posting' of feminism – as 'anti'-feminism; it glosses over some of the overlaps and contradictions that mark postfeminist contexts, thereby foreclosing the interpretative possibilities of postfeminism. In this book, we endeavour to present a more nuanced and productive interpretation of the prefix 'post' and its relations to feminism, whereby the compound 'postfeminism' is recognised as a junction between a number of often competing discourses and interests. We understand postfeminism's plurality and 'impurity' as symptomatic of a contradiction-prone late modernity and a changed social/cultural environment characterised by complex discursive and contextual interactions. For example, we are interested in the intersection of feminism with popular culture/politics and we pose a number of questions propelled by these positionings: what does the category of popular feminism imply? Can feminism be political and popular at the same time? Once feminism has become a commodity, does it still have the power to enforce social change? What kind of politics can appear in a 'representation nation' where media display is paramount (Klein)? Likewise, we also investigate the convergence of feminism with a range of anti-foundationalist movements – including postmodernism and postcolonialism – and we examine the identity, gender and agency positions available to individuals in a critical and cultural space that is no longer circumscribed by fixed boundaries and hierarchies and by universalist concepts of truth and knowledge – what John Fekete calls the 'Good-God-Gold standards' (17). In this sense, our discussion of how the prefix 'post' affects and modifies feminism will also necessarily involve a consideration of contemporary forms of agency and constructions of identity as well as a much wider examination of how we conduct critique, use definitional strategies and analytical structures to (re)present the self and/in society.

Postfeminism's frame of reference opens out to include not just – as the term suggests – a conceptual and semantic bond with feminism but also relations with other social, cultural, theoretical and political areas – such as consumer culture, popular media and neo-liberal rhetoric – that might be in conflict with feminism. Hence postfeminism is not the (illegitimate) offspring of – or even a substitute for – feminism; its origins are much more varied and even incongruous, addressing the paradoxes of a late twentieth- and early twenty-first-century setting in which feminist concerns have entered the mainstream and are articulated in politically contradictory ways. In what follows, we seek to locate postfeminism contextually in order to circumscribe a postfeminist landscape made up of an array of relationships and connections within social, cultural, academic and political arenas. Within these contexts, postfeminism acquires diverse and sometimes contradictory meanings – for example, it is often assumed that postfeminism as a descriptive popular category is conceptually inferior to and more conservative than theoretical versions associated with a postmodern challenge to identity politics.[3] While we examine the intricacies of these postfeminist sites, we also argue against the establishment of separate and detached postfeminist versions and locations (academia and media) that runs the risk of recreating the artificial partition between the academic ivory tower and popular culture. As Genz argues, 'this distinction signals an unwillingness to engage with postfeminist plurality and is viable only as a disclaimer to ensure that postfeminism remains easily categorized and contained in well-defined boxes' ('Third Way/ve' 336).

The fact that postfeminism cannot be delimited in this way and defined with a clear sense of finality and certainty points towards its *interdiscursivity* and *intercontextuality*, which inevitably take the form of boundary-crossing. Patricia Mann offers a useful description by identifying postfeminism as a 'frontier discourse' that 'bring[s] us to the edge of what we know, and encourages us to go beyond': 'Postfeminism is a cultural frontier resulting from the breakdown of previous social organizing structures that continue to exist only in various states of disarray' (208). For Mann, taking up a postfeminist position is a precarious, risky task that seeks to capture the changing quality of our social, cultural and political experiences in the context of the more general process of women's social enfranchisement (114). Postfeminism comes to be seen as a 'fertile site of risk' that transcends the confines of a feminist audience and admits a 'bricolage of competing and conflicting forms of agency' and 'multiple subject positions' (207, 31, 171). In the following chapters, we will elaborate on and discuss this notion of postfeminist agency in popular, theoretical and political terms and we will describe various embodiments of the 'unmoored' postfeminist subject – from the hybrid form of the 'postfeminist man', who blends metrosexual appeal with sexist laddishness, to the 'gendered micro-politics' of the neo-liberal entrepreneur (1).

Our usage and understanding of postfeminism are motivated less by an attempt to determine and fix its meaning than by an effort to acknowledge its plurality and liminality. We believe that postfeminism is a more complex and productive concept than many of its common usages suggest. For us, the problem surrounding postfeminism is not so much choosing between its various appropriations and imposing a 'tick list' that approves or invalidates certain postfeminist strands. Rather, we endeavour to provide a more expanded and nuanced analysis of the 'post-ing' of feminism that allows for polysemy or multiple meanings. Postfeminism is not a 'new feminism' in the sense that it represents something radically revolutionary and ground-breaking – indeed, we will later discuss the notion of 'new feminism' that has been employed by a number of writers to describe the state of contemporary feminisms and is often dependent on a consumerist and individualist logic. Our intention here is not to argue the case of postfeminism as either a new utopia or the trap of nostalgia, but to discover a postfeminist liminality that 'moves us from the exclusionary logic of either/or to the inclusionary logic of both/and' (Rutland 74). Postfeminism is both retro- and neo- in its outlook and hence irrevocably post-. It is neither a simple rebirth of feminism nor a straightforward abortion (excuse the imagery) but a complex resignification that harbours within itself the threat of backlash as well as the potential for innovation.[4] This double movement is at the root of the difficulty of attributing *a* meaning to postfeminism and containing it within a definitional strait-jacket; a futile endeavour in our view that ultimately serves only as a critical shortcut. It is important for us to avoid this definitional trap, which might supply us with some appealing conclusions and neat answers at the expense of more complex and thought-provoking questions.

At the same time, our acknowledgement of postfeminist multiplicity and liminality does not imply that we are unaware of or forgetful about postfeminism's limitations and demarcations. Most postfeminist expressions that we address in this book undoubtedly arise in a late twentieth-century Western context characterised by the proliferation of media images and communication technologies and a neo-liberal, consumerist ideology that replaces collective, activist politics with more individualistic assertions of (consumer) choice and self-rule. In today's consumer culture, the notion of freedom is often directly tied to the ability to purchase, with people's agency premised upon and enabled by the consumption of products and services. Moreover, postfeminism has also been criticised for its exclusions in terms of class, age, race and (to some extent) sexuality, whereby the ideal postfeminist subject is seen to be a white, middle-class, heterosexual girl.[5] Quoting bell hooks' precept that 'feminism is for everybody', Yvonne Tasker and Diane Negra suggest that 'postfeminism is in many ways antithetical to the notion of an open society in which all members are valued in accordance with their distinct identities' (2). By contrast, we do not ascribe to this idea of a 'closed', exclusive postfeminism and we purposefully introduce theories and case studies that transcend the limits of white, adolescent, heterosexual and middle-class femininity. We are equally interested in the yet unexplored categories of the postfeminist man and cyborg, queer and ethnic variations of postfeminism and politicised interpretations of it.

However, we do not presume that this examination of postfeminist facets is all-encompassing and we do not at any rate expect to deliver the final answer and solution to the contemporary postfeminist conundrum. Importantly, this book does not provide a sociological investigation, and more work needs to be done into how postfeminism functions across a range of markers of differentiation and diversity. Let us assure our readers as well that our analysis is not intended as an attack on the feminist movement and its important fight for women's emancipation and social equality.[6] In our eyes, postfeminism cannot be understood as an alternative to feminism and its social and political agenda. Postfeminism does not exist in this bounded and organised form as a political and social movement, and its origins are more impure, emerging in and from a number of contexts (academia, media and consumer culture) that have been influenced by feminist concerns and women's enfranchisement. At this point it is also worth remembering that, as Nancy Whittier reminds us, the 'postfeminist generation is not a homogeneous, unified group' (228). Postfeminism – in its current late twentieth- and twenty-first-century manifestations – has had almost thirty years to solidify into a conceptual category and develop a critical history in its own right that spans the backlash years of the 1980s, the Girl Power 1990s and the uncertain, post-9/11 years of the new millennium. Some of the postfeminist texts and theories that we discuss can undeniably be considered conservative, retrogressive and even anti-feminist, while others hold the potential for innovation and progress. What makes the postfeminist phenomenon so conflict-ridden but also exciting and compelling is precisely that it does not conform to our definitional frameworks and our preconceptions of where the boundaries of academia, politics and popular culture should lie. As Sarah Projansky has recently observed, 'postfeminism is by definition contradictory, simultaneously feminist and antifeminist, liberating and repressive, productive and obstructive of progressive social change' (68). Whether critics see feminism or anti-feminism as more dominant, she continues, is in the end 'a matter of interpretation and degree'. We want to go a step further by not just positioning postfeminism in relation to (and against) feminism but also contextualising it in popular culture, academia and politics. In this way, we hope to trace a *genealogy* of postfeminism that explores its pluralistic constructions, locations and meanings, its overlapping understandings and paradoxical critical practice. The 'post-ing' of feminism thus posits a challenge to cultural critics to investigate the inescapable levels of contradiction and diverse points of identification and agency we are confronted with in late modern Western societies. At the same time, the postfeminist phenomenon also demands that we interrogate and possibly re-imagine how we carry out critique, apply analytical frameworks and draw conclusions in a contemporary context that defies the logic of non-contradiction.

We begin by looking in more detail at the intersections of feminism and postfeminism and by situating the latter in relation to earlier/other forms of feminism. In order to unravel the interpretative openness and the multifaceted nature of postfeminism, the interconnections between 'post' and 'feminism', prefix and root, have to be examined. The relationships between feminist and postfeminist discourses are multiple and varied. Confusion rules as postfeminism is variously identified or associated with an anti-feminist backlash, pro-feminist third wave, Girl Power dismissive of feminist politics, trendy me-first power feminism and academic postmodern feminism. There seems to be a simultaneous denial, use and misuse of feminism, an unscrupulous embrace of contradiction and ambiguity that negotiates areas of tension that, we maintain, can be used productively within postfeminist practice and theory.

Even though postfeminism became concretised as a cultural phenomenon and discursive system in the late twentieth century, it is interesting to note that its first reference appeared much earlier, at the beginning of that century, after the vote for women had been gained by the suffrage movement. As Nancy Cott writes in *The Grounding of Modern Feminism* (1987):

> Already in 1919 a group of female literary radicals in Greenwich Village . . . had founded a new journal on the thinking, 'we're interested in people now – not in men and women.' They declared that moral, social, economic, and political standards 'should not have anything to do with sex', promised to be 'pro-woman without being anti-man', and called their stance 'postfeminist'. (282)

This initial mention of postfeminism relied on the supposed success and achievements of the 'first wave' of the feminist movement that culminated with women's suffrage, whereby the 'post' is understood in evolutionary terms as a progression of feminist ideas.[7] Yet it is fair to say that this early twentieth-century manifestation of postfeminism did not materialise or develop in any specific and tangible ways – cut short as well by important historical developments such as the outbreaks of both First and Second World Wars – and it was not until the early 1980s that the next significant appearance of postfeminism occurred. This time, it was the popular press that brought back postfeminism into the cultural limelight, where it was mostly discussed as exemplary of a reaction against second wave feminism and its collective, activist politics.[8] Postfeminism – denoting in this case post-second wave – came to signal a generational shift in feminist thinking and in understanding social relations between men and women, beyond traditional feminist politics and its supposed threat to heterosexual relationships.[9]

Approached in this way, postfeminism could be interpreted as a cyclical process of feminist rejuvenation – emerging after momentous and organised stages (or 'waves') of feminist activism and politics – and be discussed as 'post-revolutionary' in its shift away from the collectivist mobilisation that characterised both first and second waves of feminism (Stacey 8). As Julie Ewington suggests, 'it is not feminism that we are "post" but one historical phase of feminist politics' (119). Postfeminism encourages feminism to develop an understanding of its own historicity, 'an account of its own temporality that does not simply mimic the modernist grand narrative of progress' (67). It attributes a historical specificity to second wave feminism, for, as Charlotte Brunsdon asks, 'why should 1970s feminism have a copyright on feminism?' (*Screen Tastes* 101). In this chronological sense, the term 'postfeminism' is employed to describe a critical position in relation to the feminism of women's liberation, signifying both the achievements of and challenges for modern feminist politics. Postfeminism's interrogative stance could thus be read as a healthy rewriting of feminism, a sign that the women's movement is continuously in process, transforming and changing itself. This is what Ann Brooks implies in her re-articulation of postfeminism as 'feminism's "coming of age", its maturity into a confident body of theory and politics, representing pluralism and difference' (1).[10] Feminism has undoubtedly gone through a range of significant changes since its second wave heyday in the 1960s and 1970s: conceptual transformations 'from debates around equality to a focus on debates around difference'; a shift away from collective, activist politics; an increasing mainstreaming of feminism; and the appearance of a new generation of women who redefine the movement's goals and identity (Brooks 4). These intergenerational relations are characterised by connection but also, necessarily, by discontinuity and discrepancy, as young women becoming conscious of feminism in the 1980s and 1990s are embedded in an altered social, cultural and political context and climate. Nancy Whittier explains that 'just as the links between political generations grow from structural and social relations . . . so, too, are the differences grounded in the changing social structures and cultural contexts that organise the lives of women at different times' (235–6). Not surprisingly, Whittier adds, this 'postfeminist generation' has different experiences and outlooks from those of 'longtime feminists' who 'acquired a sense of the world and themselves in a different era' (226).

Importantly, for a post-1970s generation of women/feminists, feminism exists not only – or indeed, some might argue, less – as a political and social movement but also as a distinct identity position or, worse, a stereotype, most vividly expressed in the iconic figure of the humourless and drab 'bra-burner'. As we will discuss shortly, this negative representation of feminism can be attributed both to an unsympathetic mass media – which has propagated images of the bra-burning, mannish and fanatic feminist for a long time[11] – and to radical feminism's own rejection of femininity and beauty practices. Many women coming of age in a post-second wave environment have reacted against the image of 'the women's libber' that they perceive as inadequate and restrictive, and they have adopted postfeminism – in particular those postfeminist strands (like Girl Power) that embrace femininity/ sexuality as an expression of female agency and self-determination – as it 'appears not only as more rewarding but also as a lot more fun' (Budgeon, 'Fashion Magazine Advertising' 60). In these circumstances, postfeminism comes to be seen as 'the new and improved mind of feminism', a feminism fit for the new millennium, whereas 1970s second wave feminism is described as 'embarrassingly out of touch', 'no longer moving, no longer valid, no longer relevant' (Cacoullos 80).

In our opinion, this definition of postfeminism as a self-critical, evaluative mode is simply too optimistic, as in the end postfeminism is always more than a straightforward criticism of a specific feminist phase. As Lynne Alice notes, the 'inflammatory myth of new beginnings and revisionings' disguises the fact that postfeminism can 'operate like a chimera, or perhaps even a conceit', misrepresenting and undermining feminist politics and reducing all feminisms – and their long and diverse histories – to a caricaturised version of 1970s feminism (26). In some critical investigations, the 'post-ing' of feminism is denounced as an invasion of the feminist body and a vicious attempt to debilitate and sabotage the women's movement. In particular, this is the case in examinations and critiques of 1980s backlash culture that turns feminism into a 'dirty word' associated with a number of female crises and predicaments, from work-induced stress and loneliness to insanity and psychosis. In this book, we suggest that postfeminism's appropriation of feminism is more complex and subtle than a simple rewriting or modernisation, and it can even harbour anti-feminism. In its various manifestations, postfeminism exhibits a number of relations to feminism ranging from complacency to hostility, admiration to repudiation. In its most denunciatory expressions, postfeminism clearly misreads and classifies feminism as a monolithic movement that is archaic, binaristic and unproductive for the experiences of contemporary women. In order to position themselves against a supposedly unified and old-fashioned feminist entity, some postfeminists end up distorting and reducing feminism's diversity. Other postfeminist versions celebrate and reinforce their connections with earlier forms of feminism and open up 'the possibilities of finding and understanding feminisms in places and in ways very different from . . . that earlier period' (Braithwaite 27). From this perspective, post-feminism is indicative of a broadening of feminist issues and areas of interest – in Misha Kavka's words, postfeminism provides 'a focal point for articulating the meaning . . . and constituencies of feminism today' (29).

In effect, we argue that the entanglements of feminism and postfeminism are multiple and diverse and – as a debating couple – they should not be viewed reductively in opposition, nor in terms of a linear progression. In our understanding, feminist and postfeminist stances are allied and entwined, creating a dynamic and multifaceted context that is made up of various stand-points and theories.[12] However, these interconnections have often been over-looked and passed over in many critical studies in an attempt to establish two different and easily categorised positions. Much pro- and contra- postfemi-nist rhetoric relies on a reductive binary structure in order to conjure up a pole of negativity against which postfeminism can be defined and lay bare the faults of feminist orthodoxy; or, alternatively, reminisce nostalgically about a mythical feminist past characterised by a homogeneous and unified women's movement. Jane Kalbfleisch's discussion of the feminism–postfeminism coupling is instructive in this respect, as she analyses a number of rhetorical positions that underlie different articulations of postfeminism and render abstract – and almost non-existent – the potential for overlap, the ambigu-ity between the two groups and the possibility of conflict within each one. Kalbfleisch describes how the 'rhetoric of opposition' effects a polarisation of feminism and postfeminism that is based on the assumption that the two are fully distinguishable and distinct. In this sense, 'postfeminist' denotes a non-feminist stance that can be read as a term of negation. This rupture can be interpreted positively as liberation from old and constraining conditions and an affirmation of new developments; or it can be read as a deplorable regres-sion and a loss of traditional values and certainties. The rhetoric of opposition thus takes the form of both anti- and pro-postfeminism, either rejecting the term as an opportunistic move on the part of patriarchy or embracing it and thereby denouncing earlier feminist movements.

On the pro-postfeminist side of the debate, there is a group of young women who appear to speak from somewhere outside and above feminism. The term 'postfeminism' is used to suggest that the project of feminism has ended, either because it has been completed or because it has failed and is no longer valid. The most prominent advocates of this standpoint – Naomi Wolf, Katie Roiphe, Natasha Walter and Rene Denfeld – support an indi-vidualistic and liberal agenda that relies on a mantra of choice and assumes that the political demands of first and second wave feminism have now been met (enfranchisement, equal pay, sexual liberation etc.).[13] It is argued that 'all ha[s] been achieved, in fact over-achieved' to the extent that 'feminism has . . . become irrelevant to the lives of young women today' (Coppock et al. 3; Sonnet 170). Accordingly, Rene Denfeld starts her book *The New Victorians* (1995) with the observation that '[f]or women of my generation, feminism is our birthright . . . . We know what it is to live without excessive confinement. We are the first generation to grow up expecting equal opportunity and equal education, as well as the freedom to express our sexuality' (2). Denfeld defines feminism as the 'New Victorianism' that 'has become as confining as what it pretends to combat' and is totalitarian and inflexible in its upholding of views that are reminiscent of those of an earlier age (2, 5). The implicit assumption is that feminism no longer needs to be enforced politically as it is now up to individual women and their personal choices to reinforce those fundamental societal changes. In this case, the meaning of 'post' becomes equivalent to both 'anti' and 'after': 'postfeminism is that which both comes after and rejects . . . earlier feminism – it is the successor "feminism" to a now surpassed, and now unnecessary, prior feminism' (Braithwaite 24).

While Denfeld's account relies on a dualistic and hierarchical narrative structure that, as Deborah L. Siegel notes, might be summarised as 'Down with the "bad" feminism and up with the good!' ('Reading' 67), other – perhaps less antagonistic – descriptions highlight a generational divide between second wave mothers and postfeminist daughters. As Rebecca Walker – daughter of Alice, the author of *The Color Purple* – notes in her introduction to the anthology *To Be Real: Telling the Truth and Changing the Face of Feminism* (1995):

> Young women coming of age today wrestle with the term [feminist] because we have a very different vantage point on the world than that of our foremothers . . . . For many of us it seems that to be a feminist in the way that we have seen and understood feminism is to conform to an identity and way of living that doesn't allow for individuality, complexity, or less than perfect personal histories. We fear that the identity will dictate and regulate our lives, instantaneously pitting us against someone, forcing us to choose inflexible and unchanging sides, female against male, black against white, oppressed against oppressor, good against bad. (xxxiii)

A critical as well as temporal distance is established between the 'new feminists' – who discard what they see as uptight, establishment feminism (or, in some cases, 'victim feminism') in favour of ambiguity and difference – and the 'old' second wavers who hold on to a dated, old-guard and rigid feminism. As Imelda Whelehan explains this generational conflict: the daughters 'want to point out to these feminist mothers that the world has changed quite considerably since they were young feminists . . . [W]hen it comes to feminism . . . young women assuredly do not want the "rules" perceived to be handed down from the motherhood' (*Feminist Bestseller* 168, 179–80). Here, the persona of the second wave feminist appears as a historical figure whose time has now passed, a 'rather unpleasant gatekeeper to the secrets of political freedom' (180) – or, as Angela McRobbie puts it, 'a psychic policewoman, disallowing girls from the pleasure of imaging the pleasures of pre-feminist womanhood' ('Mothers and Fathers' 135). This familial logic is common among both a range of 'new feminists' who want to reframe and re-animate feminism with twenty-first-century meaning, relevance and above all, sex appeal and a 'third wave' of feminists who do not necessarily reject their second wave mothers but insist on accommodating contradictions and diversity.

In response – and very much on the anti-postfeminist side of the divide – the feminist 'foremothers' attacked their 'daughters' for their historical amnesia and misappropriations of the feminist/familial legacy. According to Lynne Segal, this new breed of feminists 'were able to launch themselves and court media via scathing attacks on other feminists' – even worse, this kind of feminism has been 'appropriated by a managerial elite' that works in the service of neo-liberal values and is 'eager to roll back welfare for workfare' ('Theoretical Affiliations' 152). Segal declares that by the 1990s the radical spirit of feminist politics had waned and there was 'a kind of cultural forgetting of the intellectual legacies of feminism', even as 'its more radical residue lingers for those who wish to find it' (Adkins 428; Segal, 'Theoretical Affiliations' 152). These anti-postfeminist critics define postfeminism as a sexist, politically conservative and media-inspired ploy that guts the underlying principles of the feminist movement. In line with this viewpoint, the advent of postfeminism has engendered not the eradication of sexism but its transformation into a more indirect and insidious form. Postfeminism is depicted as 'a hegemonic negotiation of second-wave ideals', 'working with "patriarchal" theory' and employing feminist notions of equality and agency for non-feminist goals (Dow 88; de Toro 16). In particular, the popular media is criticised for co-opting feminism's language of choice and empowerment and selling women an illusion of progress that ends up subjugating and oppressing them even further and on more unconscious levels.

This stance has notably been taken up and examined by the American journalist Susan Faludi, who portrays postfeminism as a devastating reaction against the ground gained by the second wave, and implicates the work of younger feminists (Wolf, Roiphe, etc.) in a backlash against feminism.

Quoting an article from the *Guardian*, Faludi is resolute that 'post-feminism is the backlash. Any movement or philosophy which defines itself as post whatever came before is bound to be reactive. In most cases it is also reactionary' (*Backlash* 15). Rather than being a full-blown attack on feminism, '[t]he backlash is at once sophisticated and banal, deceptively "progressive" and proudly backward' (*Backlash* 12). It does not refuse women's rights and equality outright but redefines them in terms of a liberal individualist politics that centres on lifestyle choices and personal consumer pleasures. In this instance, the prefix 'post' occupies an uneasy position suggesting an invasion and appropriation, a 'parasite riding on the back of the original movement which benefits from the ground it has won but uses this for its own means' (Kastelein 5). As Ann Braithwaite describes this process, 'feminism is "written in" precisely so it can be "written out"; it is included and excluded, acknowledged and paid tribute to, and accepted and refuted, all at the same time' (25).[14] Ultimately, however, we are advised to be suspicious of this 'undoing of feminism' that precisely appears to participate in an inclusion of feminist ideologies only to commodify, invalidate and repudiate feminist critiques (see McRobbie, 'Notes'). As Tania Modleski insists, 'texts . . . in proclaiming . . . the advent of postfeminism, are actually engaged in negating the critiques and undermining the goals of feminism, in effect, delivering us back into a prefeminist world' (3).

In what follows, we will discuss in more detail these notions of appropriation, incorporation and commoditisation that underlie many articulations and assessments of mostly popular forms of postfeminism. What interests us at this stage is the rhetoric of opposition deployed by both pro- and anti-postfeminist camps that presents the relationship between feminism and postfeminism as mutually exclusive and incompatible. This *either/or* formulation implies that only one term can subsist by obliterating the other: postfeminism can only exist to the exclusion of feminism, and feminism can only exist to the exclusion of postfeminism. Rather than situating feminism and postfeminism antithetically, the second rhetorical position that Kalbfleisch identifies, 'the rhetoric of inclusion', relies on a polarisation of a different kind to eradicate the overlap between feminism and postfeminism. In this case, postfeminism is pitted against some 'Other' (for example, postmodernism and poststructuralism) in a move that allows for the presumed commonalities among feminists and postfeminists while effectively erasing their potential differences (258). The rhetoric of inclusion displaces the polarisations from within the (post)feminist coupling to the relationships of (post)feminism and other discursive frameworks. The critical tension between feminism and postfeminism is defused in this way as the two terms are conflated into one and incorporated into another discursive project.

Academic circles in particular have adopted this theoretical approach, discussing postfeminism as 'a pluralistic epistemology dedicated to disrupting universalising patterns of thought, and thus, capable of being aligned with postmodernism, poststructuralism and postcolonialism' (Gamble 50). As Keith Green and Jill LeBihan note, postfeminism marks 'the involvement of feminism with other "post" discourses' and addresses 'one of the most pressing current concerns for academic feminism': 'the question of what to do with "post" discourses' (253–4). Within academia, postfeminism is defined as the outcome of feminism's intersection with these anti-foundationalist movements whereby the 'post-ing' is seen to denote a shift in feminist thinking and, specifically, in the way in which 'woman' as the subject of feminism is conceptualised. Postfeminism is employed as a theoretical or philosophical term that relates to the problematic search for a unifying cause of and common solution to women's subordination and a rejection of the assumption that feminism is based on a unified subjectivity, a universal sisterhood.

There is no shortage of debate on these diverse 'post' derivatives and the interactions of feminism with postmodernism especially are fraught with difficulties, with the problem of subjectivity as the point of contention and division. Indeed, we will later discuss the intricacies of a postmodern feminism that attempts to combine anti-foundationalist theories that emphasise 'the death of the subject' with a collective understanding of a feminist 'we'. While we do not deny the importance of these 'Other' discourses for the development of the postfeminist venture, we are also mindful of the fact that a purely theoretical conception of postfeminism is insufficient and inadequate. The absorption of postfeminism into postmodernist cultural critique runs the risk of repressing its importance in other domains, specifically its place in the public debate on feminism and the modern woman.[15] In our understanding, postfeminism exists as a descriptive popular category and an academic theoretical tendency as well as a political phenomenon prevalent in late modern, Western societies, and, even within these situated contexts, it does not necessarily aim for coherence. We argue against a bifurcation of postfeminism that splits it into a number of distinct, disconnected and competing strands – almost as if it were leading separate lives in popular culture, academia and politics.[16] This not only leads to oversimplified postfeminist meanings but also denies the overlaps between these postfeminist contexts, as well as the possibilities inherent in the (post)feminist coupling.[17]

Ultimately, postfeminism's complexities can be explained by neither oppositional nor inclusive rhetorical stances. Adopting Kalbfleisch's terminology, we seek to interpret postfeminism through the lens of a 'rhetoric of anxiety' that foregrounds 'conflict, contradiction and ambiguity' (259). We want to re-articulate the questions of ownership and definition that have dominated – and at times hampered – examinations and critiques of postfeminism, and to introduce a contextual approach that highlights postfeminism's multiplicity and intersections. Rather than polarising specific sites/strands of postfeminism, we retain the idea of a multifaceted postfeminist landscape that crosses the boundaries between popular culture, academia and politics. Our objective is not so much to establish and fix the meaning of postfeminism as to explore the postfeminist 'frontier' and the ongoing struggle over its contents. In this sense, we agree with Ien Ang that 'critical research' cannot be built around a 'fixed, universal yardstick' and should not 'allow itself to rest easily on pre-existent epistemological foundations' (37). In the following sections, we will situate postfeminism contextually in order to avoid the pitfalls of reductive strategies of definition, and we will investigate the emergence of late twentieth-century postfeminism in a number of cultural, theoretical and political sites.

POSTFEMINISM IN POPULAR CULTURE

The existence of postfeminism as a cultural media phenomenon is undisputed; after all, it was the popular press that resurrected the term in the 1980s in order to indicate a shift from – and at times also enact a ritualistic denunciation of – second wave feminism. Since then, the term 'postfeminism' has been used widely in popular culture, in particular as a descriptive marker for a range of female characters, from Helen Fielding's heroine Bridget Jones to the Spice Girls and the cyberbabe Lara Croft. Yet the resolutely popular character of postfeminism has often been criticised for somehow lessening its analytical potential and undermining more thorough and systematic social and academic movements. As Yvonne Tasker and Diane Negra note, postfeminism (as a popular idiom) has been 'generated and primarily deployed outside the academy, [and therefore] lack[s] the rigor we expect of scholarly work' (19). For them, postfeminism is by definition 'middle of the road, middle-class' and it is particularly treacherous in its 'pervasive insistence on the bleakness and redundancy of feminism'. In fact, 'postfeminist culture works . . . to incorporate, assume, or naturalize aspects of feminism; crucially it also works to commodify feminism' (2). The merits of such a popular postfeminist position are rather limited, for – 'as we might expect of a popular mode' – postfeminism rejects 'the supposed difficulty of feminism, its rigidity and propensity to take things "too far"' (19).

Several points are noteworthy here: Tasker and Negra not only locate postfeminism within the popular realm but also infer a value judgement that belies both the complexities of postfeminism and popular culture; they uphold a dualistic conception of feminism and academia on the one hand – as more effective and 'rigorous' sites of criticism – and postfeminism and popular culture on the other; from this perspective, the negotiation of feminism with the popular has to be considered with the utmost caution – as Tasker and Negra write, 'our responsibility as feminist critics is to approach the popular with a sceptical eye' (21). This perception of postfeminism is common among a number of (mostly feminist) critics who view the exchanges of feminism and popular culture not only with scepticism but sometimes even with hostility. Consequently, the media-friendly postfeminist stance is interpreted as an abatement and depoliticisation of the feminist movement, whereby feminism's entry into the popular is represented as a damaging attempt to manage and contain the revolutionary potential of the feminist enterprise. In this process of co-option, feminism has supposedly been made safe while its more attractive elements and terminology of liberation and emancipation have been preserved and accommodated.[18] As Joanne Hollows and Rachel Moseley comment, '[f]rom such a position, popular feminism is feminism tamed and divested of its radical meaning' (10).

In effect, postfeminism has often been discussed in these circumstances as emblematic of the debates surrounding the relationship between feminism and popular culture and the viability of the category of 'popular feminism'. As many contemporary commentators have acknowledged, feminism is now part of the cultural field and its meanings are increasingly mediated. Hollows and Moseley, for example, note that 'most people become conscious of feminism through the way it is represented in popular culture' and 'for many women of our generation, formative understandings of, and identifications with, feminist ideas have been almost exclusively within popular culture' (2). Similarly, in her attempt to settle the question 'what is feminism?' Rosalind Delmar proposes that 'it is, in practice, impossible to discuss feminism without discussing the image of feminism and feminists' (8). Delmar's comment points to the practical impossibility of experiencing and identifying an authentic feminism, unadulterated by the often conservative forces of cultural representation. In this way, 'feminism is never available in some pure or unmediated form' and instead, our understanding of feminism is filtered through the media, forming and shaping our ideas of what it means to be a feminist (Moseley and Read 234). As a result, feminist discourses cannot be comprehended as simply being outside and independent critical voices, as they are now part of a global-based media landscape. In other words, popular culture comes to be seen as a critical location for the constitution of the meanings of feminism, a site on, through and against which the contents and significations of feminism are produced and understood (Moseley and Read; Brunsdon). This engenders many different explanations and discussions about incorporation and recuperation while also prompting other questions about the nature of the media itself and the role of the feminist cultural critic. In her book *Gender and the Media* (2007), Rosalind Gill asks whether the media have been 'transformed by feminism' and 'become – in significant ways – feminist' (41). She also debates the function and responsibilities of feminist critics who can either celebrate women's choices, look for strands of resistance or formulate alternative representational strategies. As Gill rightly says, in an increasingly diverse media culture saturated by information and communication technologies, 'the "obviousness" of what it means to do feminist intellectual work breaks down' and we are left with a 'messy contra-dictoriness', a clear sign that gender relations and media representations – as well as the feminist frameworks used to understand and critique them – are constantly changing in contemporary Western societies (22, 2).

However, even if, as Gill says, 'most feminism in the West now happens in the media', this does not imply that the idea of 'feminism in popular culture' – to borrow Hollows' and Moseley's title of their collection of essays – is clear and uncontested (Gill, *Gender and the Media* 40). Quite the contrary: what happens to feminism within the popular – and how popular culture reacts to the mainstreaming of feminism – has been a major concern of feminist critics ever since the second wave's prime in the 1960s. While contemporary accounts of popular feminism have frequently oversimplified the intercon-nections between feminism and the media and the complex ways in which feminism and the feminist have been envisaged within popular culture, the early days of second wave feminism were characterised by a determinedly anti-media attitude, foreclosing even the possibility of the category of 'popular feminism'. The women's movement – along with other political groups at the time – conceived of itself as 'outside' the dominant culture and offering an alternative to the predominantly stereotypical images perpetuated by/in the 1960s and 1970s media. In this period, feminism was more visible as a vibrant social and political movement engaged in struggles over a range of issues related to women's unequal position in society. From this perspective, popular culture was criticised for its cultural representation and reproduction of gendered inequalities, and as such, it was rejected as 'a sort of ideological machine which more or less effortlessly reproduces the dominant ideology', 'little more than a degraded landscape of commercial and ideological manip-ulation' (Storey 12, 129). It was seen as an inherently compromised site that merely serves 'the complementary systems of capitalism and patriarchy, ped-dling "false consciousness" to the duped masses' (Gamman and Marshment 1). Consequently, one of the most well-known and characteristically second wave strategies, 'consciousness-raising' (or, in shorthand 'CR'), was designed to get to the core of women's subjugated state, in society as well as in their own home and bodies.[19] Female revolution in consciousness was deemed to be the crucial first step to a wider social revolution, facilitating an awakening of previously brainwashed women.

Second wave feminist critics often employed what Ang calls 'the crude hypodermic needle model of media effects' that relies on the assumptions that 'mass-media imagery consists of transparent, unrealistic messages about women whose meanings are clearcut and straightforward' and 'girls and women passively and indiscriminately absorb these messages and meanings as (wrong) lessons about "real life"' (111). This became known as the 'images of women' debate: the idea that the media socialises women/girls into consuming and accepting 'false' images of femininity and traditional sex roles which tell them to 'direct their hearts towards hearth and home' (Hollows and Moseley 4). Accordingly, it was the feminist critic's responsibility to assume the social function of demystifier in an attempt to enlighten 'ordinary' women who – it was suggested – indiscriminately and passively absorb these images and therefore suffer from a 'false consciousness'. As Imelda Whelehan advocates, the only way out of this media absorption is to separate fact from fiction: 'the role of the feminist . . . is to prove herself equal to demythologising the powerful and ever-changing myths about the female self and nature perpetuated in the mass media and other state apparatuses' (*Modern Feminist Thought* 229). In order to show 'real' images of women, second wave feminism thus had to intervene in popular culture and produce its own alternative, countercultural descriptions.[20] In this way, much second wave feminist work presumed the authority to designate what were correct portrayals and ways of seeing for all women (Hollows and Moseley). What underpinned these analyses was not only a hostility towards the popular but also an opposition between the feminist – whose 'raised consciousness' allows her to see through the mystifications of popular culture[21] – and 'ordinary' women – also referred to in some second wave tracts as 'token women' and 'parasites' (Daly; de Beauvoir) – who necessitate a feminist makeover. It was this notion of an elitist feminist 'club' that can illuminate the obfuscated and silent majority of women, and the idea of an unadulterated, media-hostile feminism, that were to be challenged by later (post)feminists who argue for a different conceptualisation of popular culture and put forward the possibility of a popular kind of feminism.

Second wave feminists also raised other objections with regard to the media which related not only to the misrepresentation of women as a whole but specifically to the depictions of feminism and feminists in popular culture. The media was condemned for launching an assault on feminism and fostering 'debilitating caricatures, allowing the culture at large to dismiss and discount it' (Mascia-Lees and Sharpe 191). In particular, the media was credited with the invention and circulation of 'the mythical, and most persistent, icon of second-wave feminism: the bra-burner' (Hinds and Stacey 156). The figure of the bra-burning, mannish and fanatic feminist has dominated popular representations of feminism 'so long as to have become one of the most familiar symbols in the contemporary political landscape and cultural imagination' (153). This negative stereotype has been propagated as a metonym for the feminist movement, with the result that 'we all know what feminists are' (Douglas 7). As Susan Douglas summarises, 'they are shrill, overly aggressive, man-hating, ball-busting, selfish, hairy, extremist, deliberately unattractive women with absolutely no sense of humor who see sexism at every turn' (7). Paradoxically, the image of the bra-burner was also the inadvertent outcome of one of the earliest and most iconic events that brought second wave feminist activism to public awareness: the demonstration that feminists staged at the Miss America beauty pageant in Atlantic City in 1968.[22] The protest symbolically enacted the rejection of oppressive ideals of womanhood, and was an attack on male-defined femininity and on the notion that women were objects to be consumed. It was also a carefully planned publicity stunt and an attempt at collective consciousness-raising: it was hoped that the media would act as a mouthpiece for the feminist movement and disseminate its messages of female emancipation to a wider audience.

However, media reports of the event were less than favourable, as much of the national press coverage depicted the demonstration in ways that made the emerging movement seem ludicrous.[23] The media stereotype of the feminist bra-burner soon took root in the popular imagination – undermining to a large extent feminists' efforts to target the public consciousness and implant their own ideas – and, even until today, such assumptions persist.[24] This incident reveals the uneasy relationship with the media that was going to characterise much of second wave feminism. While feminists were sure of their own motives for the protest and were evidently frustrated by the media's negative depictions, they were also reluctant to court the media in order to get their message across. As Imelda Whelehan writes, the second wave did not want to enter into 'the spin game': the media liked to deal with spokespeople (preferably someone attractive and eloquent) and feminists were opposed to the development of a 'star system' within their ranks and demanded a rota for media appearances (*Feminist Bestseller* 138, 46–7).[25] This did not fulfil the media's desires, nor did it enable the feminist groups to present themselves (and their message) in the most favourable manner.

Moreover, the figure of the unattractive bra-burner also cemented into the public's mind the perception of feminism as anti-feminine. Press coverage of the early 1970s reflects this media tendency to depict 'the women's libber' as an unfeminine, ugly woman.[26] As Hinds and Stacey argue, 'there is no doubt that the persistent media characterisation of the feminist, from the bra-burner onwards, condenses a range of characteristics antithetical to conventional definitions of desirable femininity' (161). Feminists are characterised as 'enemies of the stiletto heel and the beauty parlor – in a word, as enemies of glamour', and feminism is depicted as the preserve of 'only the unstable, mannish, unattractive woman who has a naturally difficult relationship to her own femininity' (Bartky 41; Whelehan, *Overloaded* 18). This media argument against feminism insistently proclaims that women who (collectively) adopt a feminist outlook and engage in feminist politics will effectively be desexed, threatening the prospective feminist with an unwelcome masculinisation.

While the view of feminism as a defeminising force can clearly be identified as a distorted media refraction and propaganda, it is important to note that the sense of incongruity between feminism and femininity was not only publicised by the contemporary media but was also present in many feminist writings of the time. In *Feminism, Femininity and Popular Culture* (2000), Joanne Hollows describes how the notion of a feminist movement and the assertion of a feminist identity are often predicated on a rejection of femininity: 'feminist critiques . . . are often dependent on creating an opposition between "bad" feminine identities and "good" feminist identities' (9). In feminist thinking – from Mary Wollstonecraft in the late eighteenth century to Naomi Wolf in the late twentieth – women's quest for femininity and beauty is often constituted as a 'problem' and a major cause of women's oppression.[27] This anti-feminine trend reached its peak during the 1960s and 1970s, when second wave feminist texts concretised the dichotomy between feminism and femininity by establishing the figure of 'the feminist heroine' in opposition to 'the feminine anti-heroine' (Hollows 17). For example, in her landmark book *The Feminine Mystique* (1963), Betty Friedan famously declared that women's enslavement to femininity gives rise to 'the problem that has no name, a vague, undefined wish for "something more"' beyond the 'genteel prison' of their suburban homes (54–5, 83). In the more radical *Gyn/Ecology* (1978), Mary Daly rejects femininity as a 'man-made construct' and 'a male attribute' that blinds women and lures them into forgetting its 'falseness' (68–9). In Daly's eyes, patriarchy has colonised women's heads to such an extent that it 'prepossesses' them and inspires them with 'false selves' (322). She condemns these 'moronized' women as 'man-made', 'painted birds' who have been incorporated into the 'Mystical Body of Maledom' and succumbed to the patriarchal invitation 'to become "living" dead women' (5, 334, 67).

After the politically charged and heady days of the 1960s and 1970s, these sometimes revolutionary and extremist perceptions were to be disputed by a number of women/feminists who could not reconcile the perceived feminist 'rules' with their experience of 'growing up female and feminist' in the 1980s and 1990s (Hollows and Moseley 8). Second wave feminists themselves were going to be troubled by a range of questions posed by their anti-media and anti-feminine stances as well as their supposed enlighten-ment vis-à-vis 'ordinary' women. As a number of critics have emphasised, Daly's feminism, for example, seems to have given up on most women and instead concentrates on a 'chosen few' (Hollows, *Feminism, Femininity and Popular Culture* 15). Her distinction between 'real women' and feminine dupes is bound to alienate those who conceive of their femininity (and feminism) in different, more diverse, terms and who do not agree with this polarity. In years to come, new (post)feminist voices would emerge to support a re-articulation of femininity and popular culture that takes into account their complex interactions with feminism. In effect, from the 1980s onwards, the relationship between feminism and the popular – and, associated with this, femininity – was reconceptualised, and new terms like popular feminism, postfeminism and third wave feminism started to appear to mark a changed social, cultural and political context. What characterises these post-second wave positions is exactly the way they locate themselves within popular culture and inside the realm of cultural representation. While negative readings of the popular are still prominent – for example, Susan Faludi's description of postfeminism as backlash very much keeps alive the suggestion that representations of feminism within the popular are anti-feminist – there have also been concerted efforts to re-imagine popular culture as a potentially liberating and innovative site that puts forward the possibilities of active consumption and the popular consumer as a creative and productive agent.

Various topics we discuss in the main body of this book challenge the view of women as passive victims of an inexorably sexist media and affirm the notions of consumer agency and popular resistance. Numerous examina-tions and articulations of postfeminism – from Girl Power to micro-politics – acknowledge their insider position within popular culture and highlight alternative modes of production/consumption that combine cultural confi-dence with feminist awareness. Empowerment and agency – goals that both second wave feminists and postfeminists claim – are envisaged differently, and thereby second wave notions of collective, activist struggle are replaced with more individualistic assertions of (consumer) choice and self-rule. As Sarah Banet-Weiser notes, within this contemporary context, 'empower-ment cannot be theorized as separate from market strategies but is rather a *constitutive* element in these strategies' (216; emphasis in original). In effect, in many recent analyses, the opposition between feminism and popular culture – fundamental in and constitutive of second wave critiques – is displaced onto the relationship between feminism and consumer culture. The debates centre on the commoditisation of feminism and the specific forms of consumption that come to the fore in contemporary culture and society. Banet-Weiser, for example, suggests that feminism has been 'rescripted' so as to 'allow its smooth incorporation into the world of commerce and corporate culture' (209). For her, the end result is 'commodity feminism' – also referred to as 'free market feminism' (Whelehan, *Feminist Bestseller* 155) – that constructs women as both subjects and consumers through an individualist rhetoric. Tasker and Negra follow a similar line of argument by placing postfeminism within the context of the 1990s 'New Economy' and 'the displacement of democratic imperatives by free market ones' (6).[28] In the course of this interaction with the market, feminism is supposedly in danger of losing its radicalism as its ideas of 'liberation', 'freedom' and 'independence' become detached from their feminist roots and 'now postulate many media forms because they sell' (Hollows, *Feminism, Femininity and Popular Culture* 194).

In this rapidly changing cultural and economic landscape, feminism's role and situation have certainly changed, and there have been many discussions as to whether it can still exist as a discrete politics once it has been incorporated into popular/consumer culture. The move towards individual, consumer-oriented empowerment has propelled the consideration of several complex questions regarding the compatibility of feminism's popular and political dimensions. In the following chapters, we examine the intricate and complex intersections of feminism and popular culture and the emergence of a postfeminist politics of representation and (controversially) emancipation. Unlike other critics, we do not interpret feminism's entry into the popular as necessarily a depoliticisation and dilution – although some popularised forms of feminism are undoubtedly conservative and retrogressive – nor do we adhere to the notion of postfeminism as apolitical and 'non-democratic'. We maintain that popular/consumer culture should be reconceived as a site of struggle over the meanings of feminism and the reconceptualisation of a postfeminist political practice that, unlike second wave feminism, does not rely on separatism and collectivism – indeed, postfeminism should not be considered along the same lines as the second wave as an activist social politics – and instead highlights the multiple agency and subject positions of individuals in the new millennium.

Many of the postfeminist stances that we examine are resolutely and unapologetically popular in the sense that they arise from and within popular culture. In this way, it is no longer possible for contemporary critics to adopt a binary framework that sets up a contrast between feminism and popular culture, 'real' feminism and 'fictional' feminism (Dow). At the same time as emphasising the importance of the popular, we also want to steer clear of a kind of populism – most famously discussed by John Fiske – that celebrates popular culture as a paradise of free choice.[29] Importantly, we do not pursue the themes of popular pleasure and empowerment to the point at which, as Angela McRobbie writes, 'anything which is consumed and is popular is also seen as oppositional' (*Postmodernism and Popular Culture* 39). Popular culture is not 'a playground for everyone', a utopian site that fosters a cultural democracy of consumers (Hollows, *Feminism, Femininity and Popular Culture* 129). In this book, we do not herald the sovereignty of the consumer or 'the freedom to play with lifestyles' and we are careful not to oversimplify the complexities of popular culture and the act of consumption (Hollows, *Feminism, Femininity and Popular Culture* 133). We do not support populist arguments that understand popular culture as 'a supermarket of meanings' from which consumers can 'cook up . . . their own culture' (Fiske 132). The problem with this viewpoint is that it presumes an autonomous popular space of liberal pluralism that is formed 'in reaction to [but] never as part of the forces of domination' and 'exist[s] in some relationship of opposition to power' (43, 49).[30] This can amount to an apologetic '"yes, but . . ." discourse' that does not situate the popular in relationship to a social and political context and downplays the structural oppressions in favour of the representation of 'a rosy world "where there's always a way to redemption"' (Ang 139).

By contrast, we define the popular domain not as an autonomous space in which free choice and creativity prevail but as a contradictory site that interlaces complicity and critique, subordination and creation. As David Gauntlett writes, '[a]lthough we may occasionally find ourselves saying that "the mass media suggests" a particular perspective or point of view, the truth is that not only is "the mass media" wildly diverse, but that even quite specific parts of media culture put out a whole spectrum of messages which cannot be reconciled' (255). Storey agrees, noting that 'popular culture is a concept of ideological contestation and variability, to be filled and emptied, to be articulated and disarticulated, in a range of different and competing ways' (202).[31] This also implies a reconsideration of the concept of 'choice' as an ideological discourse in which, as Ang says, 'the rhetoric of the liberatory benefits of personal autonomy and individual self-determination has become hegemonic' (13). This has important reverberations for popular feminism and/or postfeminism which rely on consumerist notions of choice in order to promote and propagate individualist ideas of empowerment and agency. In this sense, the postfeminist consumer is endowed with contradictory forms of subjectivity and agency that allow for 'choice', but not within the same terms of emancipatory politics that characterised the second wave – indeed, we will revisit these ideas in more theoretical examinations of

postfeminism that are concerned with the dichotomy between the 'constituted' and 'constituting' self. We argue that the most challenging representations of postfeminist subjectivity depict the double bind of consumption
and the struggle of a 'free-yet-bounded' self who is both subject and object,
active and passive, complicit and defiant (Ang 170). These contradictions are
an inevitable by-product of contemporary Western media forms that have
integrated feminist messages, and mobilise a diverse range of representations that strive to remake social relations beyond the oppositional logic of
female powerlessness and male power, feminist enlightenment and feminine
victimisation, popular indoctrination and feminist emancipation.

POSTFEMINISM IN ACADEMIA

As we have seen, articulations of postfeminism in popular culture are often
preoccupied with notions of co-option and appropriation: feminism's conjunction with the media has hardly ever been interpreted as a beneficial
exchange of ideas, values and theories, and instead, it has been conceptualised
as a takeover or subsumption whereby feminism is seen to lose its autonomous status by becoming incorporated into the popular mainstream. Similar
concerns resurface in discussions of academic strands of postfeminism that
locate it within a range of anti-foundationalist movements, including postmodernism, poststructuralism and postcolonialism.[32] In *Postfeminisms* (1997)
for example, Ann Brooks discusses postfeminism as a theoretical movement
associated with deconstructive challenges to identity politics: 'Postfeminism
expresses the intersection of feminism with postmodernism, poststructuralism and post-colonialism, and as such represents a dynamic movement
capable of challenging modernist, patriarchal and imperialist frameworks'
(4). For Brooks, postfeminism denotes the culmination of a number of
debates within and outside feminism, emerging from the juncture of feminism with elements of cultural theory – particularly postmodernism – and
theoretical/political issues arising around postcolonialism, that gives voice to
marginalised, colonised and indigenous women who question the possibility
of a universal feminist 'sisterhood'. She is adamant that postfeminism is not
about a depoliticisation of feminism but a political move in feminism's conceptual and theoretical agenda. As such, postfeminism represents feminism's
'maturity into a confident body of theory and politics, representing pluralism
and difference and reflecting on its position in relation to other philosophical and political movements similarly demanding change' (1). Postfeminism
questions the notion of feminist consensus and effects a shift from within
feminism from debates around 'equality' to a focus on 'difference' (4). Brooks
clearly envisages postfeminism as post-second wave, and thereby occupying

'a similar "critical" position in regard to earlier feminist frameworks at the same time as critically engaging with patriarchal and imperialist discourses' (2). In her analysis, feminism becomes the subject of postfeminist critiques that cast doubt on a singular and uniform conception of the feminist movement, emphasising instead the multiple and varied ways of being 'feminist' and understanding 'feminism'. In this sense, postfeminism can be considered as a movement of feminist pluralisation and diversification, making room in its ranks for a more diverse 'we'. It engages with the postmodern notion of the dispersed, unstable subject and opens up the feminist realm for the articulation of 'other' voices and identities.

Postfeminism can thus be discussed in relation to deconstructive theories that undermine the concept of an essential female/feminist identity from two critical directions: postmodernism's deconstruction of the subject category is reinforced by anti-essentialist feminists for whom 'woman' as a monolithic term is unable to address the complexity of gender in relation to other aspects of identity, including race, ethnicity, class, sexuality and age. As Deborah Siegel notes, there are 'two very different modes of deconstructive feminist theorising', two different taxonomies that can be oversimplified as 'multiculturalist' and 'postmodernist' (Siegel, 'The Legacy' 60). While postmodernist critics destabilise the idea of a universal and unified subject (including feminist subjects), multiculturalist feminists concentrate on material exclusions and examine how gender is constructed across a range of identity markers, beyond the limits of Western, white, heterosexual and middle-class female experience – indeed, we will later examine the intricacies of 'postmodern feminism', 'postcolonial feminism' and 'queer feminism' that complicate such terms as 'oppression', 'patriarchy' and 'identity' as used by second wave feminists. In place of an identity politics of feminist solidarity against male oppressors, the pluralistic postfeminist stance that comes to the fore in postmodern, postcolonial and (to some extent) queer analyses puts forward the idea of multiple oppressed subjectivities rather than privileging any one site of oppression. In effect, postfeminism denotes 'a context in which the feminism of the 1970s is problematized, splintered, and considered suspect, one in which it is no longer easy, fun, empowering, or even possible, to take a feminist position' (Mascia-Lees and Sharpe 3). It facilitates a broad-based, pluralistic conception of feminism that rejects the ideas of a homogeneous feminist monolith and an essential female self.

This theoretical/academic positioning of postfeminism is appealing, for it 'insists that we listen to the voices of those who dispute the terms of representation and who say "this is not us"' (McRobbie, *Postmodernism and Popular Culture* 7). In many ways, postfeminism can be said to respond to the theoretical and political challenges facing feminists in a post-second wave environment 'of moving feminism, as a political movement *without the fixity of a single feminist agenda* in view, into the next millennium' (Siegel, 'The Legacy' 56; emphasis added). Yet the understanding of postfeminism as feminist pluralism also highlights the fact that, with the advent of the postmodern era, any illusions of feminist unity have to be interrogated and ultimately discarded.[33] It is argued that feminism can no longer rely on the notion of an authentic and unanimous feminist realm or 'outside' and has to renounce the idea of a detached and untainted feminist identity.[34] This engenders a number of difficulties and problems for the conceptualisation of feminism as a social/political movement that is seemingly dependent on the notion of a feminist self on which to base its collective, activist politics. As Amelia Jones observes, 'the most important question . . . is whether . . . feminism is co-opted by being harnessed to other discourses which neutralize its radical potential' ('A Remasculinization' 7). While multiculturalist feminists actively counter mainstream feminist investigations (including the umbrella term 'sisterhood' that, they argue, does not account for all women/feminists and fails to address the needs and demands of marginalised and colonised women), there is also concern in some feminist quarters that 'the intersection of feminism and postmodernism might result in feminism . . . losing its distinctive character as a body of critical theory and practice' (Brooks 36). Feminism is said to be co-opted by 'other' discourses that undermine its radical politics and splinter its separate (if illusory) singular identity. As Frances Mascia-Lees and Patricia Sharpe deplore, this makes it 'both difficult, and often, undesirable to distinguish it [feminism] from endeavors with close affinities: poststructuralism, cultural studies, critical theory, and postcolonial or subaltern studies' (3).

The central questions raised by feminist critics revolve around issues of agency and the specific nature of political action that feminists can pursue in the absence of a single feminist agenda and identity. By providing a conceptual repertoire centred on deconstruction and anti-essentialism, postmodernism highlights feminism's own foundational discourses bounded by the concept of 'woman' and its epistemological entailments. In its attempts to posit a unified identity as its underpinning, feminism – in particular in its second wave manifestations – is often compelled to exclude fragmented or multiple identities from its ranks. Postmodernism calls on feminists to relinquish their foundational goals and focus on the differences between women. For feminist theorists, the attraction of postmodern critiques of subjectivity can be found in the promise of an increased freedom for women and 'the "free play" of a plurality of differences unhampered by any predetermined gender identity' as formulated by either patriarchy or feminism itself (Alcoff 418). Yet some feminists are also concerned that they cannot afford the luxury of rejoicing in 'the death of the subject' for 'if woman is a fiction . . . then the very issue of women's oppression would appear to be obsolete and feminism itself would have no reason to exist' (de Lauretis, 'Upping' 83). Feminism is said to be pulled in two opposing directions: in order to be effective as an emancipatory and political movement designed to increase women's access to equality in male-dominated cultures, it supposedly needs to rely on an essentialist definition of woman.[35] At the same time, feminism cannot deny the importance of anti-foundationalist theories that dismiss (or decentre) the concept of the autonomous subject. Thus, at the moment when 'postmodernism is forging its identity through articulating the exhaustion of the existential belief in self-presence and self-fulfilment and through the dispersal of the universal subject of liberalism', feminism is ostensibly engaged in assembling its cultural identity in what appears to be the opposite way (Waugh, *Feminine Fictions* 6). According to this logic, the postmodern notion of the 'subject in process' cannot be embraced whole-heartedly by feminism as this implies the loss of political agency and action. As Linda Nicholson asks, 'does not the adoption of postmodernism really entail the destruction of feminism, since does not feminism itself depend on a relatively unified notion of the social subject "woman", a notion postmodernism would attack?' (Nicholson, 'Introduction' 7).[36]

Postfeminism – interpreted in this academic context as the intersection of postmodernism/multiculturalism and feminism – is the battlefield on which these debates are fought out, as it attempts to negotiate between the destabilisation of the notion of *a* feminist self and the historic mobilisation of a politically engaged feminist *we*. There is a significant conceptual overlap between postmodern feminism and postfeminism, and the latter clearly participates in the discourse of postmodernism as it discredits and eschews the ideas of discursive homogeneity and a unified subjectivity. It understands that postmodernism's fracturing of the universal subject pertains to feminism's own identity, and it rejects the concept of the essential and coherent sovereign self in favour of a selfhood that is contradictory and disjunctive. Postfeminism thus embraces a complexity of vision and gives vent to the multivalent, inharmonious and conflicting voices of contemporary women, including the 'other' voices of feminists themselves. The postfeminist movement insists that feminism has to be viewed pluralistically, and in this way, it 'establish[es] a dynamic and vigorous area of intellectual debate, shaping the issues and intellectual climate that has characterized the move from modernity to postmodernity in the contemporary world' (Brooks 210).

The shift to the 'post' – for example, in postfeminism and postmodernism – has been discussed in terms of a nascent 'post-theoretical' movement that reconfigures the limits of theory, politics and (feminist) critique/practice. As Fernando de Toro observes in 'Explorations on Post-Theory':

> Something has happened. In the last two decades, before the end of this [twentieth] century, we have witnessed the emergence of the *Post*. This is a symptom of a society and a culture unable to name what is taking place in the very crux of its activity. The *Post*, then, comes to replace that which we know is there, but which we do not quite manage to signal. (9; emphasis in original)

According to de Toro, 'Western culture has entered a New Age, one which is still searching for its name' and he defines these new times as 'post-theoretical' in their introduction of a new strategy and awareness and in their 'search for a "beyond", a third theoretical space' (9, 10). As he explains, 'post-theory' implies 'exploiting the in-between spaces . . . a transitory space, a space other, a third space that is not here/there, but both' (20). Post-theory emerges from the 'deconstruction of current hegemonic systems, as well as the new knowledge being generated from the margins, or rather, from different centres' (16). This deconstructive move implies the disintegration of the tenets of dominant culture along with an attack on universalist and essentialist thinking – importantly, this also involves a critique of the foundationalist premises of patriarchy and feminism, as well as the deconstruction of their relevant subject categories, 'man', 'woman' and 'feminist'. The destabilisation of totalising and homogenising systems can be interpreted positively as a democratisation of opinion, as 'the epistemological space has been pried open, dissected, dismembered' and all privileged points of view have become obsolete, along with the dominant position which allowed the establishment of hierarchies of interpretation (12). As de Toro notes, it is, 'precisely, the de-centring of the West that has made it possible to integrate within one simultaneous space apparently diverging epistemologies' (12). Thus, he continues, '"post-theory" entails a simultaneous convergence of theories emanating from diverse epistemological fields and disciplines with the goal to analyse given cultural objects from a plurality of perspectives' (10). Advocates of post-theory maintain that this stance – and the ensuing dissolution of disciplinary and discursive boundaries – should be welcomed as 'experimentation in the combinatory mode', transcending the limits and rigidity of binary models and frameworks (Rutland 74). As de Toro puts it, what becomes important within post-theory 'is not so much *what* divergent theories say, but *what* we can do with them' (12; emphasis in original).

This examination of the 'post' as a point of conjuncture between a number of often competing interests and agendas is particularly pertinent in the case of postfeminism, which exists and moves across a number of disciplines and contexts, including popular culture, academia and politics. In this way, Christine di Stefano identifies 'a postfeminist tendency' as 'an inclination fostered by a refusal to systematically document or privilege any particular form of difference or identity against the hegemonic mainstream' (73). However, rather than rejoicing in the plurality of differences made possible by this post-theoretical/postfeminist condition, di Stefano is uncertain about the benefits of deconstructive critique that has potential anti-political and anti-feminist implications.[37] Craig Owens is equally doubtful, noting that 'pluralism . . . reduces us to being an other among others; it is not a recognition but a reduction to difference to absolute indifference, equivalence, interchangeability' (88). In effect, critics are concerned that an abstract celebration of difference might encourage cultural relativism and political passivity. It is argued that the elimination of all totalising and essentialist discourses and the ensuing post-theoretical positions – such as postfeminism – cause a perplexing multitude of differences. As a result of this multiperspectival stance, the post-theoretical subject is seen to be stranded in a decentred realm of detachment and apathy in which taking a position becomes an almost impossible task.

Post-theory is criticised for adopting the 'fantasy of capturing . . . heterogeneity in [its] "readings" by continually seeking difference for its own sake' (Bordo 39). This line of reasoning is prevalent in discussions of postmodernism as a theoretical invocation of diversity, far removed from practical contexts and pragmatic considerations of how this theoretical position can be transformed into an effectual critique and politics of change. Susan Bordo, for example, maintains that the postmodern enactment of plurality and fragmentation is animated by the 'dream of everywhere' but unfortunately, this 'new, postmodern configuration of detachment', this 'new imagination of disembodiment', slips into 'a fantasy of escape from human locatedness', a retreat from an embodied point of view (217, 226–7). The problem with these supposedly theoretically pure, postmodern readings is that 'they often present themselves as having it any way they want' as they 'refuse to assume a shape for which they must take responsibility' (228). In its abandonment of all universalist patterns of thought, postmodernism is seen to display a political naivety and inefficacy as it does not posit theoretical stopping points, nor does it reserve practical spaces for a generalised critique and for attention to nuance.[38]

Similar concerns reappear in examinations of postfeminism, which is often taken to task for its supposed indifference towards (or worse, opposition to) a collective, pragmatic and activist feminist politics, as well as its irreverent 'boundary-crossing' and bricolage of competing forms of agency. Critics have mulled over postfeminism's contents, uses and meanings that seem to arise in so many, seemingly irreconcilable contexts. Some have dismissed the postfeminist phenomenon outright for its embrace of contradiction and *intercontextuality* – suggesting, for example, that postfeminism is 'hampered by the need to meet the dual demands of theoretical consistency within the terms of poststructuralism and the wider feminist project' (Kastelein 27). In its various cultural, theoretical and political guises, postfeminism has often been criticised for its individualistic/anti-essentialist tendencies, which are seen to harbour the threats of political disablement and depoliticisation for the feminist movement.[39] In the attempt to do justice to heterogeneity, postfeminism is perceived to be in danger of becoming trapped in 'the endless dance of non-commitment' and losing the potential to operate as a 'theoretical enterprise motivated by critique' (Brooks 155). It is argued that 'just as postmodernism depoliticises political activity, so post-feminism depoliticises feminism' (Davies 6). In the following section, we will investigate the idea of a postfeminist politics and provide a political reading of postfeminism that does not eschew the possibilities of change and resistance. We propose that postfeminism can act in politically and theoretically engaging and challenging ways that do not presuppose the end of critical production and politics. In its most constructive sense, postfeminism offers a different conceptual model to understand political and critical practice – it is not so much a depoliticisation or trivialisation of feminism as an active reinterpretation of contemporary forms of critique and politics that take into account the diverse agency positions of individuals today. As we will see, it has now become essential to rethink (political/feminist) agency in the context of recently destabilised identity categories and gender relationships as well as the mainstreaming and commoditisation of feminism in late twentieth- and twenty-first-century culture and society.

POSTFEMINISM IN POLITICS

In some ways, the heading of this section, 'postfeminism in politics', can be considered controversial, as for many critics, the postfeminist phenomenon epitomises an inherently apolitical/non-activist stance that at its best is simply apathetic and narcissistic, and at its worst acts as a retrogressive and reactionary backlash that undermines the gains of the feminist movement/politics and returns women (and men) to the limited gender roles of a bygone era. Yvonne Tasker and Diane Negra, for example, take the distinction between 'feminist politics' and 'postfeminist culture' as the starting point for their collection of essays, *Interrogating Postfeminism* (2007), as well as the title of their introduction. As they argue, 'the transition to a postfeminist culture involves an evident erasure of feminist politics from the popular, even as aspects of feminism seem to be incorporated within that culture' (5). From their perspective, postfeminism is not only intrinsically 'middle of the road' but also works to 'invalidate systematic critique' by transforming the postfeminist subject into a 'silent' consumer (19, 3). Consequently, as they suggest, postfeminism should be differentiated from feminism, which fundamentally operates as a political and critical movement, emphasising 'the operations of power, whether economic, social, ideological, or representational' (16). In effect, Tasker and Negra define postfeminism as 'a set of assumptions . . . having to do with the "pastness" of feminism' as 'it is precisely *feminist* concerns that are silenced within postfeminist culture' (1, 3; emphasis in original). Underlying this division is not only a perception of incongruity between feminism and postfeminism – and to some extent, politics and culture – but also a strong sense of hesitation and distrust vis-à-vis the latter – as Tasker and Negra write, their analysis can be situated within a body of work that 'names' postfeminism but ultimately 'remains unsure about its material, limits and theoretical territory' (11).

By contrast, in this book we seek not only to politicise postfeminism but also to offer an interpretation of postfeminist politics that allows for the multiple agency and subject positions of individuals in a late twentieth- and twenty-first-century context. We want to complicate the critical understanding of postfeminism as a depoliticised and anti-feminist backlash, and we endeavour to advance a more complex and diversified interpretation of the postfeminist phenomenon that acknowledges contemporary feminisms' varied relationships with Western politics and media structures. We suggest that postfeminism responds to the changing qualities of both female and male experiences in a late liberal society in which people are less willing to become ideologically identified with any political movement, even though at the same time they are still encountering gendered struggles in their private and public lives. As Patricia Mann notes in *Micro-Politics: Agency in a Postfeminist Era* (1994), '[g]iven the chaotic state of individual motivations and responsibilities in this scenario, it may be wholly [*sic*] unrealistic to expect anyone to worry very much about establishing firm social identities' (115). Moreover, importantly, we do not understand postfeminism as an alternative to feminism and its political struggle, nor do we wish to discuss it as a bounded philosophy and an organised political movement that gains its force through activist lobbying at grass-roots level. Instead, we maintain that postfeminism pushes us, in Mann's words, to 'reach beyond the boundaries of a feminist audience' and address the fact that feminist concerns have entered the mainstream and are articulated in politically contradictory ways (118). The approach that we put forward involves not only a reconsideration of postfeminism and its political dimensions but also a reconceptualisation of political and critical practices.

As Mann rightly observes, it is now necessary 'to expand the vocabulary of political actions in order to make sense of individual agency in moments of discursive uncertainty and political change' (17).

Of course, this also has reverberations for our discussion and perception of feminist politics and critique, which have historically been dependent on separatist, collective and activist practice. At the end of the twentieth century and the beginning of the new millennium, feminism has undoubtedly gone through a paradigm shift that problematises political action as conceived by second wave feminism – the Miss America demonstration that we mentioned in the previous section is a representative example of the kind of direct and collective campaigning that underlies much of second wave politics. As Michèle Barrett writes, feminism has undergone a 'turn to culture' whereby 'there has been an increasing tendency in feminism to think about politics through the medium of cultural debate' (22). This move towards the cultural arena 'has come at a time when there is quite rightly much less confidence than there once was in the standing and methodology of the traditional critical disciplines' (23). Barrett argues that feminism's turn to culture has created a more critical and reflexive feminism, whose initial 'consensus and confidence around issues of "patriarchy", distinctions along sex/gender lines, as well as issues of "subject" positioning and sexuality' are cast into doubt by the emphasis on deconstruction and difference (Brooks 38). Other critics are less positive about this emergence of 'cultural politics', and they have focused on feminism's 'crisis of activism' and the 'dissolution of feminism as theory and practice' as a result of its intersection with cultural theory (Stuart 40; Walters, 'Premature Postmortems' 105). As Andrea Stuart asks, how do we now go about changing oppressive situations 'without some sort of campaigning "movement"' (40)?

In effect, in these circumstances, the idea of a collective 'sisterhood' – a united feminist 'we' and, related to this, a collective politics of engagement – becomes not only dubious but almost impossible. Sarah Banet-Weiser notes that the complexity of the current feminist landscape means that 'the idea that "we" all share a feminist politics, that we all "want the same thing", is highly problematic. Not only does this propagate the mistake made by many second-wave feminists, who insisted on a universal feminist standpoint, but it also functions as a kind of refusal to identify what it is we all apparently want' (210). In other words, Banet-Weiser continues, 'if "we" all want the same thing in feminism, what is it: a liberal version of equality, a more radically configured understanding of liberation from patriarchy, or simply a more frequent and "positive" media appearance?' (210). This struggle over territory has often resulted in a kind of 'turf war', with different factions and, over longer periods of time, 'waves' of feminism debating the meanings, uses

and goals of feminism. The politics of feminism has undeniably changed
for a post-second wave generation, and both postfeminism and third wave
feminism, for example, are produced in an altered cultural and political
climate than were 1960s and 1970s strands of feminism. What makes the
current historical moment and political field so challenging – and perhaps
disconcerting for some – is that it is impossible to amalgamate contemporary
versions of feminisms into a singular 'movement'.[40] Instead, as Banet-Weiser
suggests, 'feminisms exist in the present context as a politics of contradiction
and ambivalence' (210).

Shelley Budgeon characterises this shift as a move from modernity to
postmodernity:

> Feminism is fundamentally an emancipatory discourse as it has its
> origins in modernity and a liberal humanist political philosophy which
> emphasizes universal rights to equality, but as movement is made towards
> postmodernity, increasing differentiation problematizes the notion of
> universality itself, resulting in fragmentation and the questioning of
> unity. There is still an emphasis on the right to self-determination and
> the right to choose but it becomes increasingly difficult to prescribe in
> advance the answers to questions about how to live and how to navigate
> those choices. ('Emergent Feminist (?) Identities' 21)

As Budgeon writes, 'the problem of difference within the category "woman"'
has revealed that 'there are as many ways of becoming a feminist as there are
of becoming a woman' (23). Added to this escalation of difference between
women is the fact that many feminist ideas have become part of the mainstream and common sense of today's consumer culture to the extent that, at
times, those ideas are expressed in a form that does not necessarily correspond
with 'traditional' feminist methods and critiques. The questions that arise
for contemporary critics then have to do with how we can formulate and
articulate a politicised agency within the conditions of late modernity, and
how we can theorise the politics of contradiction that emerge in the context
of consumerism and individualism – indeed, at a later stage in this book, we
will engage in more detail with the notion of 'micro-politics', which recon-
ceptualises the political sphere in more dynamic and flexible terms and as part
of neo-liberal, consumer culture.

Postfeminism appears at the centre of the discussions on the state of twenty-
first-century feminisms and politics as it has been defined as an inherently
individualist and consumer-oriented stance that works to incorporate, com-
moditise and disperse feminism's fight for female emancipation and equal
opportunities. Postfeminism is said to effect a decollectivisation of the feminist
movement as it translates feminist social goals and political ideas into matters

of individual choice or lifestyle. Some, mostly feminist, commentators take a unanimously negative view of postfeminism's individualistic stance, arguing that 'the political is personal' as 'the distinction between feminist politics and feminist identity is in danger of completely disappearing' (Dow 210, 209). This ironic reversal of the well-known feminist adage illustrates post-feminism's individualistic agenda, which problematises notions of a collective feminist identity or sisterhood.[41] Critics insist that, with the emergence of postfeminism, 'feminist politics become feminist identity' as feminism's political theory and practice are transformed into a set of personal attitudes and any emphasis on organised intervention is regarded as misguided (Dow 209). It is feared that the implicit assumption is that feminism has become anachronistic and therefore should be rejected in its state of collectivity. The reasons for this dismissal are highly varied, ranging from a theoretical questioning of the concepts of unity and coherence – for example, in examinations of postmod-ernism – to the argument voiced in some media quarters that equality has been achieved and hence, women can relax in their organised struggle and concentrate on the real work ahead – individual goals.

The popular press provides the most explicit portrayal of this postfeminist utopia in which women can do whatever they please, provided they have sufficient will and enthusiasm. According to this optimistic formulation, women choose the life they want and inhabit a world centred in what Elspeth Probyn calls *choiceoisie*, which envisions all major life decisions as individual options rather than culturally determined or directed necessities. This post-feminist version of the American dream (with its celebration of individual-ism) is seen to be entirely available to those who work hard enough. 'Being empowered' becomes synonymous with 'making the most of oneself' and 'pleasing oneself' and in this way, the second wave's challenging collec-tive programme of equal opportunity is transformed into atomised acts and matters of personal choice. As Susan Douglas writes, 'women's liberation metamorphosed into female narcissism unchained as political concepts and goals like liberation and equality were collapsed into distinctly personal, private desires' (246). This 'narcissism as liberation' equates women's eman-cipation with their ability to do whatever they want, whenever they want, no matter what the expense. The comforting message propagated by this individualist rhetoric appears to be that women's collective victimisation has ended and/or is exaggerated by feminist orthodoxy – indeed, this idea resurfaces later in this book in our discussion of 'power feminism', which views feminism's emphasis on women's subordinated status as disempower-ing and even oppressive. Instead, women are presented as having freedom of choice to pursue their ambitions actively and take up the opportunities that a postfeminist *choiceoisie* puts at their disposal.[42]

Some critics are adamant that the notion of 'narcissism as liberation is liberation repackaged, deferred and denied' as the most basic and revolutionary principles of feminism are distorted and undermined (Douglas 265). As Nancy Cott notes, as much as feminism asserts the female individual, 'pure individualism negates feminism because it removes the basis for women's collective self-understanding or action' (6). For her, the threatening outcome of this emphasis on personal choice is an excessively individualist feminism that obliterates the political. The danger lies not in postfeminism's celebration of the personal struggles and triumphs of women, but rather in mistaking these often quite satisfying images 'for something more than the selective, partial images that they are' (Dow 214). In favouring individual effort rather than group struggle, a token is held up 'not as exception but as proof that egalitarianism (the fully functioning American Dream) was present all along' (Helford 292).[43] The rhetoric of tokenism redefines oppression and structural disadvantage as personal suffering while reframing success as an individual accomplishment, faith and self-determination. The implication is that choice has supposedly always been there, in reach for the right person who knows how to work within the system for personal improvement. According to this viewpoint, postfeminism is seen to be driven by representational concerns for a more attractive and easily sellable image and is no longer on the defensive, as its individualistic credo domesticates feminism's critical stance. While focusing on the strong individual's will, the tokenism inherent in postfeminism displaces the importance of the group nature of the adversity as it obscures the collective nature of oppression and the need for organised action to remedy social injustice. Moreover, critics maintain that postfeminism's individualism points towards its exclusivity, whereby it is only appealing to 'young women professionals imbued with confidence, an ethic of self-reliance and the headstart of a good education' (Kaminer 23). However, this brand of feminism does not ensure that all women should receive ample opportunities and choices and, in so doing, it guarantees that a power and privilege imbalance persists to exist among them. As Janet Lee suggests, postfeminism's individualist discourse is 'a luxury the majority of women can't afford' and the postfeminist woman, 'if there is one, is rich' and 'she can afford to consume clichés' (172).

Ultimately, for these anti-postfeminist critics, 'postfeminism takes the sting out of feminism', 'confusing lifestyle, attitudinal feminism with the hard political and intellectual work that feminists have done and continue to do' (Macdonald 100; Dow 214). Abandoning the structural analysis of patriarchal power, postfeminism is seen to mask the larger forces that continue to oppress many women's lives and re-inscribes their marginality by undercutting the possible strategic weight of feminist collectivities for change. Assuming rather than questioning equal opportunity for women, postfeminist individualism is criticised for depoliticising feminism and undermining the collective nature of women's liberation while directing them to personal goals. As Dow writes, the notion of postfeminist *choiceoisie* is 'at base, a rhetorical fiction' under whose guise the term feminism – as well as the patriarchy it tries to combat – becomes anachronistic and sometimes is scorned as reductive (194). Critics are concerned that this scorn for a perceived anachronism may even enable the patriarchal order to operate all the more smoothly within postfeminist discourse. Adopting this outlook, Helford concludes that 'postfeminism leaves patriarchy in place, denouncing the idea that women are oppressed as a group and that the "personal is political" in an attempt to avoid all forms of direct struggle against male domination' (293).

While we do not wish to invalidate these critiques and we do not deny that patriarchal ideology is a component of the postfeminist phenomenon, we object to the critical suggestion that postfeminism is an integral part and creation of patriarchy. Nor do we adhere to the view that postfeminism is automatically apolitical or guided entirely by an individualist ethic in the pursuit of personal goals, just because it does not comply with feminism's definition of what constitutes activism – that is, engagement in collective action. In our opinion, the second wave's interpretative framework and models of political action need to be expanded in order to include the multiple agency and subject positions that individuals take up in twenty-first-century culture and society. This also involves a reconsideration of the concept of the individual, not as a self-absorbed narcissist or 'token' who is a secret agent of patriarchy but as an engaged agent – or, in Patricia Mann's words, a 'conflicted actor' who is 'capable of individually integrating diverse desires and obligations on a daily basis through creatively reconfiguring [his or her] practices and relationships' (32). Instead of conceiving postfeminism merely in terms of an exclusionist and exclusive viewpoint – appealing only to cliché-loving, privileged women – we contend that its individualism highlights the plurality and contradictions of contemporary female (and male) experience. We suggest that postfeminism gives rise to a contradictory and potentially problematic stance that is doubly coded in political terms – being able to act in both conservative and subversive ways, while also repudiating 'traditional' activist strategies and communal demonstrations. As we will shortly discuss, some versions of postfeminism – in particular those related to 1980s backlash culture and new traditionalism – are undoubtedly retrograde and can be linked to the conservative politics of the right. More recently, postfeminism has also been aligned with 'Third Way' politics, adopted by centre-left governments throughout the 1990s in Europe and North America as a progressive alternative to the worn-out dogmas of liberalism

and conservatism (Giddens, *Third Way*; Genz, "Third Way/ve'). While postfeminism's adoption of Third Way principles is controversial – some critics
argue, for instance, that the Third Way's emphasis on market-based policies
results in a 'politics for women without feminism' (McRobbie, 'Feminism
and the Third Way' 99) – it has also been interpreted more productively as a
renewal of feminist policies and a reconceptualisation of the political sphere
(see Genz, 'Third Way/ve').

In effect, we propose that postfeminism adopts a politically 'impure' stance
between complicity and critique. Several cultural/political commentators
have sought to discuss the contradictions of the contemporary political field:
Shelley Budgeon, for example, refers to a postfeminist 'politics of becoming'
while Geraldine Harris discusses 'a politics of undecidability' that 'acknowledges the impossibility of theoretical purity or perfectly politically correct
practices' ('Emergent Feminist (?) Identities' 22; *Staging Femininities* 186).
The politics of undecidability does not depend on *a priori* laws, pre-existing
assumptions, universal truths or appeals to absolute authorities. Instead,
it promotes a double movement of exploitation and contestation, use and
abuse, rupture and continuity. This form of politics accepts the necessity
of working within what already exists and forging a future from resources
inevitably impure. As Harris notes, the politics of undecidability strives to
discover a position between 'wild hope and total pessimism', in order to deal
pragmatically with the fact that 'we are always within that which we would
criticize without falling into passivity or relativism' (180). Similarly, Judith
Butler designates 'a politics of discomfort' as a 'politics of both hope and
anxiety' whose key terms are not fully secured in advance and whose future
form cannot be fully anticipated (*Excitable Speech* 161). She forges the notion
of 'living the political *in medias res*' in order to describe this 'reconfiguration
of our "place" and our "ground"' ('For a Careful Reading' 131).

These variously named politics acknowledge that a transformation of
the political is taking place and its outcome cannot be fully explained or
decided upon from within the present without limiting the possibilities
of this transformation. This need not imply a politics of pure flux and
ceaseless change but means that, ultimately, there are 'no rules for subversion or resistance, no guarantees of efficacy, only a process of . . . making
provisional decisions, which are always invested with power relations
. . . always haunted by their own internal contradiction' (Harris 187).[44]
Countering critiques that insist that postfeminism is an apolitical or politically one-dimensional (and mostly conservative) phenomenon, we interpret postfeminism as an inherent component of the transformed political
sphere in contemporary Western societies. Throughout this book, we seek
to trace the varied and often conflicting influences, texts and contexts that

make up the postfeminist landscape – beyond the benchmarks and dualities of feminism and patriarchy, right and left ideology, popular culture and academia, feminism and femininity. Postfeminism responds to and is emblematic of the paradoxes of modern-day politics and culture, seeking to reconcile feminist ideas of female emancipation and equality, consumerist demands of capitalist societies and media-friendly depictions of feminine/masculine empowerment. For us, it makes more sense to examine how power functions in contradictory ways in postfeminist discourses and how engaged individuals rework notions of agency in the context of postfeminist politics. In this way, while we do not engage in a simple celebration of postfeminism and its representations, we hope to provide a critical analysis that elicits and reveals both its drawbacks and possibilities, its transgressive and retrogressive dimensions.

NOTES

1. As Rostislav Kocourek has discussed in his examination of the prefix 'post' in contemporary English terminology, 'an expression "post" + X can either be X or non-X, or both at the same time, which makes the derivative motivationally ambiguous' (106). This programmatic indeterminacy and interpretative openness are inherent in all 'post' terms – most notably, postmodernism and post-structuralism – to the extent that they become issues of debate about whether the prefix signifies an end of a particular type of influence or a recognition of the fundamental importance of the latter.

2. On 29 June 1998, *Time* magazine's front cover featured a row of black-and-white photos of three famous white feminists (Susan B. Anthony, Betty Friedan and Gloria Steinem) and a colour portrait of fictional television lawyer Ally McBeal (Calista Flockhart), along with the caption 'Is feminism dead?'. In the accompanying article, journalist Ginia Bellafante bemoaned the state of contemporary feminism that is 'wed[ded] to the culture of celebrity and self-obsession' (57). In fact, as the *Independent*'s columnist Joan Smith argues, obituaries for feminism appear so regularly in the press that they have come to constitute a specific genre:

    'False feminist death syndrome', as it is known, has been around for a very long time, ever since the late Victorian press described campaigners for women's rights as 'a herd of hysterical and irrational she-revolutionaries' . . . We vividly recall *Newsweek* declaring 'the failure of feminism' in 1990; *The New York Times* assuring its readers that the 'radical days of feminism are gone' in 1980; and *Harper's* magazine publishing a 'requiem for the women's movement' as early as 1976.

3. Another distinction that underlies a number of critiques is between 'feminist politics' and 'postfeminist culture' (see, for example, Yvonne Tasker's and Diane Negra's introduction in *Interrogating Postfeminism* [2007]).

4. The notion of resignifiability is important for our understanding of post-feminism, as it opens up the process of meaning construction and allows for multiplicity without foreclosing any interpretations. Following the theorist Judith Butler, meaning can never be fully secured because 'signification is not a founding act' but a site of contest and revision that accommodates the possibility of resignification, a citational slippage or deviation that creates new and unanticipated meanings (*Gender Trouble* 145).

5. As Sarah Projansky has recently discussed, 'postfeminism depends on girlness, is defined by it in fact' (43). Postfeminism's focus in girlness and youthful femininity – most vividly expressed in 1990s versions of Girl Power – has been criticised by commentators as a historicising and generationalising strategy that disempowers feminism: 'the new female subject is, despite her freedom, called upon to be silent, to withhold critique, [in order] to count as a modern sophisticated girl' (McRobbie, 'Post-Feminism and Popular Culture' 258, 260). Girl Power thus presents itself as youthful and energetic while installing an image of feminism as 'old'. At the same time, in its celebration of young femininity and its application of the term 'girl' to adult women, Girl Power is seen to infantilise and belittle women of all ages by treating them as children or adolescents. As Yvonne Tasker and Diane Negra have argued, in these circumstances, girlhood is imagined as 'being for everyone; that is, girlhood offers a fantasy of transcendence and evasion, a respite from other areas of experience' (18).

6. Crucially, we do not want to write out of feminism women's struggles in non-Western parts of the world, say the global South or the former Soviet bloc states, which would find it difficult to relate to postfeminism's consumerist, individualist notions of empowerment.

7. The 'first wave' of US and British women's movements generally refers to the surge of feminist activism in the late eighteenth and nineteenth centuries. The issue of women's suffrage was raised from the 1830s onwards, but it was not until 1918 that the vote was won for women over thirty and 1928 that women were enfranchised on the same terms as men (1920 in the United States).

8. The 'second wave' – that we now mostly associate with feminism – denotes the resurgence of women's activism and organising in the 1960s. The term 'second wave' was coined by Marsha Weinman Lear in a 1968 article in the *New York Times Magazine* ('The Second Feminist Wave') and refers to an increased feminist activity in North America and Europe from the 1960s onwards. Linda Nicholson points out that 'something important occurred in the 1960s . . . That occurrence was a new intensity in many societies in the degree of reflection given to gender relations' ('Introduction' 1). Nicholson goes on to say that in the United States, the beginnings of these changes can be seen in two, originally separate, political movements: The first was the Women's Rights movement that emerged in the early 1960s and was composed largely of professional women, who put pressure on government institutions to end discrimination against women as they entered the paid labour force; the second movement

   – the Women's Liberation Movement – grew out of the civil rights and New Left movements in the late 1960s. While Women's Rights has been the more politically widespread movement, 'expressing an ideology more in accord with that of the population as a whole', the Women's Liberation Movement has produced most of the theoretical works of the second wave (1–2). In her discussion of the feminist bestseller, Imelda Whelehan puts an end date on the second wave of 'around 1975': 'It wasn't that Second Wave feminism died in 1975 . . . yet, nonetheless, the heady period of activism was on the wane and intra-feminist groupings were becoming more clearly demarcated than they had been' (*Feminist Bestseller* 42).

9. For an early 1980s account of postfeminism, see Bolotin's *New York Times Magazine* article discussing young women's attitudes to feminism. One of Bolotin's interviewees is characteristic in her dismissal of feminism: 'Look around and you'll see some happy women, and then you'll see these bitter, bitter women. The unhappy women are all feminists. You'll find very few happy, enthusiastic relaxed people who are ardent supporters of feminism. Feminists are really tortured people' (31).

10. Similarly, Ann Braithwaite argues for an alternative understanding of postfeminism that takes into account that 'the breadth of feminist issues is now much broader than ever before, across a range of political, social and cultural issues, and intersecting with a variety of theories about gender, race and ethnicity, sexuality, class, and even corporeality' (27).

11. See, for example, Claudia Wallis' *Time* cover story of 4 December 1989, which proclaims that 'hairy legs haunt the feminist movement; as do images of being strident and lesbian' (quoted in Jones, 'Feminist Pleasures' 19).

12. Here it is worth remembering that, as Sarah Gamble points out, 'there are different ways of seeing which are all feminist, allowing for diversity within disciplines and within the feminist movement itself' (231).

13. Given the statistical evidence, it is clear that such claims cannot be sustained. Women continue to earn less than their male counterparts (17 per cent less an hour if they work full-time; 36 per cent if they work part-time) and 96 per cent of executive directors of the UK's top 100 companies are men, while only 20 per cent of MPs are women. For more facts about gender inequality, visit www. fawcettsociety.org.uk (accessed 15 February 2008). As Vicki Coppock comments, 'this is not to say that nothing has changed for women and some aspects of women's daily experiences can be defined as "progressive." . . . While things may be different for women, this does not guarantee, nor translate into equality or liberation' (Coppock et al. 180).

14. Similarly, Angela McRobbie uses the phrase 'taken into accountness' to illustrate 'the co-existence of feminism as at some level transformed into a form of Gramscian common sense, while also fiercely repudiated, indeed almost hated' ('Post-Feminism and Popular Culture' 256).

15. As Amelia Jones suggests, 'the incorporation of one particular kind of feminism into a broadly conceived . . . project of postmodernist cultural critique

tends to entail the suppression of other kinds of feminist practices and theories'
('Feminist Pleasures' 22).

16. Some critics contend that there are separate and easily distinguishable post-
    feminist strands, most commonly defined in terms of a popular, mainstream
    backlash on the one hand – which incorporates postfeminism's political
    dimensions as part of a conservative reaction against feminism – and academic
    'post' discourses on the other. As Deborah Siegel and Ann Cacoullos note,
    'when invoked by the popular press, "postfeminism" smugly refers to an era
    in which feminist movement is no longer necessary' whereas in academia, 'it
    refers to the challenging ways poststructuralist, postmodernist and multicul-
    turalist modes of analysis have informed feminist theory and practice' (Siegel,
    'The Legacy' 53; Cacoullos 80). Postfeminism is condensed and defined as
    either popular feminism or postmodern/poststructuralist feminism respec-
    tively and it is suggested that these two postfeminist contexts should be kept
    apart and considered separately. Accordingly, Ann Brooks points out in her
    theoretical exploration *Postfeminisms* (1997) that 'popular "post-feminism's"
    conceptual repertoire provides a useful point of distinction from the way
    postfeminism is framed within the feminist academic community', and she
    centres her discussion on the 'conceptual equivalence in postmodern feminism
    and postfeminism' (4, 6). Amelia Jones, conversely, focuses on the widespread
    popular conception of postfeminism as a result of the term's appropriation
    by the media, noting that 'the popular deployment of . . . postfeminism . . .
    involves invidiously redefining femininity, feminism and even masculinity'
    ('Feminist Pleasures' 21).

17. As Genz notes in relation to the often-cited distinction between popular and
    theoretical postfeminisms: 'This dualistic conception relies on the assumption
    that postmodern postfeminism is non-hegemonic and inclusive whereas popular
    media postfeminism depicts a hegemonic negotiation of second wave ideas'
    ('Third Way/ve' 337).

18. Joanne Hollows and Rachel Moseley note that 'this idea of co-option is a central
    one in many debates about the relationship between feminism and popular
    culture, whereby it is frequently claimed that those elements of feminism that
    can be "sold" – for example, ideas of liberation, independence and freedom – are
    appropriated by consumer culture but, in the process, become detached from
    the feminist discourses that anchored their radical meaning' (10).

19. Inspired by the black power movement, feminists adapted CR strategies to
    encourage women to identify the social, psychological and political origins of
    their personal problems. One of the main second wave slogans ('the personal is
    political') illustrates this scheme: 'the personal is political' implied that every-
    day interactions between men and women (sex, family life, household chores)
    were no longer simply private matters but implicated in the exercise of institu-
    tionalised power. Women were meant to become aware of this power through
    consciousness-raising sessions which involved sharing experiences with a small
    group of other women and simultaneously learning about their experiences. It

was hoped (and envisaged) that these personal acts of liberation would lead to a collective politics and activism. The anonymous essay 'Consciousness Raising' published in the 1973 collection *Radical Feminism* provides some insights into the workings and aims of the process: the guidelines suggest that a period of three to six months should be spent articulating the members' personal experiences, before they are analysed in 'feminist' terms. This was then followed up by activities and self-help groups as well as organised protests (quoted in Whelehan, *Modern Feminist Thought* 72).

20. An example of such feminist intervention is feminist documentary film-making that is seen to offer an alternative to the 'false' images of women perpetuated by Hollywood. As Annette Kuhn writes, the aim is to represent women, and feminism, with more 'accuracy' and 'honesty', which often means telling 'real women's' stories through an 'autobiographical discourse' (148).

21. In fact, Betty Friedan's *The Feminine Mystique* (1963) – a landmark text of liberal feminism – examined the role the media played in socialising women into restrictive images of femininity, in particular the 'happy housewife' myth. The ideology of the 'feminine mystique' convinces women that they should 'desire no greater destiny than to glory in their own femininity' and it uses the media, growing consumerism – and its associated forms of advertising and shopping – and fashionable psychoanalysis to bring about 'the sexual sell' (13, 181). Friedan was resolute that women's confinement in the 'genteel prison' of the feminine mystique has life-threatening consequences and amounts to a 'slow death in mind and spirit' and a 'progressive dehumanisation' (83, 245). She was adamant that women can only break this cycle of 'helpless conformity' through a realisation of 'the emptiness of the housewife's role': a woman 'must unequivocally say "no" to the housewife image' (164, 212, 297). For a detailed analysis of Friedan's text and liberal feminism, see Genz's chapter 1 in *Postfemininities* (2009).

22. For a detailed analysis of the Miss America protest, see Genz's chapter on the bra-burner in *Postfemininities* (2009).

23. For example, TV stations added imaginary flames in their reports in an attempt to ridicule the demonstrators, while the *Times* salaciously referred to the 'bra-burnings' (though, in reality, no bras had been burnt, in accordance with Atlantic City police's request not to endanger the wooden walkway). As Hinds and Stacey comment, 'what is striking about the persistence of this icon is that bra-burning seems never to have happened':

> bras were not burnt, but were just one of many items – including corsets, suspender belts, high heels and hair rollers – to be cast into the 'freedom trash can' . . . [as] part of the women's liberation protest against the sexism and racism of beauty contests staged the day before the Miss America pageant in Atlantic City in 1968. (157)

24. A 2003 study on men's and women's attitudes to equality in Britain (commissioned by the Equal Opportunities Commission [EOC]) found that feminism is regarded virtually unanimously in negative terms, from old-fashioned to 'ball

breaking'. Other research also suggests that 'the label "feminism" operates as a negative cognitive frame' which might reduce women's support for the feminist movement in the future (Hall and Rodriguez 898).

See www.equalityhumanrights.com/Documents/EOC/PDF/Research/talking_equality _ report.pdf.

25. Whelehan discusses second wave feminism's refusal to play the media game, whereby 'the Movement went into defensive retreat' and 'feminists weren't beyond expelling people summarily if they were felt to have betrayed the central principles of feminism' (*Feminist Bestseller* 138). Rosalind Miles clearly expressed this anti-media, anti-consumerist attitude in *The Fiction of Sex* (1974): 'there are always the commercially-minded who are quite ready to climb up on their sisters' backs to make their impact (and their fortunes)' (quoted in Whelehan, *Feminist Bestseller* 138).

26. For example, a *Times* article from 1971 laments that 'some women's liberation girls decide against caring for their looks. The movement rejects the artificiality of bras, deodorants, depilatories and other wonders of twentieth-century technology which they feel exploit women commercially and debase them into sex objects' (quoted in Hinds and Stacey 161).

27. In the proto-feminist classic *A Vindication of the Rights of Woman* (1792), Mary Wollstonecraft writes that 'taught from infancy that beauty is woman's sceptre, the mind shapes itself to the body and roaming round its gilt cage, only seeks to adorn its prison' (113). Similarly, in *The Beauty Myth* (1991), Naomi Wolf suggests that 'we are in the midst of a violent backlash to feminism that uses images of female beauty as a political weapon against women's advancement: the beauty myth' (10).

28. Thomas Frank uses the term 'market populism' that upholds the concept of the market as proof of social egalitarianism: 'Markets were serving all tastes . . . . they were extinguishing discrimination; they were making everyone rich'; in this way, market populism identifies 'the will of the people with the deeds of the market' (quoted in Tasker and Negra 6–7).

29. In *Understanding Popular Culture* (1989), John Fiske champions popular culture as a creative site where the popular consumer actively and *producerly* negotiates the potentially oppressive effects of power structures. Fiske rejects the notion of the cultural dupe as 'the victim of the system', and instead stresses 'how people cope with the system' and how they employ their resourcefulness and creativity to 'make do with what is available' (162, 105, 5). He seeks to unpack the term 'consumer' and reveal the productivity involved in the act of consumption, advocating 'an entirely different kind of production called "consumption"' that uses 'the products of capitalism [as] the raw materials, the primary resources of popular culture' (142). In effect, Fiske makes a case for 'active consumption' or the 'semiotic activity' of the consumer who acts as a 'poacher, encroaching on the terrain of the cultural landowner . . . and stealing what he or she wants without being caught and subjected to the laws of the land' (142, 143). In Fiske's eyes, the consumer's raids or *guerrilla tactics* point towards the progressive

political potential of popular culture that finds its expression on the micro-political level: 'the politics of popular culture is micropolitics, for that is where it can play the greater part in the tactics of everyday life' (56). The politics of popular culture takes as its object the individual's resistances and evasions in the minutiae of everyday life through which she or he constructs meanings and creates a sense of identity.

30. In his exploration of popular culture, Fiske focuses on 'those moments where hegemony fails, where ideology is weaker than resistance, where social control is met by indiscipline' (177).

31. The concept of articulation refers to the process of 'establishing a relation among elements such that their identity is modified as a result of the articula-tory practice' (Ang 122). Stuart Hall develops the theory of articulation in order to account for the double way in which texts work in popular culture: a text-centred way and a reader-centred way. John Fiske summarises the argument: 'to *articulate* has two meanings – one is to speak or utter (the text-centered meaning) and the other is to form a flexible link with, to be hinged with (the reader-centered meaning in which the text is flexibly linked with the reader's social situation)' (146). The theory of articulation maintains a balance between seeing the text as a producer of meaning and seeing it as a cultural resource, open to a range of creative uses. The notion of articulation discusses the ways in which 'meaning is a social production, a practice' that arises from 'a struggle to articulate, disarticulate and rearticulate cultural texts and practices for particular ideologies, particular politics' (Storey 128–9). In other words, no articulation is ever definitive or absolute but it is always unfinished and subject to continual re-articulation and reproduction. This dynamic process of fixing and fitting together is never final or total but always 'inexorably contextual' (Ang 122).

32. Following Steven Best's and Douglas Kellner's *Postmodern Theory* (1991), we interpret poststructuralism as a subset of a broader range of theoreti-cal, cultural and social tendencies that constitute postmodern discourses. Poststructuralism forms part of the matrix of postmodern theory and can be described as 'a critique of modern theory and a production of new models of thought, writing, and subjectivity, some of which are taken up by postmodern theory' (25). Indeed, 'postmodern theory appropriates the poststructuralist critique of modern thought, radicalizes it, and extends it to new theoretical fields' (25–6).

33. Patricia Waugh writes that the first phase of post-1960s feminism was charac-terised by a desire to experience a 'whole', 'unitary' or 'essential' subjectivity. In fact, 'if women have traditionally been positioned in terms of "otherness", then the desire to become subjects . . . is likely to be stronger than the desire to deconstruct, decentre, or fragment subjectivity' (*Feminine Fictions* 12). Feminism passed through 'a *necessary* stage' of pursuing a unitary essential self in order that women 'might fully understand the historical and social construction of gender and identity':

> Certainly, for women in the 1960s and early 1970s, 'unity' rather than dispersal seemed
> to offer more hope for political change. To believe that there might be a 'natural'
> or 'true' self which may be discovered through lifting the misrepresentations of an
> oppressive social system is to provide nurturance and fuel for revolutionary hope and
> practice. (13)

Feminist thinkers thus endeavoured throughout the 1960s and 1970s to produce
expansive social theories that could explain the basis for male/female inequalities. In the process, they often reified female differences through essentialist
(or universal) categories that excluded the determinants of race, class or sexual
preference.

34. Fredric Jameson articulates this idea when he explains that 'the luxury of the
    old-fashioned ideological critique . . . becomes unavailable' as 'distance in general
    (including "critical distance" in particular) has very precisely been abolished in the
    new space of postmodernism' ('Postmodernism, or The Cultural Logic of Late
    Capitalism' 85, 87). Accordingly, the position of 'the cultural critic and moralist'
    has to be interrogated as we come to realise that 'we . . . are all somehow secretly
    disarmed and reabsorbed by a system of which . . . [we] might well be considered
    a part, since . . . [we] can achieve no distance from it' (85, 87).

35. As Toril Moi writes, 'it still remains politically essential for feminists to defend
    women as women in order to counteract the patriarchal oppression that precisely
    despises women as women' (quoted in Waugh, *Feminine Fictions* 25).

36. Christine di Stefano expresses similar doubts concerning the supposedly
    destructive encounter of feminism and postmodernism, stating that 'the post-
    modernist project, if seriously adopted by feminists, would make any semblance
    of a feminist politics impossible' (quoted in Cacoullos 92–3).

37. According to di Stefano, the 'postfeminist tendency' is a problematic side-effect
    of feminist postrationalism or postmodernism. In her discussion of the debates
    on gender differences, she distinguishes three strategic forms for posing the
    relationship between contemporary Western feminism and the Enlightenment
    legacy of humanistic rationalism: (1) feminist rationalism, (2) feminine anti-
    rationalism and (3) feminist postrationalism. (1) Feminist rationalism uses a
    minimalist notion of gender difference and enables a critique of sexism as an
    irrational and hence illegitimate set of beliefs and practices. (2) Feminine anti-
    rationalism, committed to a stronger version of difference, levels its protest
    against the rational/masculine and irrational/feminine construct and attempts
    to revalorise, rather than to overcome, traditional feminine experience. Di
    Stefano criticises both rationalist and anti-rationalist frameworks: With regard
    to rationalism, equality is constituted within a set of terms that disparage things
    female or feminine. '*She*' dissolves into '*he*' as gender differences are collapsed
    into the (masculine) figure of Everyman. Anti-rationalism, on the other hand,
    attempts to revalorise the feminine but fails to criticise it, sliding into anti-femi-
    nism. (3) Feminist postrationalism seems to provide the only way out as it rejects
    the terms and strategies of the previous two stances and argues that feminism

must initiate a break with the rationalist paradigm. Eschewing a position either within or outside of the rationalist framework – for or against difference – postrationalism attempts to transcend the discourse of rationalism and to offer new, decentred narratives of opposition. Hence, difference is simultaneously upheld and deconstructed as a proliferation of differences is counterposed to the singular difference of gender. While this strategy is theoretically appealing, di Stefano notes that it is also complex and unnerving, inhabiting a constantly shifting ground of emerging and dissolving differences. With postrationalism, '*she*' dissolves into a perplexing plurality of differences, none of which can be theoretically or politically privileged over others.

38. In Bordo's words, 'any attempt to do justice to heterogeneity . . . devours its own tail. For the appreciation of difference requires the acknowledgement of some point beyond which the dancer cannot go. If she were able to go everywhere, there would be no difference, nothing that eludes' (228).

39. The notions of postfeminist individualism and anti-essentialism resurface in popular, academic and political investigations of postfeminism, which highlight the plurality and contradictions inherent in contemporary Western societies. The ideas and beliefs conglomerated under the heading of postfeminism are characterised by an anti-universalist stance that betrays an awareness of the limitations of identity politics. For example, third wave feminism heralds the 'return to the personal' whereas power feminism and Girl Power embrace a 'theory of self-worth' and a vision of self-help (Siegel, 'The Legacy' 51; hooks, 'Dissident Heat' 63). Similarly, academic versions of postfeminism reject the category of 'woman' altogether by challenging and deconstructing the humanist subject, who is no longer conceptualised as a fixed entity, a manifestation of essence. Viewed as a whole, the different facets of postfeminism question the possibility of a singular and coherent identity, a common ground from which to construct a collective politics and criticism. Popular postfeminism's return to the 'I' and academic postfeminism's deconstruction of the universal subject thus undermine the assumption that there is a continuous field of experience shared by all – women, men and feminists alike.

40. In *The Feminist Bestseller* (2005), Imelda Whelehan charts the transformations and developments that feminism has undergone since its second wave heyday, whereby from the mid-1970s onwards 'there was a gradual shift away from radicalism and activism' (159). As Whelehan notes, certainly by the 1980s, 'there could no longer be any belief that feminism spoke for all women . . . that moment of radical utopianism had passed where the problems that united women coming out of a male-dominated political framework seemed larger and more urgent than those which spoke to other aspects of a woman's identity' (160–1).

41. The second wave slogan 'the personal is political' describes women's relation to patriarchy and encapsulates the idea that women's personal, individual problems can be traced to their political living in a male-dominated and male-defined society. The adage sums up the way in which second wave feminism strove not just to extend the range of social opportunities open to women, but also,

through intervention within the spheres of reproduction, sexuality and cultural representation, to change their domestic and private lives.

42. Tellingly, in the best-selling *Fire with Fire: The New Female Power and How It Will Change the 21st Century* (1993), Naomi Wolf urges her reader 'to claim her individual voice rather than merging her voice in a collective identity', reminding her that 'making social change does not contradict the principle that girls just want to have fun' (136, 138). Wolf adopts a feminist terminology but discards the more radical aspects of the second wave centred in sexual politics and a profound awareness of power differences between the sexes at all levels and in all arenas. Feminist commentators deplore the fact that this personalised stance results in a postfeminist movement that can 'embrace everyone, since it has no overt political tenets' (hooks, *Outlaw Culture* 98). The resort to individualism produces outstanding models of personal accomplishment but cannot engender a programme for change in the position of women as a group. As Susan Douglas notes:

> instead of group action, we got escapist solitude. Instead of solidarity, we got female competition over men. And, most important, instead of seeing personal disappointments, frustrations and failures as symptoms of an inequitable and patriarchal society, we saw these . . . as personal failures, for which we should blame ourselves. (265)

43. Dana Cloud explains that 'a token is a cultural construction of a successful persona who metonymically represents a larger cultural grouping': 'in popular culture . . . a token can be defined as a persona who is constructed from the character and life of a member of a subordinated group, and then celebrated, authorized to speak as proof that the society at large does not discriminate against members of that group' (122–3).

44. Geraldine Harris refers to Derrida in order to explain that the politics of undecidability 'does not mean that decisions cannot or should not be made' but highlights 'the process of negotiation by which they are and *must* be made' (180; emphasis in original). As Derrida points out, undecidability is always a 'determinate oscillation between possibilities, possibilities which themselves are highly determined in strictly defined situations' (148). Thus, the politics of undecidability does not offer absolution from the responsibility of making decisions, but it accepts that these cannot be made by applying a pre-existing law.

1

Backlash and New Traditionalism

In this chapter we examine one of the key strands of postfeminism, a largely pessimistic position that equates postfeminism with an anti-feminist and media-driven backlash characterised by a rejection of feminist goals and an attempt to turn the clock back to pre-feminist times. Emerging at the close of Reaganite America and Thatcherite Britain, such approaches interpret postfeminism as primarily a polemical tool with limited critical and analytical value. Famously discussed by the American journalist Susan Faludi in her 1992 bestseller, the backlash is seen to be fuelled by an entirely hostile media that blames feminism for a series of female illnesses and troubles, from burnout and infertility to depression and mental health problems. Feminism is depicted as 'women's own worst enemy' and they are admonished that they cannot 'have it all' and must choose between private and public life, home and career (Faludi, *Backlash* 2). While backlash fears are pervasive in many popular narratives and representations of women – including Bridget Jones's desperate search for 'Mr Right', narrated in her fictional diaries – the back-lash scenario has been most vividly depicted in the 1987 film *Fatal Attraction*, which stages the dichotomy between the unmarried businesswoman and her apparent opposite, the homemaking wife, and reaffirms the patriarchal family by eliminating the single woman.

Related to the backlash is the notion of 'new traditionalism', which articulates a vision of the home as women's sanctuary from the stresses of their working lives. The new traditionalist discourse centralises and idealises women's apparently fully knowledgeable choice to abstain from paid work in favour of hearth and family. The domestic sphere is rebranded as a domain of female autonomy and independence, far removed from its previous connotations of toil and confinement – a view advanced by mostly second wave critiques of domesticity. In particular, the female homemaker is no longer portrayed as a political prisoner held captive in what Betty Friedan called, in her 1963 landmark text *The Feminine Mystique*, the 'comfortable concentration camp' of the family. Instead, home becomes the site of 'mystique chic' – 'an illusory refuge from the drudgery of the corporate workplace' (Kingston 66). We will analyse late twentieth- and twenty-first-century versions of domesticity through case studies on the 1987 film *Baby Boom* and the television series *Desperate Housewives* (2004–).

FEMINISM AND THE BACKLASH

Throughout the twentieth century and into the early twenty-first, the feminist movement has been troubled by the fear of backlash. Indeed, some feminist critics argue that a period of female/feminist advancement is almost invariably accompanied by a following stage of backlash – a reverse movement that is a reaction to, or a counterassault on, feminism. This was certainly the case in the 1950s and early 1960s when, after the tumultuous years of the Second World War had opened millions of jobs to women to support the war effort, there was a postwar backlash that saw industry, government and media converge to force a female retreat from the public sphere. During the 1950s, women (and men) were encouraged to adopt more conservative positions and roles as advertisers reversed their wartime message (that women could simultaneously work and enjoy a family life) and claimed that women must choose the home while men were meant to go out to work. Home was once again regarded as the proper haven for women and feminism was pushed further out of women's lives.

This mid-twentieth-century backlash acted as an impetus for the emergence of second wave feminism in the late 1960s and 1970s (the 'first wave' of feminism having come to an end before the war and culminated with women's suffrage in the 1920s in the United States and the UK). Second wave feminism attacked the 'cult of the housewife', illustrated for example by popular television programmes such as the 1960s American sitcom *I Dream of Jeannie*, in which a female genie (played by Barbara Eden) confined to living in a bottle becomes the servant (and later wife) of an American astronaut. Betty Friedan's *The Feminine Mystique* (1963) was instrumental in the exposure of the 'happy housewife' myth (what she also termed 'the problem that has no name'). Friedan described the housewife as the epitome of female non-identity and passivity, and was adamant that the very condition of being a housewife has a progressively dehumanising effect on women: 'I am convinced', Friedan writes, 'there is something about the housewife state itself that is dangerous. In a sense that is not as far-fetched as it sounds, the women who "adjust" as housewives . . . are in as much danger as the millions who walked to their own death in the concentration camps' (264–5). Friedan, a journalist and founder of NOW (National Organisation for Women), admitted that she herself had helped to create this image: 'I have watched American women for fifteen years try to conform to it. But I can no longer deny my own knowledge of its terrible implications. It is not a harmless image . . . what happens when women try to live according to an image that makes them deny their minds?' (quoted in Whelehan, *Feminist Bestseller* 33). Friedan's book tackled many of the issues that were to characterise much of second wave politics in the latter part of the 1960s. The second wave encouraged women to develop an understanding of their subjugated status in a patriarchal society and embark on a 'consciousness-raising' journey, through dedicated sessions in women-only discussion groups, public acts and demonstrations, and other forms of collective campaigning.

As a number of critics have suggested, the heady, politically charged days of the second wave came to an end by the late 1970s and certainly the 1980s, when the media fostered an anti-feminist backlash that worked to revoke the gains made by the feminist movement (see Whelehan, *Feminist Bestseller*). The 1980s are generally seen as a difficult decade for feminism, in terms of popular representations as well as inner divisions that – although present from the beginning of the second wave – were causing rifts within the women's movement and fracturing the communal ideal of sisterhood. Nancy Whittier describes 'the Eighties' as a 'grim symbol of antifeminism' and 'a tough period of retrenchment': 'the 1980s contained massive opposition and setbacks for feminism that drove longtime activists out of social movement organisations and into more individual forms of agitation. "Feminism" became a dirty word in many circles' (191, 194). In effect, feminism lost much of its core position and identity as it was pulled in two directions by internal and external forces: on the one hand, feminists were confronted with a wider range of issues, which meant that more attention had to be paid to diversity and differences among women, particularly in terms of racism, classism and heterosexism. As Whittier summarises, 'in short, feminist collective identity, or how participants understood what it meant to be a feminist, changed in the 1980s', with the result that '"[f]eminist" came to mean something quite different by 1990 than it had meant in the 1970s' (196, 191). On the other hand, feminism also became less tangible and distinct in the ways that it was perceived from without. Feminism lost much of its outsider status as many feminist activists entered more institutionalised professions in the 1980s and feminist ideas of emancipation and empowerment were appropriated and adopted by popular culture (see Whittier 204–11).

This is not to say that the second wave's demise and the 1980s backlash were caused solely by internal fractures and divisions. On the contrary, by the time Margaret Thatcher was voted into power in the UK in 1979, feminism was facing a very different political climate and profound changes in the social, economic and cultural environments of Britain and the US. In her bestselling book *Backlash: The Undeclared War against Women* (1992), the American journalist Susan Faludi locates a backlash against feminism in 1980s politics and media. As she explains, the 1980s saw 'a powerful counter-assault on women's rights, a backlash, an attempt to retract the handful of small and hard-won victories that the feminist movement did manage to win for women' (12). The thesis originated in the United States, with the ascendancy of the 'New Right' and a shift in a more conservative direction that was to typify the Reagan era. The backlash soon made its way into media discourses that, Faludi maintains, work hand in hand with a right-wing political ideology to launch an attack on the core beliefs and politics of the women's movement and to re-articulate conventional versions of femininity and domesticity. Faludi outlines the backlash tenets that were propagated by a range of media texts in the 1980s and early 1990s and that are based on the assumption that female identity is troubled and tormented:

> Professional women are suffering 'burnout' and succumbing to an 'infertility epidemic'. Single women are grieving from a 'man short-age' . . . Childless women are 'depressed and confused' and their ranks are swelling . . . Unwed women are 'hysterical' and crumbling under a 'profound crisis of confidence' . . . High powered career women are stricken with unprecedented outbreaks of 'stress-induced disorders' . . . Independent women's loneliness represents 'a major mental health problem today'. (1–2)

As Faludi explains, these so-called female crises have been laid at the door of the feminist movement, which has supposedly 'gone too far', provid-ing women with more independence and choice than they can handle and thereby wrecking their relationships with men (xiii). Feminism is said to be responsible for 'the sad plight of millions of unhappy and unsatisfied women' who, thinking they could combine career and family, have jeop-ardised an essential part of their femaleness (Walters, *Material Girls* 119). Suzanna Danuta Walters summarises the backlash argument whereby femi-nism 'promised more than it put out': 'we thought we wanted equality, but realize instead that we cannot have it all' (121). Attempting to live up to an ambitious 'Superwoman' image, working women have been positioned in a no-win situation as they are either condemned to a 'double-day/second-shift' existence or recognise that their professional success has come at the cost of relationships and marriage (122). Backlash propaganda aims to dichotomise women's private and public, feminine and feminist aspirations, splitting their 'lives into half-lives' (Faludi, *Backlash* 491). Moreover, the backlash not only warns women that they cannot 'have it all' and must choose between home and career, but also makes the choice for them by promoting wedded life and domesticity as a full and fulfilled existence. In other words, women are told that 'if they gave up the unnatural struggle for self-determination, they could regain their natural femininity' (490).

Faludi directly links the conservative 1980s backlash to, in her opinion, an equally retrograde postfeminism that lures women into an apathetic silence and inaction: 'Just when record numbers of younger women were support-ing feminist goals in the mid-1980s . . . and a majority of all women were calling themselves feminists, the media declared that "post-feminism" was the new story – complete with a younger generation who supposedly reviled the women's movement' (14). In her eyes, postfeminism does not refer to a changed social context in which 'women have arrived at equal justice . . . but [means] simply that they themselves are beyond even pretending to care. It is an indifference that may, finally, deal the most devastating blow to women's rights' (95). She is adamant that the backlash/postfeminism can be attributed to an entirely hostile media that acts as an anti-feminist force to damage and undermine the women's movement and slander it as 'women's own worst enemy' (2). In particular, single professional women are targeted by the popular press and pilloried for their unmarried state and the error of their independent ways. Working single women are cautioned that, unless they hurry and change their overly liberated lives, they are going to end up loveless and manless as 'single women are "more likely to be killed by a ter-rorist" than marry' (124). In fact, 'to be unwed and female' comes to be seen as an 'illness with only one known cure: marriage' – tellingly, these backlash fears continue to circulate in popular culture well into the 1990s when thirty-something Singleton Bridget Jones is told by her 'Smug Married' friends that she is an 'old girl' whose 'time's running out' and biological clock is ticking away (Faludi, *Backlash* 122; Fielding, *Bridget Jones's Diary* 40–1). Unattached career women are pathologised and defined as abject and deficient, selfish and emotionally stunted, and ultimately regretful about neglecting their essential roles as wives and mothers. As Faludi observes, single women are taught to see that 'what they think is a problem with the man is really something inside them', and therefore that it can only be dealt with through individual, rather than collective, responsibility (*Backlash* 376). Backlash texts thus try to con-vince their readers/viewers of the impossibility and undesirability of being

Superwomen as, in the attempt to juggle job and family, they jeopardise their feminine appeal and sign up to an exhausting existence filled with pain and guilt. The stigmatisation of working womanhood is particularly deprecatory in the case of single women who dare to diverge from homely femininity in search of a career. In the most one-dimensional backlash scenarios, the unattached and childless professional woman is portrayed as a figure of evil and a neurotic psychopath, designed to deter women from seeking public success and neglecting their feminine duties.

CASE STUDY: *FATAL ATTRACTION* (1987)

The 1980s backlash and the fears associated with it have been vividly portrayed in the now classic film *Fatal Attraction*, which condemns the figure of the liberated and unmarried businesswoman. The film's villain, Alex Forrest (Glenn Close), embodies all that counters the dominant patriarchal structure: she is an independent career woman and an autonomous free spirit, maintaining a large apartment in Manhattan's meat-packing district and living out her sexuality and her emotions aggressively and excessively. Alex knowingly enters into a weekend affair with married lawyer Dan Gallagher (Michael Douglas) but then refuses to obey 'the rules', overstepping her assigned patriarchal position as the temptress/mistress and attempting to 'have it all'. Pregnant with Dan's child, she is resolute that she will not be 'ignored' or treated 'like some slut'. However, the film forcefully undercuts the single woman's position and desires by depicting Alex as a madwoman and specifically a 'bunny-boiler' who, having been spurned by her lover, is determined to have her revenge and will not stop at anything, even boiling a pet – the gruesome image of Dan's daughter's favourite rabbit simmering in a pot upon the stove has proven so powerful and influential as to have become part of our cultural knowledge/language, deserving its own entry in the *Oxford English Dictionary*. Following her vicious killing of an innocent animal, Alex came to be seen by moviegoers and journalists as an embodiment of evil, with one tabloid even dubbing Glenn Close's character the 'MOST HATED WOMAN IN AMERICA'. The film works to trivialise Alex's anger by focusing on her increasingly psychotic behaviour, and to obscure Dan's paternal duties by siding overwhelmingly with him and favouring his life inside the established family unit.

In fact, *Fatal Attraction* enacts a well-established dichotomy between what the screenwriter James Dearden calls 'the Dark Woman and the Light Woman', or in this case, the raving single woman and the dutiful wife, the sexualised temptress and the good mother (quoted in Faludi, *Backlash* 149). Any overlap or similarity between Alex and Beth Gallagher (Anne Archer) is denied, and ultimately it is the wife's responsibility to act as the final arbiter of familial justice and destroy her unmarried nemesis. Confirming Bromley and Hewitt's assertion that 'in the 1980s the single career woman must be killed in order to preserve the sanctity of the family', Beth defeats her arch-enemy in a bloody finale and shoots the she-monster Alex has become in her intrusive and violent quest to find an avenue into Dan's life (23). The brutal killing in the film's final scenes is depicted as a justified act of self-defence and an overdue punishment for the mad seductress who unlawfully tries to enter the family entity. The backlash thus succeeds in firmly relegating women to their conventional gender roles as wives/mothers and instructing them that their desire for a place outside the home could lead to a variety of dire personal consequences and may even result in death. As Susan Faludi concludes, in 1980s cinema 'there's only room for one woman at a time' (*Backlash* 158).

NEW TRADITIONALISM

When *Cosmopolitan* magazine declared in its June 2000 issue that young twenty-something women had become the new 'housewife wannabes', the relationship between domesticity and female/feminist emancipation seemed to have been reversed (Dutton). While for the last century women had struggled to uncover and challenge the subjugation inherent in their domestic subject positions, now it appeared that they were keen to re-embrace the title of housewife and re-experience the joys of a 'new femininity'. Domesticity suddenly became a buzzword, with housewives, fictional and real, emerging in all areas of society and popular culture: from Nigella Lawson whipping up tasty treats on TV (and simultaneously managing to look infinitely glamorous) to Brenda Barnes famously giving up her job as president of Pepsi-Cola North America to spend more time with her three children, there was no denying that domesticity was re-emerging as a distinct twenty-first-century site and topic for critical investigation.

Feminist critics in particular have been wary of this return to domesticity/ femininity and they have interpreted it as an inherent part of the backlash against feminism. According to Faludi, the 'back-to-the-home movement' has to be recognised as the malicious creation of the advertising industry and, in turn, 'a recycled version of the Victorian fantasy that a new "cult of domesticity" was bringing droves of women home' (*Backlash* 77). The backlash tries to convince women of their need to scale back their professionalism and rekindle their interest in romance and marriage. In Elspeth Probyn's words, this marks the agenda of a 'new traditionalism' that articulates and naturalises a 'vision of the home to which women have "freely" chosen to return' as a site of fulfilment (149). The new traditionalist stance centralises a woman's 'choice' to retreat from the public sphere and abstain from paid work in favour of family values. Severing its previous associations with drudgery and confinement, the domestic sphere is redefined and resignified as a domain of female autonomy and independence. Many critics are concerned that this return to the domestic realm conceals a political assault on women's rights, their re-imprisonment in the home and regression to a stance of feminine passivity. As Faludi explains, new traditionalism encourages women to withdraw into the domestic shell and adopt the 'cultural myth of cocooning' that 'maps the road back from the feminist journey': whereas feminism can be discussed in terms of 'the attempt of women to grow up', cocooning's 'infantile imagery' promotes 'a retreat from female adulthood' and urges women to assume a 'false feminine vision' that circles around home and family (*Backlash* 77–8).

In *The Meaning of Wife* (2004), Anne Kingston also comments on the romanticisation of domesticity that lures late twentieth-century housewives into a 'domestic nirvana' and a dream of 'mystique chic':

> Increasingly, housework – an endeavour reviled for decades as drudgery, as the source of women's psychiatric problems, as the very root of female oppression – was presented as both fashionable and, even more perversely, a surefire route to female satisfaction. Call it mystique chic. Call it the ultimate backlash to *The Feminine Mystique*. (65)

Kingston explores how in a chiastic reversal of the home/work dichotomy, domesticity has been transformed into an idyllic space of personal satisfaction and freedom from the shackles of working life. According to the rhetoric of 'mystique chic', the workplace has switched places with the homefront as the source of female frustration, and now the corporation is presented as the same prison for women that the 1960s suburban home had once been. Whereas work outside the home is now an unavoidable economic necessity for most women, 'homework' has become the sanctuary of a few privileged, financially secure housewives – paradoxically, as Kingston points out, the domestic dream is perpetuated by a number of 'professional' housewives, like 'the voluptuous, cashmere-encased' British 'domestic goddess' Nigella Lawson and the 'hard–core careerist' and 'mass-media entrepreneur' Martha Stewart, who sell domesticity to women viewers/consumers. Kingston maintains that women's re-embrace of domesticity – and retreat from the workplace – is at best a nostalgic illusion and at worst a ruse to return women to 'the same kind of idealized domesticity that, ironically, had given rise to the twentieth-century feminist movement in the first place' (102).

More recently, critics have started to analyse the revival of domesticity in the late twentieth and twenty-first century not just in relation to a conservative and reactionary move – such as the notions of backlash and new traditionalism imply – and they have sought less prescriptive and more flexible ways to interpret postfeminist domesticity and the figure of the housewife. In their introduction to *Feminism, Domesticity and Popular Culture* (2009), Stacy Gillis and Joanne Hollows describe how in the past, the housewife has often operated as 'the feminist's "other"', on the basis of the idea that 'an investment in the domestic [is] antithetical to the ideals of feminism' (1–2). Arguing against 'a monolithic and homogeneous perspective on the relationships between feminism, domesticity and popular culture', Gillis and Hollows want to open up discussions about 'these contentious, thorny and occasionally pleasurable relationships' in order to answer the question of 'how feminism might conceptualize domesticity in different ways' (3, 9). Elsewhere, Hollows has also examined how a 'downshifting narrative' functions in contemporary literature and cinema, promising 'alternative versions of "the good life" in which a new hybrid form of domestic femininity might emerge between the feminist and the housewife' – Sophie Kinsella's bestselling *The Undomestic Goddess* (2005) and the 1987 film *Baby Boom* are representative examples of the kind of narratives in which a female protagonist gives up the joys and professional rewards of city living to retreat to the country in search of the 'freedom' of domesticity (Hollows, 'Can I Go Home Yet?' 109). In the downshifting narrative, urban femininities are abandoned in favour of rural ones and a 'work–life balance' is seen to be available through geographic relocation (108). Hollows acknowledges the problems and limitations of this proposed lifestyle change, which is not readily available to everyone, involving a 'profoundly classed' and 'thoroughly commodified' narrative that centres on 'choices for those who inhabit specific middle-class femininities' (110–11). However, she also emphasises that – while 'it would be very easy to read the key downshifting narrative as a classic backlash tale', depicting what could be seen as women's 'failure of nerve' to smash the glass ceiling – downshifting can also be interpreted as 'an opportunity to interrogate the very notion of "having it all"' (107).

In her latest work on 'postfemininities', Stéphanie Genz takes this idea further by discussing the paradoxes of contemporary postfeminist femininities that reference both traditional narratives of feminine passivity and more progressive scripts of feminine agency. As Genz writes, 'postfeminism offers a new mode of conceptualising the domestic as a contested space of female subjectivity where women/feminists actively grapple with opposing cultural constructions of the housewife' ('I Am Not a Housewife, but . . .' 49–50). In particular, she continues, 'a postfeminist lens allows us to transcend a critical impasse (trapped by a dualistic logic) and re-interpret the homemaker as a polysemic character caught in a struggle between tradition and modernity, past and present' (50). In effect, depictions of twenty-first-century housewives – such as in Allison Pearson's novel *I Don't Know How She Does It* (2002) or the television series *Desperate Housewives* (2004–) – undermine static constructions of the housewife and, instead, highlight the contradictions inherent in modern-day femininity/domesticity and its complicated interactions with feminism and postfeminism. In Genz's words, domestic femininity comes to be seen as 'a site of undecidability, of meaning in question' whereby 'the figure of the housewife is inscribed with multifarious significations, vacillating between patriarchal scripts of enforced domesticity and postfeminist re-appropriations that acknowledge agency and self-determination' (50).

CASE STUDY: *BABY BOOM* (1987)

Baby Boom has often been cited as representative of 'new traditionalism' and the backlash idea that, as Susan Faludi points out, 'babies and business don't mix' (*Backlash* 159). The film's main protagonist, high-flying Manhattan career woman J.C. Wiatt (Diane Keaton), is converted to the joys of motherhood after she 'inherits' a toddler from a distant relative. Initially characterised by her business panache and single-minded pursuit of her professional ambitions – tellingly, J.C. is also known among her colleagues as the 'Tiger Lady' – she tries to combine motherhood with a high-powered job in the city but soon comes to realise that she must choose between 'the corner office' and 'the cradle' (Faludi, *Backlash* 159). It appears that, as her boss (Sam Wanamaker) tells her, caring for a child has made J.C. 'lose her concentration' and 'go soft'. In a 'downshifting' move, she quickly retreats to the country, where, after an initial phase of boredom, she enters into a fulfilling relationship with the local vet and even founds a baby-food empire. At the end of the film, when J.C. is presented with the possibility of reclaiming her identity as a savvy businesswoman – her former associates are bidding to buy her new company in a multimillion-dollar deal – she turns down the offer and with it, her previous way of life and objectives: 'I'm not the Tiger Lady anymore . . . I don't want to make . . . sacrifices and the bottom line is nobody should have to.'

In her discussion of the film, Faludi criticises *Baby Boom* for its reductive, backlash-inspired emphasis on women's private matters and family relationships at the expense of public, professional achievements, culminating in 'a dewy-eyed reverie about the joys of rural living' (*Backlash* 161). Similarly, Walters argues that Diane Keaton's character in *Baby Boom* 'lets us all know the deep dissatisfaction of women at work and lays bare the budding mama behind every gleaming corporate desk' (*Material Girls* 125). More recent examinations, on the other hand, highlight the film's attempt to find a compromise between domesticity and professionalism. As Joanne Hollows suggests, while *Baby Boom* has frequently been discussed as one of the 'quintessential backlash texts', 'by now it is beginning to look like it captures an emergent structure of feeling', considering 'what emerges between the feminist and the housewife' ('Can I Go Home Yet?' 105).

CASE STUDY: *DESPERATE HOUSEWIVES* (2004–)

When *Desperate Housewives* first aired in 2004 in the United States and the UK, the show became an instant success and pop culture phenomenon on both sides of the Atlantic, with even First Lady Laura Bush confessing to being a huge fan of the series. Blending a number of generic forms and conventions – including soap opera, murder mystery, family drama and romantic comedy – the series' focus is on the suburban lives of five women – Susan Mayer, a divorced single parent; domestic goddess Bree Van de Kamp; working mother Lynette Scavo; adulterous ex-model Gabrielle Solis; and serial divorcee Edie Britt. While its title seems to conjure up visions of the pre-feminist housewife – whose 'desperate' state encouraged second wave feminists like Betty Friedan to unmask the 1950s American home as a 'comfortable concentration camp' – *Desperate Housewives* has been credited with catching the twenty-first-century female zeitgeist, with its characters and plots discussed in wider culture and the main actresses featured on the covers of glossy magazines and fronting high-profile advertising campaigns. The premise of the series revolves around the suicide of a seemingly happy housewife, Mary Alice Young, who becomes the show's omniscient narrator from beyond the grave, commenting on the trials and tribulations of her neighbours on Wisteria Lane. As the series' creator Marc Cherry – who, as critics never fail to mention, is (seemingly paradoxically) both homosexual and a Republican – emphasises, the concept of *Desperate Housewives* was inspired by his own mother and reflects the desperation of women who have chosen to live in the suburbs but then realise that suburban life is not as they imagined. His reasoning on the show as a 'post-post-feminist take' captures the ambivalence of the postfeminist age: 'The women's movement said "Let's get the gals out working." Next the women realised you can't have it all. Most of the time you have to make a choice. What I'm doing is having women make the choice to live in the suburbs, but that things aren't going well at all' (quoted in McCabe and Akass 9).

The storylines are characteristically diverse, ranging from adultery and the troubles of combining motherhood with a high-flying career to murder, teenage pregnancy and cancer in the later seasons. The series has been

discussed as the antithesis of the tame 1960s suburbia portrayed in programmes such as *Bewitched!*, exposing the discontent, lust and betrayal behind
the picket fences of American suburban life. The show's feminist credentials
have also been the subject of considerable debate: Alessandra Stanley for
example is perturbed by what she interprets as a turning back of the clock to
a 'pre-Betty Friedan America' (E1), while Ashley Sayeau expresses a similar
sense of disappointment with the show's 'faux feminism', 'that subtle, yet
increasingly pervasive brand of conservative thought that casts itself as deeply
concerned with the frustrations of modern women, but can ultimately offer
no alternatives except those of a traditional stripe' (44). By contrast, other
critics have focused on *Desperate Housewives'* subversion of domesticity and
sexual norms *from within*. As Samuel Chambers suggests, the series raises
a number of controversial questions concerning the politics of gender and
sexuality, airing, for example, one of the very few kisses between two males
on network TV – Andrew Van de Kamp (Bree's son) and his friend Justin –
or displaying Rex Van de Kamp's taste for S/M role-playing ('Desperately
Straight' 73). Chambers argues that 'challenging the norm from the centre
has the potential to wield a much greater force than questioning the norm
from the margins', leading him to the 'counter-intuitive but nevertheless
powerful conclusion that *Desperate Housewives* motivates a significant cultural
politics, subversive of heteronormativity' (72–3). Anna Marie Bautista also
highlights the transgressive possibilities of the series, which subverts notions
of domestic bliss and undermines cultural myths of the 'happy housewife',
highlighting instead the contemporary homemaker's contradictory social and
cultural position. Ultimately, as Janet McCabe and Kim Akass suggest, how
best to understand *Desperate Housewives* remains 'enthralling and puzzling,
mesmerising and frustrating, in equal measure', as this 'prime-time soap bub-
bling with devilishly dark humour' is set to continue to divide its audience
and critics (14).

BEYOND THE BACKLASH

While for cultural commentators such as Susan Faludi, postfeminism is
equivalent to a media-driven backlash – and both are synonymous with a
retrogressive attack on feminism – other critics have complicated the notion
of 'backlash' and, associated with this, the view of popular culture as necessarily conservative and retrograde. Myra Macdonald, for example, observes
that 'we need to recognize the part we all play in keeping mythologies and
ideologies alive. This gets obliterated in conspiracy-theory accounts that see
the media as bastions of male privilege, spurred on by the mission of keeping
feminism at bay' (11). More recently, Ann Braithwaite has argued for a more

expanded and nuanced understanding of the backlash (and postfeminism) that goes beyond 'a simple anti-feminism . . . of being against women's rights' (22). According to Braithwaite, the above interpretation of the backlash offers a delimited understanding of feminism, femininity and popular culture that overlooks their diverse relationships and engagements with one another. As she writes, 'the politics of backlash thus become a politics of rejection' and 'a kind of shorthand for a distinction between a more "authentic" feminism on the one hand, and a suspect, tainted, and usually commercialized rendition of feminism on the other' (26). Rather than focusing on how the backlash (re)acts against feminism, Braithwaite suggests that one might alternatively take into account 'how much something about feminism has instead saturated pop culture, becoming part of the accepted, "naturalized", social formation' (19). By revisiting terms (like 'backlash') that seemingly foreclose different, more productive meanings, Braithwaite seeks to open up the possibility of 'seeing how they in fact articulate continuities in feminist thinking and the current status of feminism throughout popular culture' (20). In many ways, this book is motivated by a similar concern for a more complex understanding of postfeminism that highlights the breadth of feminist issues and the contradictions inherent in a twenty-first-century 'post-ing' of feminism.

RECOMMENDED FURTHER READING

Braithwaite, Ann. 'Politics and/of Backlash.' *Journal of International Women's Studies* 5.5 (2004): 18–33.

Genz, Stéphanie. '"I Am Not a Housewife, but . . . ": Postfeminism and the Revival of Domesticity.' In *Feminism, Domesticity and Popular Culture*. Eds Stacy Gillis and Joanne Hollows. New York and London: Routledge, 2009. 49–62.

Gillis, Stacey, and Joanne Hollows, eds. *Feminism, Domesticity and Popular Culture*. Abingdon and New York: Routledge, 2009.

Probyn, Elspeth. 'New Traditionalism and Post-Feminism: TV Does the Home.' *Screen* 31.2 (1990): 147–59.

2

New Feminism: Victim vs. Power

OVERVIEW

In this chapter we examine the notion of 'new feminism', prominent in the 1990s, that focuses on a younger generation of women who express their desire to fashion new styles of feminism. Marked by an interest in 'power feminists' – including a revisionist reading of Margaret Thatcher as a free market feminist – new feminism provides an optimistic and celebratory picture of a confident, assertive group of young women who are reporting high levels of achievement and success across private and public sectors. 'New feminist' texts – such as Natasha Walter's *The New Feminism* (1998) – address the relationship between women and power, arguing that new feminism must reclaim the early women's movement's focus on material issues of inequality. A key move of new feminism is a decoupling of the personal from the political, signalling a break with second wave feminism which, Walters maintains, was too preoccupied with sexual politics and reductive accounts of female victimhood. Other writers (like Naomi Wolf, Katie Roiphe and Rene Denfeld) also discuss the distinction between 'victim feminism' and 'power feminism', suggesting that women have the power for self-definition and simply need to exploit it. The second wave's reliance on women's victim status as a unifying political factor is seen as disempowering and outdated and therefore should be replaced with 'power feminism' that is 'unapologetically sexual', 'free-thinking', 'pleasure-loving' and 'self-assertive' (Wolf, *Fire with Fire* 149, 180). We will examine the dichotomy between victim feminism and power feminism through a case study on the television series *Ally McBeal* (1997–2002).

NEW FEMINISM

If during the 1980s, the prevailing mood surrounding the feminist movement was one of disillusionment and backlash, then the following decade came to represent a more upbeat and 'popular' – though by no means uncontested – version of feminism. It was during this time that postfeminism became more recognisable and concretised as a cultural phenomenon and journalistic buzzword, as the 1990s saw a veritable explosion of 'new' kinds of feminism: 'do-me' feminism, power feminism, raunch feminism and, perhaps most famously, Girl Power – indeed, we will discuss in more detail some of these categories that are part of a late twentieth-century postfeminist discourse that blends mainstream and individualised forms of feminism with a range of sexual/feminine markers. In an attempt at renovation and possibly renewal, feminism is reconstructed – and its language refurbished – by prefixing it with another (mostly 'feminine') classifier, sometimes resulting in oxymoronic formulations like 'raunch feminism', 'bimbo feminism' and 'babe feminism', which revolves around the simplistic idea that 'Good Feminism = Great Sex' (Siegel, *Sisterhood, Interrupted* 10; Quindlen 4). Importantly, in this book, we acknowledge the significance and prevalence of some of these 'new feminist' strands for the development of the postfeminist phenomenon but we argue for a more complex interpretation of the 'post' that goes beyond a straightforward narrative of progression. As we have proposed, postfeminism is not a 'new feminism' in the sense that it represents something radically revolutionary and pioneering that transcends the feminist past; instead, the 'post-ing' of feminism involves a process of resignification that harbours the threat of backlash as well as the potential for innovation.

Contrastingly, the term 'new feminism' indicates a more definitive rupture and distinction from an 'old' kind of feminism considered outdated, unfashionable and, in most cases, obsolete. In fact, Natasha Walter starts her book *The New Feminism* (1998) with the question 'Has feminism had its day?' and immediately provides the answer: 'It often seems as if a movement for women's rights must be a thing of the past' (1). Walter is characteristically optimistic in her belief that, as women, 'we've never had it so good': 'Everywhere you look, you see individual women who are freer and more powerful than women have ever been before' (197, 1). As the title of Walter's text implies, the focus is on a younger generation of women who confidently 'down pints in pubs', 'pay their own bills' and 'walk down streets with a swing in their strides' (1). According to Walter, these are 'new times' characterised by modernisation and detraditionalism as well as an increasing dissonance of the political and cultural lives of a new generation of women with those of their (feminist) mothers. The 'raw, uncharted newness' of contemporary women's experiences makes 'the old certainties of feminism' look outmoded as the new breed of women 'are beginning to move somewhere without any markers or goalposts. Although they have heroines, they are making up their lives as they go along. No one before them has ever lived the lives they lead' (2).

However, this does not mean – Walter is careful to point out – that feminism has no role to play in modern-day female existence. On the contrary, 'feminism is still here, right at the centre of these new lives' where it is needed to address a central paradox of this 'brave new world' (3). In effect, *The New Feminism* presents a contradictory picture of unprecedented female freedom and independence coupled with continuing blatant inequalities, manifestly portrayed by young women's transition from being 'top of the class' at school to confronting the glass ceiling in the workplace. The average woman, 'with all her new dreams and beliefs', still faces a number of concrete, economic and social injustices, such as a drop in pay after having children and an increased chance of living in poverty (3). In response, Walter advocates that the new feminism should reclaim the early women's movement's focus on material inequalities. For her, second wave feminism lost its way by shifting to an exclusive concern with sexual politics and culture in the mid-1970s. One of the key aspects of the second wave that she most emphatically discards is its politicising of the personal: 'the slogan "the personal is the political" sprang up in the seventies in debates about abortion, sexual harassment, rape and the division of domestic labour, often to good, and even revolutionary effect. But identifying the personal and the political in too absolute and unyielding a way has led feminism to a dead end' (4). Walter is adamant that the time has come to disentangle the personal from the political and move beyond the constraints and 'spectre of political correctness' which a post-second wave generation of women no longer identifies with (4).

By accentuating younger women's desire to free themselves from the normative demands of a feminist 'straitjacket', *The New Feminism* resonates with other, late twentieth-century descriptions of individual agency that encourage contemporary subjects to engage in what Anthony Giddens calls the 'reflexive project of the self' and forge their identities beyond/outside established social categories: as Walter explains, the new feminists are 'combining traditionally feminine and traditionally masculine work and clothes and attitudes. They are wearing a minidress one day and jeans and boots the next' (Giddens, *Modernity and Self-Identity*; Walter 2). In her account, feminism – or rather, the second wave – is depicted as an elitist and dictatorial 'club' that forces its potential members to learn 'a set of personal attitudes' before being admitted (5). Even worse, the image that feminism has – 'man-hating' and 'intolerant', 'angry rather than optimistic', 'whingeing rather than buoyant', 'negative rather than positive' – often alienates younger women who do not want to become feminist 'outsider[s]' (36). Walter maintains that the new feminism must not be trammelled by rigid ideology and must find a vocabulary that combines social and political equality with personal freedom relevant for diverse constituencies of feminists, including men and women who 'flirt' (5). In her opinion, pragmatism, not purity, is the watchword of a flexible, contemporary kind of feminism that focuses on political, social and economic reforms and is not framed in 'the reductive language of victim or oppressor' (9).

In this way, as Diane Richardson notes, new feminism wants to present itself as 'more popularist, more inclusive, more willing to embrace power, more tolerant in crossing political boundaries, a feminism that belongs to men as well as women, conservatives as well as socialists' (5). The main principle underlying this feminism's 'newness' is one of innovation, renovation and resignification. As Deborah Siegel observes, 'new feminists came up with new names for everything. They wanted to refurbish the language, the ideas, and the face. New names were necessary – strong and edgy names' (*Sisterhood, Interrupted* 116). However, critics remain divided over how successful and 'new' this resignificatory strategy is and how damaging the revamping of 'the "F" word' can be for the feminist movement: while some have championed new feminism as a pertinent example of recent shifts in gender lifestyles and women's relation to power – Helen Wilkinson, for example, declares that we are all power feminists now and offers a revisionist reading of former British prime minister Margaret Thatcher, who, through her single-minded vigour and efficient leadership, provides a pertinent model of female power and a 'road map' for women, 'a route to follow, a vantage point from which to strike out in a new direction' (31; see also Walter 172–6) – new feminism also received much criticism from feminist commentators for its misrepresentation of feminism and its lack of political analysis. Imelda Whelehan contends that new feminism is about 'the individual consumer making choices to improve their own life' but in such a way that 'the cost to themselves is minimal' (*Feminist Bestseller* 166). Even though *The New Feminism* asserts the need for continuing political, social and economic reforms – exemplified by five concrete goals that conclude the text: the reorganisation of the workplace, childcare, male inclusion in domestic life, the opening of the poverty trap and support for female victims of violence – the book's individualist and consumerist bias is encapsulated by the epilogue in which Walter celebrates the 'ordinary freedoms' of sitting in a London café, wearing a trouser suit and paying for her drink 'with my own money, that I earn from my own work' (256, 255). While Walter's goals have a solid policy foundation, her dismissal of a collective women's party or network and her embrace of individualism are seen to put into question the implementation of these objectives. As Lynne Segal writes:

> But quite how (new) feminism will manage to deliver, once it remedies its ways and adopts 'a new, less embattled ideal', remains mysterious. Walter's analysis promotes no particular collective political formations or affiliations. We are simply told: 'We must understand that feminism can give us these things now, if we really want them'. Fingers crossed! (*Why Feminism?* 228)

For Segal, new feminism lacks the very thing it hopes to promote: political seriousness, a point which is reinforced by Diane Richardson in her definition of new feminism as 'feminism without the politics: feminism-lite' (7). Rather than a politically active individual, the new feminist is often dismissed as no more than, in Melissa Benn's words, a 'young-ish and pleasant-ish, professional woman' who 'is interested in designer clothes', 'goes to the gym', 'likes sex' and 'gossips a lot with her girlfriends' (224). Critics are also concerned that through its emphasis on and celebration of female power, some versions of new feminism may in effect work to deny female victimisation and vulnerability.

POWER FEMINISM VS. VICTIM FEMINISM

In *Fire with Fire* (1993), Naomi Wolf argues that a 'genderquake' has taken place in the late twentieth century and women have now reached 'an open moment' when they can begin to 'balance the imbalance of power between the sexes' (xvi). However, before they can grasp authority from men and embrace their own power, women have one important obstacle to overcome, which is their belief in their own victimisation. According to Wolf, women who flaunt victim status – a realisation crucial for second wave feminist politics and its emphasis on collective activism and 'consciousness-raising' – have made themselves impervious to the power actually available to them. She distinguishes two traditions of feminism that she designates 'victim feminism' and 'power feminism': one tradition is 'severe, morally superior and self-denying' while the other is 'free-thinking, pleasure-loving and self-assertive' (180). As she explains, victim feminism is 'when a woman seeks power through an identity of powerlessness. This feminism takes our reflexes of powerlessness and transposes them into a mirror-image set of "feminist" conventions' (147). Casting women as 'sexually pure' and 'mystically nurturing', victim feminism stresses 'the evil done to these "good" women as a way to petition for their rights' (xvii). While useful and necessary in the past, these victim feminist 'assumptions about universal female goodness and powerlessness, and male evil, are unhelpful in the new moment', for they exalt what Wolf calls 'trousseau reflexes' – 'outdated attitudes women need least right now' (xvii). In effect, it is feminism's adherence to a victim-focused stance that has made women turn away from the feminist movement. In Wolf's eyes, feminism is plagued by 'some bad habits' and 'maladaptive attitudes' that have led many women to view 'the weapon of feminist politics' with distaste (65, xvi). While feminism was triumphant in bringing about 'the most successful and least bloody revolution in human history', it now has lost touch with contemporary women who fear that it 'embod[ies] a rigid code of required attitudes and types of behaviour' (63, 66). In line with other late twentieth-century individualist narratives, Wolf is keen to point out that her own feminism (as well as that of her friends) is 'self-defined' and does not fit the list of feminist 'dos' and 'don'ts':

> 'Don't tell the sisterhood', we often joke, uncomfortably, when we are about to confide some romantic foolishness or unsanctioned sexual longing or 'frivolous' concern about clothes or vulnerability or men. We have all felt pressure to espouse a line that does not conform entirely with our true practices or desires. If you can no longer square your feminism with your real-life experience, then something has gone seriously wrong. (68)

In Wolf's account, feminism has come to represent a strict and uncompromising orthodoxy and the refuge of a minority few who are 'too proscriptive of other women's pleasures and private arrangements' (*Fire with Fire* 68). The definition of feminism has become 'ideologically overloaded' and instead of offering 'a mighty Yes to all women's individual wishes to forge their own definition', it has been disastrously redefined in the popular imagination as 'a massive No to everything outside a narrow set of endorsements'. Wolf is unwavering in her belief that victim feminism is obsolete and even harmful to the feminist cause – in effect, '[t]his feminism has slowed women's progress, impeded their self-knowledge, and been responsible for most of the inconsistent, negative, even chauvinistic spots of regressive thinking that are alienating many women and men' (147) – and therefore should be replaced with a different approach that she terms 'power feminism'. Countering notions of female collective victimisation, power feminism sees 'women as human beings – sexual, individual, no better or worse than their male counterparts – and lays claim to equality simply because women are entitled to it' (xvii). Power feminism means identifying with other women through shared pleasures and strengths, rather than shared vulnerability and pain. As such, it is 'unapologetically sexual' and 'understands that good pleasures make good politics' (149). Wolf also addresses the second wave's embattled relationship with the media, asserting that the latter is at the heart of the new power feminism and that leading power feminists include both men and women – Wolf specifically mentions a number of celebrities and public figures such as Madonna and Spike Lee. One distinguishing feature of power feminism that clearly differentiates it from earlier, second wave feminist strands is its acceptance, use and manipulation of its insider position within popular culture. Contradicting Audre Lorde's famous precept, Wolf claims that 'the master's tools can dismantle the master's house' – moreover, she is convinced that 'the genderquake should show us that it is *only* the master's tools' that can deconstruct and undermine the patriarchal power base, for '[the master] hardly bothers to notice anyone else's' (118, 59; emphasis in original). The power feminist thus has to show herself capable of rearranging these tools – among which Wolf counts the electoral process, the press and money – and 'examine closely the forces arrayed against [her] so she can exert her power more effectively' (149). In particular, some of the 'more flexible actions' Wolf advises that women should take include the 'power as consumers', as 'readers and viewers', 'the power of technology' and of controlling 'their tuition payments' (319–30).

Critics have been sceptical of this insider tactic and have censured power feminism for 'working within the status quo rather than attempting to overturn current political realities' (Whelehan, *Feminist Bestseller* 163). As Whelehan puts it, power feminism 'seems nothing more than an empty endorsement of a social meritocracy'. Sarah Gamble concurs, arguing that Wolf oversimplifies the power structures that work to constrain women and obstruct their aims of equality and economic empowerment: 'Her entire argument rests on the assumption that power is there for the taking', but, Gamble asks, 'is it, can it ever be, as easy as that?' (49). Given that power feminism centres on 'alliances based on economic self-interest and economic giving back' – in place of a sentimental 'fantasy of cosmic sisterhood' – critiques such as Gamble's that highlight Wolf's status as a white, middle-class, educated, solvent American may be justified (Wolf, *Fire with Fire* 58). Following a similar line of argument, bell hooks concludes that Wolf's 'new vision of female power works best for the middle class' and its message seems to be that 'women can be procapitalist, rich, and progressive at the same time' ('Dissident Heat' 63). However, by rejecting feminism as a collective political movement that seeks to eradicate sexism and female exploitation, power feminism can be considered, in hooks' eyes, as no more than 'a theory of self-worth' that can conveniently 'embrace everyone, since it has no overt political tenets': 'This "feminism" turns the movement away from politics back to a vision of individual self-help.'

Individualism, rather than collectivism, was to be the focus of a number of new feminist writers in the 1990s who upheld a dichotomy between the victimising politics of 'old feminism' and the powerful 'new feminism' needed to overcome the feminist 'cult of victimology' (Siegel, *Sisterhood, Interrupted* 103). In *The Morning After* (1993), Katie Roiphe focuses on the issues of rape and sexual harassment – central in second wave feminist analyses of female oppression – asserting that 'feminists are closer to the backlash than they'd like to think' (6). By overly investing in women's discrimination, feminism is charged with presenting an image of 'women as victims, offended by a professor's dirty joke, verbally pressured into sex by peers' (6). Roiphe suggests that second wave feminism was responsible for a particular form of victim feminism and a 'date rape hysteria' that, she claims, is overrunning American campuses. She argues that feminist anti-rape initiatives (like Take Back the Night marches) are self-defeating as they underline women's vulnerability and weakness instead of bolstering their strength. According to Roiphe, feminism's preoccupation with women's victimisation is fuelled by an outdated model of sexuality, 'one in which men want sex and women don't' (Siegel, *Sisterhood, Interrupted* 99).

Rene Denfeld, in common with Katie Roiphe, distances herself from collective feminist politics of the 1960s and 1970s, and she articulates a view of feminism as a totalitarian, old-fashioned and fanatic doctrine. For Denfeld, organised feminism 'has become bogged down in an extremist moral and spiritual crusade that has little to do with women's lives', and – by drifting into the realm and language of academia that is 'inaccessible to the uninitiated' – it offers a 'worldview that speaks to the very few, while alienating the many' (5). While Roiphe describes feminism as having lapsed into a 1950s image of women – characterised by passivity and 'wide-eyed innocence' (6) – Denfeld looks even further back in her description:

> In the name of feminism, these extremists have embarked on a moral and spiritual crusade that would take us back to a time worse than our mother's day – back to the nineteenth-century values of sexual morality, spiritual purity, and political helplessness. Though a combination of influential voices and unquestioned causes, current feminism would create the very same morally pure yet helplessly martyred role that women suffered from a century ago. (10)

She dubs second wave feminism the 'new Victorianism' that is bound to promote 'repressive sexual morality' by promulgating 'the vision of an ideal woman' as 'sexually pure and helpless yet somehow morally superior to men' (16). By insisting on pursuing an agenda based on female victimisation at the hands of an all-powerful patriarchy, the feminist movement that began in the 1960s with a 'fierce fight for economic, social, and political parity' has degenerated into 'a profoundly antisex, antifreedom, and ultimately anti-women's rights perspective' (216, 237). As Denfeld stresses, the 'feminist matriarchy' is in danger of duplicating 'Victorianism in all its repressive glory', whereby 'the woman [is] revered on the pedestal, charged with keeping society's moral order yet politically powerless – and perpetually martyred' (155, 16–17).

Both Denfeld and Roiphe acknowledge that they are beneficiaries of feminism's struggle to expose and combat women's oppression and victimisation – Denfeld, for example, writes that 'we have it much better now than our mothers ever did', describing feminism as her 'birthright' and herself as an 'equality feminist' – but they make a distinction between the women's movement's rightful fight in the past and its 'stagnant' present, when it is heading towards 'complete irrelevance' (Denfeld 1, 2, 267). They want to reinvent the image of feminism and turn it from 'a doctrine that dictates the most personal aspects of our lives' to a 'movement that, quite simply, represents the majority of women' (Denfeld 16, 21). Not surprisingly, this 'us' and 'them' rhetoric has been criticised for its overly simplistic rendering of the second wave and attitude towards feminism. Deborah Siegel comments on the harm performed by such sweeping analyses:

> Dissenting feminist voices participate in a much needed intergenerational conversation . . . [but] these authors' desires for mastery overwrite any attempt to keep a dialogue moving. In their incorporation of a rhetoric of repossession, in their masterful articulation of 'good' feminism, and their righteous condemnation of a monolithic 'bad' feminism, Wolf, Roiphe, and Denfeld make feminist history the story of a product rather than that of a process. ('Reading Between the Waves' 59)

Siegel is adamant that ultimately such scripts can only result in paralysis and they are noteworthy 'not so much for what [they] argue' as because they sparked 'a war between – and also among – generations of feminists' (*Sisterhood, Interrupted* 100). These disagreements were to continue in examinations of popular culture that debate the emergence of new female characters in the 1990s and their adoption of 'new feminist' strategies, such as a recourse to individualism, power through sex and working within the system to dismantle 'the master's house'.

CASE STUDY: *ALLY MCBEAL* (1997–2002)

Ally McBeal – a fictitious twenty-something Boston lawyer who is famous for her unorthodox work methods as well as her yearning to find a husband – has come to be intimately connected with the state of contemporary feminisms ever since *Time* magazine featured the television character – or rather, a colour portrait of actress Calista Flockhart, whose demonstrably anorexic-looking body has proven a topic for discussion in its own right – on its June 1998 cover, juxtaposed with a row of black-and-white photos of three renowned white feminists (Susan B. Anthony, Betty Friedan and Gloria Steinem), along with the caption 'Is feminism dead?' The article took the success of the Fox series as a sign that feminism was no longer relevant to a 1990s generation of women who, as author Ginia Bellafante bemoaned, apparently only think about their bodies and themselves. Despite feminist objections to Ally McBeal as a dubious feminist role model, the television persona has also been embraced by a predominantly female audience who strongly identify with Ally's struggles to combine a successful work life with an equally fulfilling romantic relationship.

The series has been discussed as simultaneously 'pro-woman' and 'anti-feminist' as it takes for granted women's right to education, career and wealth but repackages these feminist principles into feminine issues. As L. S. Kim notes, 1990s depictions of 'the working girl (or single girl in the city) seem to proffer a feminist tone or objective but it ultimately seems to be a false feminism' that sets up 'pro-woman' values and expressions in opposition to feminist goals (323). Kim suggests that *Ally McBeal* illustrates this pro-woman/anti-feminist stance, as the programme offers female protagonists in roles that are categorically strong and empowering but then deflates and feminises their feminist potential. Ally and her colleagues are Harvard Law School graduates, working in an up-and-coming Boston law firm and enjoying financial independence and social equality. As Ally herself puts it, 'I've got it great, really, good job, good friends, loving family, total freedom and long bubblebaths. What else could there be?' In Kim's framework, Ally's position as a liberated woman is sabotaged by her constant search for the missing element in her life: a man and a heterosexual partnership. Ally admits that, even though she is 'a strong working woman', her existence 'feels empty without a man' and, unlike her 1970s precedent Mary Tyler Moore, she 'doesn't want to make it on her own' (Kim 331; Chambers et al. 58). She clings to a fairytale notion of love and often retreats into her private fantasy world to reflect on her unmarried and childless state – the series features regular interludes that comically visualise Ally's interior monologues, such as her hallucination of a dancing baby. Following Kim's logic, Ally emerges as a 'self-objectifying, schizophrenic woman' and a 'falsely empowered image', too self-diminishing and indecisive to bear the feminist label (332, 323). The character remains trapped in 'a state of pseudoliberation', as her education and professional credentials have not gained her personal fulfilment or self-understanding and her main strategy for success and happiness is 'through sexuality' (321, 332).

Laurie Ouellette follows a similar line of argument in her discussion of the 'postvictimization premise' of *Ally McBeal*: in its construction of 'idealized postfeminist subjectivities', the programme presumes women's 'already-achieved professional and sexual gains while simultaneously affirming their right to choose femininity' (315, 332–3). In this context, Ouellette reads postfeminism in terms of a 'flexible subject position for a new era' that presupposes the success of the women's movement but, at the same time, construes feminism as '"other" and even threatening to contemporary femininity' (316). She is adamant that the 'postvictimization' discourse amounts to a depoliticisation of feminism because, 'although its proponents make compelling points, they tend to exaggerate feminism's unity . . . and advocate individual agency over collective action' (323).

Rachel Moseley and Jacinda Read also interpret *Ally McBeal* as a postfeminist text, but they go beyond a backlash reading, suggesting that Ally is 'postfeminist . . . not because she represents the death of feminism, but because she represents a period that is post-1970s feminism' (237). While other critics establish a dualistic relationship between Ally's feminine and feminist, private and public traits, Moseley and Read argue that the programme represents 'a re-evaluation of the opposition between feminism and femininity which informed much 1970s feminist thought'. Ally McBeal can be seen to deconstruct such oppositions by 'attempting to hold together the apparently incompatible' and 'have it all' – marriage, children and partnership in the law firm (239). Moreover, staging 'the coming together of "traditional" feminist values with a historically and materially different experience' of a younger generation, the series speaks to a number of women who identify with 'being female, feminist, and feminine in the late twentieth and early twenty-first centuries' (240). In particular, the articulation of Ally's interiority in the fantasy sequences is not signalled as 'manifestly unreal, but instead as *emotionally* real', making the heroine's feelings and presence 'concrete, immediate, and all pervasive' (243–4; emphasis in original). As Moseley and Read conclude, *Ally McBeal* 'encourages rejection of the monolithic definitions of femininity or feminism, allowing multiple opportunities for female identification in its dramatisation of the tensions and contradictions experienced by many young working women' (247). In this sense, Ally McBeal can be understood not so much as an imperfect feminist role model but as an embodiment of postfeminist in-betweenness and heterogeneity.

RECOMMENDED FURTHER READING

Kim, L. S. '"Sex and the Single Girl" in Postfeminism: The *F Word* on Television.' *Television & New Media* 2.4 (2001): 319–34.

Moseley, Rachel, and Jacinda Read. '"Having it *Ally*": Popular Television (Post-) Feminism.' *Feminist Media Studies*. 2.2 (2002): 231–49.

Siegel, Deborah. *Sisterhood, Interrupted: From Radical Women to Grrls Gone Wild.* Basingstoke and New York: Palgrave Macmillan, 2007.

Walter, Natasha, ed. *On the Move: Feminism for a New Generation.* London: Virago, 1999.

Whelehan, Imelda. *The Feminist Bestseller: From Sex and the Single Girl to Sex and the City.* Basingstoke: Palgrave Macmillan, 2005. 156–72.

3

Girl Power and Chick Lit

OVERVIEW

This chapter explores a key strand of power feminism that is aimed at a young generation of women/girls and is particularly pervasive in media definitions of postfeminism: Girl Power. Propagated in the 1990s by the Spice Girls, Girl Power's defining characteristic is a re-appraisal of femininity – including the stereotypical symbols of feminine enculturation such as Barbie dolls, make-up and fashion magazines – as a means of female empowerment and agency. Girl Power contains an implicit rejection of many tenets held by second wave feminists – who stressed the disempowering and oppressive aspects of femininity in a male-dominated society – and it is often considered in popular culture to be synonymous with 'chick lit', a female-oriented fiction that celebrates the pleasures of feminine adornment and heterosexual romance. Girl Power has been dismissed by a number of critics as an objectifying and commoditising trap that makes women buy into patriarchal stereotypes of female appearance and neo-liberal individualist principles. Yet Girl culture also has the potential to uproot femininity and make it available for alternative readings/meanings. Recent critiques have discussed Girl Power as a complex, contradictory discourse that provides a new articulation of young femininity and represents 'a feminist ideal of a new, robust, young woman with agency and a strong sense of self' (Aapola et al. 39). We will analyse Girl Power and chick lit through case studies on the Spice Girls and the bestselling novel *Bridget Jones's Diary* (1996), which has been credited with summoning the zeitgeist, with Bridget being hailed as a 'kind of "everywoman" of the 1990s' (Whelehan, *Helen Fielding* 12).

GIRL POWER

Publicised by the British band the Spice Girls, Girl Power refers to a popular feminist stance (common among girls and young women during the mid-late 1990s and early 2000s) that combines female independence and individualism with a confident display of femininity/sexuality. The phrase 'Girl Power' came into popular usage in 1996 when the Spice Girls used the slogan in their interviews and on their merchandise to promote female assertiveness and autonomy in lifestyle and sexuality. Girl Power can be understood as a response to longstanding feminist critiques of feminine gender roles that define femininity as a patriarchal marker of female powerlessness and oppression – in effect, second wave feminists were almost unanimous in their dismissal of femininity as an 'artificial, man-made' product and called for what radical feminist Mary Daly terms an 'undoing [of] our conditioning in femininity' and an 'unravelling [of] the hood of patriarchal woman-hood [sic]' (409) – as well as media representations of feminists, in particular the epithet of the 'bra-burner' that has been propagated in the popular press since the 1970s and caricatures feminists as mannish, aggressive and humourless (see Douglas; Genz, *Postfemininities*, chapter 2). As Hinds and Stacey note, Girlies perform a glamorous makeover of the drab and unfashionable women's liberationist of the past, effecting a 'shift from the *monstrous outsiders* of the 1960s and 1970s to the *incorporated Ms* of the 1990s' (155; emphasis in original).

Reclaiming elements of femininity and girlishness in fashion and style, Girl Power discards the notions that feminism is necessarily anti-feminine and anti-popular and that femininity is always sexist and oppressive. Instead, Girlies are convinced that feminist and feminine characteristics can be blended in a new, improved mix. As Jennifer Baumgardner and Amy Richards proclaim in their Girlie manifesto:

> Girlie culture is a rebellion against the false impression that since women don't want to be sexually exploited, they don't want to be sexual; against the necessity of brass-buttoned, red-suited seriousness to infiltrate a man's world; against the anachronistic belief that . . . girls and power don't mix. (137)

Girlies are adamant that they can compete successfully alongside their male counterparts and attain equality without sacrificing all forms of 'pink-packaged femininity' (137). On the contrary, their empowerment and assertiveness are seen to be directly linked to their feminine identities and their ability to redefine the meanings of and objects related to femininity. Insisting that they are not trapped by their femininity, Girlies want to gain control by using their insider position within consumer culture. Girl Power thus combines cultural confidence with feminist awareness, emphasising that the traditional/patriarchal connotations of girlishness can be interrupted by alternative modes of production/consumption. As Baumgardner and Richards explain, the term 'Girlie' depicts the 'intersection of culture and feminism' and allows for a productive re-appropriation of conventional instruments of femininity:

> Using makeup isn't a sign of our sway to the marketplace and the male gaze; it can be sexy, campy, ironic, or simply decorating ourselves without the loaded issues . . . . What we loved as girls was good and, because of feminism, we know how to make girl stuff work for us. (136)

The myths of femininity that have historically been imprinted on the female body as signs of passivity and subordination are revitalised in Girlie rhetoric, which establishes a gap between image and identity and, in this new signifying aperture, rearticulates feminine modes and subjectivities. The central tenet of Girl Power is that femininity is powerful and empowering, providing women/girls with the agency to negotiate the possibilities of their gender role. In this sense, women are encouraged to use their femininity to complement and even further the qualities of independence and emancipation fostered by the feminist movement. Proponents of Girl Power maintain that it offers a way out of the one-sided attention to the restrictions of feminine conventions that has obscured women's engagement in the construction of femininity. They embrace Girl Power for creating more expansive forms of femininity and a 'take-charge dynamism' that rewrites the scripts of feminine 'passivity, voicelessness, vulnerability and sweet naturedness' (Aapola et al. 19). The claim of a new meaning for old symbols opens up a space for the inventive and potentially subversive use of cultural signs and a refashioning of feminine identities. This encompasses a reconsideration of a multitude of practices and forms – including previously tabooed symbols of feminine enculturation (Barbie dolls, make-up, fashion magazines) as well as body remodelling exercises such as cosmetic surgery. Taken to its logical conclusion, Girl Power makes a case for femininity politics or 'femmenism' that implies using the signs and accoutrements of femininity to challenge stable notions of gender formations. Jeannine Delombard describes this feminine politics by alluding to Audre Lorde's famous precept: 'femmenism is using the master's tools to dismantle the master's house' – it involves 'playing up your femininity' not as a mark of oppression but in resistance to a context of prohibition (22).

While this understanding of Girl Power as a deconstructive strategy to rework gender categories from within can clearly be related to postmodern theories that interpret gender as a cultural construction and 'a doing', there have also been substantial objections to the Girlie stance and politics (Butler, *Gender Trouble* 25). Critics have argued that Girl Power's assertion of dynamic self-fulfilment and feminine self-expression is not unanimously liberating but rather conceals a trap of conformity and disempowerment. As Susan Bordo writes, 'employing the language of femininity to protest the conditions of the female world will always involve ambiguities' (177). In effect, Girl Power functions within and is animated by the same cultural imagery that transfers onto women the labels of inferiority and powerlessness. Its detractors deplore the fact that Girlies' celebrated energies and powers are channelled towards, in their opinion, a confined and limited goal, that is, the adoption and creation of femininity. Although Girlies are resolute that they are free to construct their own appearances and identities, critics are concerned that the range of their choices is suspiciously narrow as the Girlie look is similar to, if not synonymous with, patriarchal ideals of feminine beauty. As Shelley Budgeon points out, this form of agency is contingent upon 'self-objectification and dependence upon the approving gaze of others' ('Fashion Magazine Advertising' 66). In this model of social power, women are offered the promise of autonomy by voluntarily objectifying themselves and actively choosing to employ their capacities in the pursuit of a feminine appearance and a sexualised image. Rosalind Gill laments that in this way, 'sexual objectification can be presented not as something done to women by some men, but as the freely chosen wish of active . . . female subjects' ('From Sexual Objectification' 104). The focus on femininity as an avenue to self-determination is interpreted as a malicious cover-up that masks a deeper exploitation than objectification and 'a shift from an external, male judging gaze to a self-policing narcissistic gaze' (*Gender and the Media* 258). This, Gill and Arthurs argue, is representative of a neo-liberal society that constructs individuals as autonomous, free and in charge of their opportunities and destiny ('New Femininities?').

Other commentators have highlighted Girl Power's emphasis on media visibility and consumer culture and criticised its appeal as a marketing slogan aimed at a lucrative girl market. Angela McRobbie, for example, uses the term 'commercial femininities' to refer to feminine subjectivities that are produced by/in contemporary popular culture, particularly in women's magazines ('More!'). In Girlie rhetoric, the notions of emancipation and agency are often directly tied to consumer culture and the ability to purchase, with women's agentive powers premised upon and enabled by the consumption of products and services, frequently associated with femininity/sexuality. In its most commercialised forms, 1990s expressions of Girl Power combine an emphasis on feminine fun and female friendship with a celebration of (mostly pink-coloured) commodities and the creation of a market demographic of

'Girlies' and 'chicks'. The embrace of consumer culture represents a marked point of differentiation from second wave feminism, which believed in the power of separatism over what Imelda Whelehan terms 'the spin game' (*Feminist Bestseller* 138). Whelehan is sceptical of this 'free market feminism' that 'allows women to think that they can change their own lives even if they don't have the mettle to change the world' (155). In turn, Angela McRobbie underlines the individualism inherent in such commercial feminine forms, arguing that the 'over-emphasis on agency and the apparent capacity to choose in a more individualised society' shift feminism's ideas and values – along with its community-based, activist politics – into the past ('Notes on Postfeminism' 10). In these critiques, Girl Power's popularity is credited to its very lack of threat to the status quo and its individualising and commoditising effects that co-opt and undermine feminist content/politics by presenting the production of femininity as entirely self-willed and (commercially) available, and thereby refuting calls for social change.

In a similar manner, a younger generation of feminist critics/activists take issue with Girl Power's central position in the popular mainstream and argue for a diversification of Girl culture that differentiates between the marketable 'girl' – epitomised by the Spice Girls – and the non-conformist 'grrrl', who emerged in the 1990s from the US underground punk scene and the Riot Grrrl movement. Deborah Siegel explains the difference between the two:

> 'Grrl' [sic] was 'girl' with a healthy dose of youthful female rage, minus the sugar and spice. The word entered the lexicon sometime around 1991, along with the Riot Grrl movement – a loosely connected network of all-girl punk bands and their fans that started in Olympia, Washington, and Washington, D.C. . . . Not to be confused with . . . 'Girl Power' (a marketing ploy that deployed empowerment rhetoric to sell products), grrl was a grassroots popular expression engendered and disseminated by girls and young women themselves. (*Sisterhood, Interrupted* 146)

Described as 'an infusion of punk and feminism', the Riot Grrrls (exemplified by such bands as Bikini Kill and Bratmobile) staged a rebellion against dominant representations of girlhood and the patriarchal structures they encountered in the music scene (Feigenbaum 132). Addressing issues such as sexual abuse and eating disorders in song lyrics, weekly meetings and zines, the Riot Grrrls have been described as forging 'a unique feminist space for young women' that, it has been suggested, is not 'that structurally dissimilar to that sustained by the second wave consciousness-raising groups and support networks' (Gillis and Munford, 'Genealogies' 170). The structural similarities with the second wave highlight a desire to ensure a continuation of feminist principles and ideas – a desire that, as we will discuss in a later chapter, is also shared by 'third wave feminists' who adopt the Riot Grrrl movement as exemplary of their activist work and critical engagement with popular culture.

The distinction between 'girl' and 'grrrl' has been used to illustrate a common perception of a much wider division between postfeminism and third wave feminism, whereby the former is interpreted as middle-of-the-road and depoliticised while the latter is more subcultural and activist. According to Rebecca Munford, in the transition from underground music scene to mainstream culture, various 'dangers of colonisation and recircula-tion' become apparent, illustrated by the lipglossed Spice Girls who fall prey to this 'dangerous slippage between feminist agency and patriarchal recu-peration' (148, 149). As she observes, 'Spice Girls-style girl power' is often no more than a 'fashion statement', 'a ready site for postfeminist colonisation', whereas the grrrl movement can be understood as part of a 'politics of *identi-fication* that is vital to both individual and collective empowerment' (147–9; emphasis in original). Munford seeks to rescue 'Girl Power' from postfemi-nism's trivialising grip by pointing out that the phrase – although popularised by the Spice Girls in the mid-1990s – was actually coined some years earlier by members of the Riot Grrrls. Hijacked by the popular media, the term was then hollowed out and 'deprived of its radical and activist history' (Gillis and Munford, 'Genealogies' 170).

Contrastingly, Stéphanie Genz has argued against a dichotomisation of postfeminism and the third wave – and with this, 'girl' and 'grrrl'– suggest-ing that 'it might be futile to erect a line of demarcation and differentiation between what constitutes postfeminist activity and third wave activism' ('Third Way/ve' 346). Genz draws attention to 'the different dimensions of agency that women participate in', emphasising how 'micro-political forms of gendered agency . . . play to the expectations of the patriarchal gaze while hoping to rewrite [these] patriarchal codes'. In their analysis of diverse expres-sions of contemporary girlhood, Aapola, Gonick and Harris also adopt a view of Girl Power as an eclectic concept with 'various meanings and uses' that offers young women an image of femininity which is about 'possibility, limit-less potential and the promise of control over the future' (39). They propose that Girl Power's 'mainstreaming effect' does not necessarily imply 'selling feminism'; on the contrary, the resolutely popular stance brings feminist ideas 'into the lives of young women' – through music, film and television characters – and encourages a 'dialogue about feminism' that raises 'important questions about the relationships between feminism, femininity, girls and new subjectivities' (29–31, 20). Rather than espousing a singular meaning, Girl Power's implications are multiple and varied, allowing for the possibility of an altered understanding and reformulation of femininity that takes into account its relation to – rather than disconnection from – feminism and discourses of female empowerment and assertiveness. As Gillis and Munford put it, 'the "power" and the "girl" in girl power need to be interrogated rather than dismissed outright' ('Genealogies' 173).

CASE STUDY: SPICE GIRLS

The term Girl Power has often been directly linked with music culture, in particular since the arrival of the Spice Girls on the pop stage in 1996. Defining Girl Power as 'a celebration of self-belief, independence and female friendship', David Gauntlett, for example, writes that 'the Spices – driven by Geri Halliwell – really did push the "girl power" agenda for a while' (217–18). Neatly packaged into five facets of 1990s British femaleness – Sporty, Scary, Posh, Ginger and Baby – the Spice Girls (with their 'Girl Power' battle-cry) declared their intention to shake up the music scene (and society with it). The girls' message to be repeated in innumerable interviews and song lyrics (such as their debut single 'Wannabe') was about 'fulfilling your dreams, going against expectations and creating your own opportunities for success' – in tandem with the 'freedom' to flaunt their femininity/sexuality through a display of hot pants, platform shoes and Wonderbras (218). As their self-penned manifesto *Girl Power!* (1997) reveals, the Spice Girls position themselves as late twentieth-century modernisers providing an updated version of feminist empowerment: 'Feminism has become a dirty word. Girl Power is just a nineties way of saying it. We can give feminism a kick up the arse. Women can be so powerful when they show solidarity' (48).

The suggestion that feminism deserves a good shake-up (a 'kick up the arse') has been condemned by a number of critics as illustrative of an antifeminist backlash in popular culture that presents feminism as obsolete and outmoded. Imelda Whelehan, for instance, suggests that the band's comment – though a seemingly genuine gesture of pro-female camaraderie – shows 'how girl power as a rhetorical device is all too prone to appropriation for essentially patriarchal ends. It inevitably promotes the widespread view that feminism is nothing but a tangle of infighting factions who never gave serious consideration to the idea of female solidarity' (*Overloaded* 45). Whelehan argues that, at their height, the Spice Girls 'offered a vision of success, youth and vitality to the young in a world where youthful, childless, sexually attractive women are the most visible fetishised image of femininity' (46). This is at best a purely individualistic type of feminism that 'bears no relation to the "bigger" issues' as the Spice Girls 'seem to have forgotten, or remain blissfully unaware of, the social and political critiques offered by second-wave feminism' (47). Another, associated, point of contention relates to the band's commercial and mainstream appeal, which is viewed by many as a symptom of the 'selling out' of feminist principles and their co-option as a marketing device. As numerous feminists (and others) have hastened to point out, the Spice Girls are a 'manufactured' band, hand-picked by the British pop mogul Simon Fuller and 19 Management, and as such, their motivations and commitment to female emancipation have been questioned – 'empowerment' is seen to be defined merely in terms of their own financial gain. An Australian Riot Grrrl zine concisely makes the point that '[the Spice Girls'] version of lame "girl power" is so far away from our original vision of "grrrl power"; co-opted, watered down, marketable, profitable – all style and not . . . a lot of content' (quoted in Aapola et al. 25).

Contrastingly, Gauntlett maintains that – despite being 'a commercial tool' – Girl Power undeniably has had a positive effect on young women and girls: 'Whilst it was easy for cynics to criticise the "girl power" idea as a bunch of banal statements about "believing in yourself" and "doing whatever you want to do", it was still an encouraging confidence boost to young women and should not be dismissed too readily' (219–20). In her discussion of feminine adolescence, Catherine Driscoll argues that the Spice Girls might also have interesting reverberations for the circulation of the label 'feminist' and the dominant perceptions of what girls want (186). In her view, Girl Power's relation to feminism should not be conceived in too definite terms – whereby 'either it is or it isn't feminism'. Pop icons like the Spice Girls may not produce revolutionary change but they create a shift in the dominant paradigms of cultural production directed at girls (Aapola et al. 31). In a similar manner, Kathy Acker – one notable exception to the generalised feeling (within the feminist movement) of distrust towards Girl Power – highlights the band's appeal to women, beyond class and educational boundaries. In an interview she conducted with the Spice Girls for the *Guardian*, Acker describes the girls' ability to represent 'the voices, not really the voice, of young women and, just as important, of women not from the educated classes' (19). In this sense, Girl Power underscores an intellectual elitism and anti-sexual bias within feminism: 'it isn't only the lads sitting behind babe culture . . . who think that babes or beautiful lower and lower-middle class girls are dumb. It's also educated women who look down on girls like the Spice Girls, who think that because . . . [they] take their clothes off, there can't be anything "up there" [in their brains].' As Sheila Whiteley summarises the impact of the Spice Girls: 'By telling their fans that feminism is necessary and fun . . . they sold the 1990s as a "girl's world" and presented the "future as female"' (216–17). The Spice Girls prepared the stage for a number of girl bands like Destiny's Child that inherited the Girl Power mantle – although not necessarily the slogan itself – and continue the emphasis on women's (financial) self-determination and autonomy – the lyrics of 'Independent Women Part 1', for example, praise 'all the honeys makin' money' and proudly proclaim, 'I depend on me.' The Spice Girls themselves continue their celebration of 'Woman Power' after their reunion in June 2007 – following Geri's departure in 1998 and their separation in 2001 – with all the Spices now in their thirties and the majority of them being mothers/wives and having found fame in other arenas – Posh Spice, for example, is nowadays more famous for being a fashion icon and married to David Beckham. It remains to be seen whether these more mature girls will be as influential and contentious in the new millennium as they were in the last decade of the twentieth century.

CHICK LIT

If the 1990s music scene was influenced by the emergence of the Spice Girls and their popular Girl Power slogan, then the publishing industry saw a corresponding development with the arrival of 'chick lit' – a female-oriented form of fiction and a highly successful and commercial literary phenomenon. Frequently characterised by ubiquitous pastel-coloured, fashion-conscious covers, chick lit has simultaneously attracted the adoration of fans and the disdain of some critics, who have dismissed it as trashy fiction – feminist writer Germaine Greer and novelist Beryl Bainbridge, for example, have weighed in against chick lit, famously describing it as 'an updated version of the old Mills & Boon scenario' and a literary 'froth sort of thing' that 'just wastes time' (quoted in Whelehan, *Helen Fielding* 59; quoted in Ferriss and Young 1). Chick lit has come to be recognised for its distinctive subject matter, character, audience and narrative style. Suzanne Ferris and Mallory Young provide a definition of the genre: '[s]imply put, chick lit features single women in their twenties and thirties navigating their generation's challenges of balancing demanding careers with personal relationships' (3). Scarlett Thomas offers a more colourful description of chick lit as 'a "fun" pastel-covered novel with a young, female, city-based protagonist, who has a kooky best friend, an evil boss, romantic troubles and a desire to find the One – the apparently unavailable man who is good-looking, can cook and is both passionate and considerate in bed' (quoted in Whelehan, *Feminist Bestseller* 203). The origins of chick lit have been traced to Helen Fielding's *Bridget Jones's Diary* (1996), which is said to have inaugurated the genre, offering a model and formula that many other writers were to adopt. The book gave prominence to the figure of the 'Singleton' – a thirty-something woman who is employed, financially independent, sexually assertive and (unhappily) single – with Bridget Jones becoming a recognisable emblem and a point of identification for a mostly female readership. By the late 1990s and the early 2000s chick lit was well established as a genre, earning publishers more than $71 million in 2002 and occupying *Publishers Weekly* bestseller lists (see Ferris and Young 2).

Chick lit has often been likened to the traditional romance genre, which focuses on a love story and affords 'an emotionally satisfying happy ending' (Gill and Herdieckerhoff 490). Critics suggest that novels like *Bridget Jones's Diary* maintain a straightforward romance plot at their core – an argument given credence by the fact that Helen Fielding's book is, as she has openly admitted, a rewriting of Jane Austen's *Pride and Prejudice* (1813). The novel acknowledges its nineteenth-century predecessor in a number of ironic allusions, exemplified by Bridget's observation on her first meeting with her love interest Mark that 'it struck me as pretty ridiculous to be called Mr. Darcy and stand on your own looking snooty at a party' (13). Commentators have criticised chick lit's romance element, noting that 'as Bridget gets her Darcy at the end of the book, we are not only given a narrative with some structural similarities to Jane Austen's work, but some of its dominant values as well' (Whelehan, *Overloaded* 138). Chick lit is decried as 'nothing more than the contemporary version of the "How to Get Married Novel"', a 'retro form that details the search for and nabbing of a husband, any husband' (Jacobson 3). The chick lit heroine is said to embrace a passive and disempowered image of womanhood that has simply been revamped for a postfeminist era. As Imelda Whelehan argues, 'chick lit provides a post-feminist narrative of heterosex and romance for those who feel that they're too savvy to be duped by the most conventional romance narrative' (*Feminist Bestseller* 186). While 1990s characters like the Singleton are presented as independent working women enjoying financial and sexual freedom – and as such can be seen as more empowered and emancipated than their romantic forebears – they are also portrayed as neurotic and preoccupied with finding a man and scrutinising the size of their bodies – Bridget Jones's incessant calorie counting and weight monitoring at the beginning of her diary entries are pertinent examples. As Rosalind Gill and Elena Herdieckerhoff note, in this way 'the codes of traditional romance are reinstated "through the backdoor"' by pathologising singlehood and focusing women's efforts on the creation of a feminine and sexy body and on the quest for a romantic hero who can rescue the chick lit heroine from a life of spinsterhood (494).

Contrastingly, supporters claim that, unlike convention-bound romance, chick lit discards the heterosexual hero and 'offer[s] a more realistic portrait of single life, dating, and the dissolution of romantic ideals' (Ferriss and Young 3). Refuting the 'narrow-minded description of the genre' as a reprisal of some well-worn clichés, fans and authors of chick lit insist that 'these books don't trivialize women's problems' and can be designated 'coming-of-age stories, finding out who you are, where you want to go' (Jacobson 3). The genre's drawing power is said to lie in its realism and authenticity, reflecting the 'lives of everyday working young women' in 'all the messy detail' (Ferriss and Young 3). Chick lit protagonists are touted as 'bold', 'ambitious', 'witty' and 'sexy', while simultaneously being bemoaned as 'shallow', 'overly compulsive', 'neurotic' and 'insecure' (*Chick Lit USA* 1). In effect, it is the Singleton's inherent contradictoriness that makes her appealing for a 1990s generation of women who are unwilling to renounce their joint aspirations for job and romance, their feminist and feminine values. As Bridget Jones proudly proclaims, 'we are a pioneer generation daring to refuse to compromise in love and relying on our own economic power' (Fielding, *Diary* 21). As a result of her sometimes incongruous desires and choices, the typical chick lit heroine is characteristically flawed and fallible, eliciting the readers' compassion and identification and producing what Gill and Herdieckerhoff call a 'that's me' moment of recognition.

Such identification is augmented by the genre's distinctive narrative style and its use of the confessional mode, either by drawing on the diary form (as in Fielding's novel) or by employing the format of letters/emails or simply first-person narration to create the impression that the protagonist is speaking directly to readers – for example, Jane Green's *Jemima J.* (1998) and Allison Pearson's *I Don't Know How She Does It* (2002) make use of one or more of these narrative techniques. Chick lit's confessional tone has been discussed as representative of a 'return to the I' in postfeminist discourse whereby, as Daniele notes, there is an 'implosion of personal styles and narratives' in the postfeminist 'rhetoric of autobiography' (83, 81, 89). Offering an intimate engagement with and promising a closer insight into the heroines' personal life and psychological dilemmas, chick lit provides the fiction of an 'authentic' female voice bewildered by the contradictory demands and mixed messages of heterosexual romance and feminist emancipation. This reliance upon the subjective voice has been interpreted as a postfeminist re-enactment of the consciousness-raising experiences of second wave feminism. As Imelda Whelehan observes, 'chick lit has clear links with the tradition of the consciousness-raising novel in seeming to tell it like it is and to raise individual awareness of shared personal concerns' (*Feminist Bestseller* 186). The focus on the ordinary and the trivial in contemporary chick lit is 'reminiscent of the substance of early feminist criticism' and writing which asked for 'authentic images of women to counter the perniciousness' of patriarchal stereotypes of femininity (200). However, Whelehan also draws attention to the differences and shortcomings of chick lit, concluding that '[u]nfortunately, this revival of confessional writing . . . is not likely to prompt a heady renaissance of feminism along the lines of 1970s politics' (188). Deborah Siegel concurs, maintaining that postfeminist chick lit's 'personal expression . . . differs from the personalizing of the political effected through consciousness raising' ('The Legacy' 51). While fruitfully exploring the complexities of twenty-first-century femaleness, femininity and feminism, chick lit is censured for failing to move out of the protagonists' personal sphere and relate the process of confession to a wider context of female discrimination and social inequality. Critics are concerned that the return to the personal does not provide an access to feminist politics and thus risks sliding into 'lifestyle politics', confined to navel-gazing introspection rather than life-changing analysis and interrogation (Dow 209).

The case of chick lit has often been held as exemplary of the controversy regarding the distinction between feminism and postfeminism. As Ferris and Young point out:

> Reactions to chick lit are divided between those who expect literature by and about women to advance the political activism of feminism, to re-present women's struggles in patriarchal culture and offer inspiring images of strong, powerful women, and those who argue instead that it should portray the reality of young women grappling with modern life. (9)

Some critics take issue with chick lit's 'unseriousness' and supposed anti-feminism. Anna Weinberg, for instance, maintains that 'many of these titles really are trash', while writer Erica Jong laments that today's young women 'are looking for the opposite of what their mothers looked for. Their mothers sought freedom; they seek slavery' (quoted in Ferriss and Young 9; quoted in Jacobson 3). Chick lit is taken to task for not advancing the cause of feminism in a straightforward and politically evident manner and for rehearsing the narratives of romance and femininity that second wave feminists rejected. Moreover, chick lit's unashamed commercialism and concern with shopping and fashion – epitomised by Sophie Kinsella's series of *Shopaholic* novels – have also marked it for feminist disapproval and fears that see women being turned into the unwitting dupes of consumerism. As Ferriss and Young ask, '[i]s chick lit "buying in" to a degrading and obsessive consumer culture' that leads to a 'focus on skin-deep beauty' and heralds retail therapy as a means of personal fulfilment (11)?

Such charges have been answered by other, mostly younger critics as well as authors and fans of chick lit who contend that ambiguity lies at the genre's core. Countering criticisms of her novel, Helen Fielding writes with characteristic aplomb that '[s]ometimes I have had people getting their knickers in a twist about Bridget Jones being a disgrace to feminism. But it is good to be able to represent women as they actually are in the age in which you are living' (quoted in Ferriss and Young 9). She adds, '[i]f we can't laugh at ourselves without having a panic attack over what it says about women, we haven't got very far with our equality'. Examining chick lit varieties over the past decade – recent permutations include, for example, 'mumlit', 'bride lit' and black chick lit – Ferriss and Young are adamant that 'the genre is rife with possibilities and potential', raising 'issues and questions about subjectivity, sexuality, race, class in women's texts for another generation of women to ponder' (12). Even commentators who were initially dismissive of chick lit are now willing to re-examine its prospects: as Imelda Whelehan writes in her conclusion to *The Feminist Bestseller* (2005), she is 'in two minds about chick lit', and 'this uncertainty' can be discerned in her book when she 'waver[s] on both sides of the argument' (218). For her, chick lit is essentially an 'anxious genre' that 'does not know what to do' with the problems and paradoxes it unearths about contemporary women's lives and experiences (218). Ultimately, it appears that chick lit's continuing popularity and increasing variations will ensure the genre's endurance and challenge critics to take its contradictoriness as a starting point for their analyses of twenty-first-century women's fiction. As Gill and Herdieckerhoff put it, it is not enough simply to point to the coexistence of contradictory discourses in chick lit – 'what is important is the work they are doing' (500).

CASE STUDY: *BRIDGET JONES'S DIARY* (1996)

Starting life as a column in the British newspaper the *Independent*, *Bridget Jones's Diary* has often been discussed as the Ur-text of chick lit. An international bestseller and successful feature film – the 2001 film adaptation (starring Renée Zellwegger and Hugh Grant) took $160 million worldwide – Helen Fielding's novel about a British thirty-something single working woman has been credited with catching the mood of the period and summoning the zeitgeist. In this *Bildungsroman* of the single girl, Bridget struggles to make sense of her chaotic life and 'career[s] rudderless and boyfriendless through dysfunctional relationships and professional stagnation' (Fielding, *Diary* 78). She rejects the pejorative label 'spinster' and its negative connotations of unattractiveness, loneliness and social ineptitude, and redefines her status by coining the term 'Singleton' – a new, rebel identity with its own language and attitudes – and forging an unconventional and self-selected urban family of friends. While Bridget is trying to throw off the stigma attached to her single state and resignify it as a novel and rewarding subject position, she also remains ensnared and persecuted by her recurring fear and 'existential angst' of 'dying alone and being found three weeks later half-eaten by an Alsatian' (20). Fielding identifies her character's disorientation as a symptom of a postmodern era of uncertainty, explaining that 'Bridget is groping through the complexities of dealing with relationships in a morass of shifting roles, and a bombardment of idealized images of modern womanhood' (quoted in Whelehan, *Helen Fielding* 17). In these complicated times, women seem to have lost their sense of direction as they are in the process of experimenting with a new set of identities, simultaneously revolving around feminist notions of empowerment and agency as well as patriarchal ideas of feminine beauty and heterosexual coupledom. Bridget neatly expresses the tensions between the lure of feminist politics that enables her to fulfil her public ambitions and a romantic fantasy that sees her swept off her feet by a mysterious and passionate Byronic hero. Trying to combine her progressive feminist beliefs with more conventional views about heterosexual relationships, she reveals that 'confusion . . . is the price I must pay for becoming a modern woman' (119). Bridget's paradoxical outlook is summed up by her New Year's resolution not to 'sulk about having no boyfriend, but develop inner poise and authority and sense of self as woman of substance, complete *without* boyfriend, as best way to obtain boyfriend' (2; emphasis in original).

Starting each diary entry with a calorie/alcohol/cigarette count for the day, Bridget clearly intends to manage and take charge of her life, but she remains obsessed with the twin spectres of marriage and physical insecurity. Bridget's diary sets out her goals in the form of a lengthy list of New Year's resolutions, but her persistent failure to carry out her plans marks the Singleton's inconclusiveness about her position and her constant weighing of the costs and benefits of living in a postfeminist world. Bridget's fallibility and haplessness generate a number of humorous incidents and, eventually, come to be seen as the character's passport to fulfilment and happiness, securing her a partner, the appropriately named Mr Darcy. Critics have interpreted Bridget's inherent tension between the confident paragon she aspires to be and her imperfect and striving 'natural' self as a feminist/feminine, public/personal dichotomy. Accordingly, the novel's 'key contradiction' can be found in the gap between 'the autonomous career women' who populate Singleton narratives and 'the rather pathetic romantic idiots' they become in their relationships (Whelehan, *Helen Fielding* 42). As Imelda Whelehan argues, 'while the success of professional women is trumpeted . . . intimate heterosexual relationships remain unreconstructed, and people have no means of transforming their personal life to match their professional life' (42–3).

The novel poses a number of problems for critics who emphasise second wave feminism's fight for women's equality and access to professions – for example, Bridget takes her boss's email about her short skirt not as sexual harassment but as welcome opportunity for flirtation. Chick lit thus presents women as sexual agents who knowingly employ their femininity – frequently as a statement of empowerment – and do not need to be sheltered from male advances. This accords women a kind of 'sexual subjecthood' and constructs 'an articulation or suture between feminism and femininity' (Gill and Herdieckerhoff 499). As Gill and Herdieckerhoff explain, this is exemplary of a contradictory postfeminist discourse in which, in relation to sexual relationships, 'a discourse of freedom, liberation, and pleasure-seeking sits alongside the equally powerful suggestion that married heterosexual monogamy . . . captures women's real desires' (500). Bridget encapsulates this contradictoriness, which comes to be seen as her saving grace, eventually winning Mark Darcy's heart. She is wanted and desired, not despite but because of her imperfections and her persistent failure to remake herself in another image. In this way, *Bridget Jones's Diary* discards the notion of a perfect feminine or feminist identity and embraces incoherence and contradiction as the space of fulfilment.

RECOMMENDED FURTHER READING

Aapola, Sinikka, Marnina Gonick, and Anita Harris. *Young Femininity: Girlhood, Power and Social Change*. Basingstoke: Palgrave Macmillan, 2005. 18–39.

Ferriss, Suzanne, and Mallory Young, eds. *Chick-Lit: The New Woman's Fiction*. New York and London: Routledge, 2006.

Gill, Rosalind, and Elena Herdieckerhoff. 'Rewriting the Romance: New Femininities in Chick Lit?' *Feminist Media Studies* 6.4 (2006): 487–504.

Munford, Rebecca. '"Wake Up and Smell the Lipgloss": Gender, Generation and the (A)politics of Girl Power.' In *Third Wave Feminism: A Critical Exploration*. Eds Stacy Gillis, Gillian Howie and Rebecca Munford. Basingstoke: Palgrave Macmillan, 2004. 142–53.

4

Do-Me Feminism and Raunch Culture

OVERVIEW

In this chapter we consider a highly sexualised version of power feminism, so-called 'do-me feminism', that sees sexual freedom as the key to female independence and emancipation. Female sexual objectification and pornography have long been the subjects of feminist debates, from the 1970s onwards, with critics vigorously defending both anti- and pro-pornography stances. Advocated by cultural theorists like Camille Paglia, pro-sex feminism emerged as a response to the late 1970s anti-pornography movement – virtually synonymous with the work of Andrea Dworkin and Catharine MacKinnon – that put pornography at the centre of feminist explanations of women's oppression. In many ways, pro-sex feminism can be linked to 1990s expressions of do-me feminism – also referred to as 'bimbo feminism' and 'porno chic' – which addresses women as knowing, active and heterosexually desiring subjects. An important element of do-me feminism is its acceptance and use of irony as a space of playfulness and ambiguity. The increasing sexualisation of female representations in popular culture has been criticised by a number of commentators who are suspicious of the notion of sexual subjecthood. Dismissing the idea that this is a bold new face of feminism, Ariel Levy condemns the rise of 'raunch culture' and the emergence of (what she terms) 'female chauvinist pigs' who deliberately 'make sex objects of other women' and of themselves (4). Raunch culture and do-me feminism blend the sometimes conflicting ideologies of women's liberation and the sexual revolution by heralding sexually provocative appearance and behaviour (including exhibitionist stripping) as acts of female empowerment. We will investigate this sexualised feminist position through case studies on celebrity culture (Paris Hilton) and popular television (*Sex and the City*).

As we examined in the previous chapter, the last decade of the twentieth century saw a re-appraisal and new configurations of femininity in Girl culture and chick lit. The Girlie stance restyles the feminist message of female agency and independence by addressing an (often adolescent) female subject who is self-assured and comfortable with her femininity. The more sexed-up version of this position – 'do-me feminism' – made its way into popular men's magazines in the early 1990s and focuses on sexuality as a means to attain freedom and power. Exemplified in popular culture by a range of 'brainy babes' – including the television lawyer Ally McBeal and the successful Singletons of the HBO series *Sex and the City* – the 'do-me feminist' has been discussed as a 'new breed of feminist heroine' who is 'untrammeled, assertive, exuberantly pro-sex, yet determined to hold her own in a man's world' (Shalit 27). As Ruth Shalit describes:

> the do-me feminist is plucky, confident, upwardly mobile, and extremely horny. She is alert to the wounds of race and class and gender, but she knows that feminism is safe for women who love men and bubble baths and kittenish outfits; that the right ideology and the best sex are not mutually exclusive. She knows that she is as smart and as ambitious as a guy, but she's proud to be a girl and girlish. (28)

The do-me feminist consciously employs her physical appearance and sexuality in order to achieve personal and professional objectives and gain control over her life. She expresses her individual agency not by politicising her relationships with men and her status as a sexual object but primarily through the re-articulation of her feminine/sexual identity. As Angela Neustatter reveals, this sexy 'new woman' no longer requires 'any of that nasty bra-burning, butch, strident nonsense' and she has learnt to make it for herself 'feminine-style' (137). In this sense, the do-me feminist can be said to have 'a different relation to femininity than either the pre-feminist or the feminist woman' as 'she is neither trapped in femininity (pre-feminist), nor rejecting of it (feminist), she can use it' (Brunsdon 85). This 'new' kind of woman is both feminine and feminist at the same time, merging notions of personal empowerment with the visual display of sexuality. Do-me feminists (and their advocates) insist that the adoption of sexual/feminine agency is framed by 'a cultural climate in which women can now be traditionally "feminine" and sexual in a manner utterly different in meaning from either pre-feminist or non-feminist versions demanded by phallocentrically defined female heterosexuality' (Sonnet 170). As Esther Sonnet explains, the current 'return to feminine pleasures . . . is "different"' because, it is suggested, it takes place within 'a social context fundamentally altered by the achievement of feminist goals' (170). The do-me feminist does not manipulate her appearance 'to get a man on the old terms' but 'has ideas about her life and being in control which clearly come from feminism' (Brunsdon 86). Sexuality/femininity thus undergoes a process of resignification whereby it comes to be associated with feminist ideas of female emancipation and self-determination rather than its previous connotations of patriarchal oppression and subjugation.

Do-me feminists want to distance themselves from feminist positions that have been deemed 'anti-sex' by celebrating the pleasures of feminine adornment and sexuality. Do-me feminism bears obvious resemblances to earlier 'sex-positive' feminist stances that argue for sexual empowerment and subjecthood. Sex-positive (or pro-sex) feminism stands in marked contrast to 'sex-critical' feminist analyses that focus on the degrading and exploitive aspects of (hetero)sexuality. Taking its cue from the US grass-roots anti-violence movement, much second wave feminist activism was geared to highlighting women's encounters with sexualised violence – for example, through consciousness-raising sessions that were meant to politicise women's individual experiences and private lives. Many second wave writers and activists were interested in how ideological constructions of gender and sexuality participate in naturalising and perpetuating acts of violence against women. Heterosexual practices were criticised for objectifying and subjugating women, and gradually, voices emerged – in particular in some radical feminist quarters – that urged women/feminists to unseat normative heterosexuality, through, for instance, 'political lesbianism', celibacy and anti-pornography legislation (Whelehan, *Feminist Bestseller* 132; see also Genz, *Postfemininities* chapter 2).

These sex-critical viewpoints reached their most radical height in the late 1970s and early 1980s with the 'pornography wars', which saw two distinct oppositional factions develop: on one side, the anti-pornography and pro-censorship camp – influenced by the writings and political activism of Andrea Dworkin and feminist law professor Catharine MacKinnon – argued that sexually explicit, pornographic material was inherently defamatory to women, encoding misogyny in its most extreme form. As Dworkin writes, '[t]he oppression of women occurs through sexual subordination', as '[i]n the subordination of women, inequality itself is sexualized: made into the experience of sexual pleasure, essential to sexual desire' ('Against the Male Flood' 30). Dworkin identified pornography as 'the material means of sexualizing inequality', revealing an ideology of male domination that posits men as superior to women. Postulating a causal link between pornography and violence

– in accordance with Robin Morgan's famous slogan 'porn is the theory, rape is the practice' – anti-pornography activists protested against commercial sex and aimed at banning it. To this effect, Dworkin and MacKinnon drafted a series of anti-pornography ordinances in the mid-1980s with the intention of making pornography a civil rights issue – rather than a moral one – and giving victims of pornography the right to legal redress. Dworkin and MacKinnon sought to change the legal definition of pornography, and succeeded in getting anti-pornography ordinances passed in some American states, to be overturned later by the US Supreme Court on the grounds that they were in opposition to the constitutional right to free speech.

Many feminists shared this view and saw anti-pornography legislation as an instance of censorship. Anti-pornography perspectives were also denounced for not engaging with female and non-heterosexual desires as other than expressions of pornography's objectifying ideological function. In much anti-pornography rhetoric, porn is depicted as a fixation of straight men and this – pro-pornography campaigners suggest – leaves out both lesbian and pro-pornography women. Arguing that the view of women as passive sufferers and dupes is insufficient, these campaigners are adamant that attention should be given to meanings attached to pornography by women who draw on and get pleasure from it. Following this line of argument, the use of pornography encompasses a number of perspectives on female sexuality: some women might see their consumption of pornography as a source of sexual pleasure and an affirmation of their sexual identities, as well as an exercise of freedom of choice. Instead of understanding women simply as victims, pro-pornography proponents assert that women are capable of placing their own meanings on pornographic material. Anti-pornography feminists are criticised for relying on one-dimensional definitions and readings of pornography/sexuality as operations of male power and female oppression while also simplifying questions of representation, desire and fantasy (see for example, Rubin).

Reacting against the interpretation of sexually explicit material as inherently demeaning and disempowering, sex-positive feminists want to dissociate themselves from what they perceive as puritanical and monolithic feminist thinking. Principally, sex-positive feminism maintains that 'women have the right to determine, for themselves, how they will use their bodies, whether the issue is prostitution, abortion/reproductive rights, lesbian rights, or the right to be celibate and/or asexual' (Alexander 17). Combining sexual empowerment with feminist emancipation, sex-positive feminism emerged from two distinct but closely linked revolutionary movements of the late 1960s and 1970s: women's liberation and the sexual revolution. As Ariel Levy has recently discussed, these two important twentieth-century cultural movements initially overlapped – with many of the same people involved in both causes – but ultimately a schism would form between them (53–4). Many second wave feminist writers originally understood sexual revolution as an integral component of feminism's struggle for women's equality and freedom. For example, Kate Millett's feminist classic *Sexual Politics* (1970) called for a 'fully realized sexual revolution . . . [to] end traditional sexual inhibitions and taboos . . . [as well as] the negative aura with which sexual activity has generally been surrounded' (24, 62). She continues, '[t]he goal of revolution would be a permissive single standard of sexual freedom, and one uncorrupted by the crass and exploitative economic bases of traditional sexual alliances' (62). On a more literary level, this sexualised feminist position is perhaps best represented by Erica Jong's bestselling novel *Fear of Flying* (1973), which follows its heroine, Isadora Wing, on her search for the now infamous 'zipless fuck' – the ultimate 'platonic ideal' of passionate and commitment-free sex (11).

Yet radical and mainstream feminists soon became critical and suspicious of the alliance between women's liberation and the sexual revolution. In *The Dialectic of Sex* (1970), Shulamith Firestone was already expressing her scepticism, commenting that 'women have been persuaded to shed their armour' 'under the guise of a "sexual revolution"' (127). Firestone argued that the sexual revolution 'brought no improvements for women' but proved to have 'great value' for men: by convincing women that 'the usual female games and demands were despicable, unfair . . . and self-destructive, a new reservoir of available females was created to expand the tight supply of goods available for traditional sexual exploitation' (127–8). More contemporary commentators, such as Ariel Levy and Imelda Whelehan, have reinforced the distinction between feminist emancipation and liberation as conceived by the sexual revolution. As Whelehan explains, the sexual revolution might have announced a sea change in social attitudes but it did not automatically alter 'women's sexual identity or their power relationships with men'; sexual revolution thus came to be seen as a 'chimera where women were being sold the idea of sex as liberation but often it cast them in just as strong a thrall to men, with new pressures to perform sexually at every occasion' (*Feminist Bestseller* 109).

By contrast, sex-positive feminists remained faithful to a libertine notion of sexuality well into the 1980s and 1990s, celebrating sexual energy, power and strength. In *Sexual Personae* (1991), Camille Paglia contends that we need to recall the principles of the global consciousness of the 1960s and in particular the sexual revolution in order to enable a new mode of feminism that 'is open to art and sex in all their dark, unconscious mysteries' (vii). Speaking from a late twentieth-century perspective, Paglia adds that 'the feminist of the *fin de siècle* will be bawdy, streetwise, and on-the-spot confrontational, in the prankish sixties way' (vii). Her model of a 'true feminist' is Madonna, who, in Paglia's eyes, has 'taught young women to be fully female and sexual while still exercising control over their lives' (*Sex, Art and American Culture* 4). Controversially, Paglia also argues against feminist involvement in policing sexual relationships, including the issue of sexual harassment and date rape. This aligns her with 'new feminists' like Katie Roiphe who criticise feminism's prudery and focus on female victimisation through exaggerating the dangers of date rape.

More recently, the possibility of a feminist sexuality has been instrumental in the formation of a new feminist culture that brings together a younger group of 'third wave' feminist writers and activists who reject anti-sex forms of feminism and embrace the notion of sexual power. In her introduction to her anthology of personal essays *Jane Sexes it Up* (2002), Merri Lisa Johnson proposes that sexual bravado is part of a contemporary kind of feminism – part of what she terms the 'Jane generation's' revamping of feminism. In Johnson's rhetoric, the phrase 'Jane generation' denotes a new type of woman who is 'lodged between the idea of liberation and its incomplete execution' and wants to reconnect with the feminist movement through exploring the pleasures and dangers of sexuality (1). Her attitudes towards sex and power are in marked contrast to earlier sex-critical feminist stances that now appear unappealing and rigid to a new generation of sexually assertive women. As Johnson provocatively puts it, women of the 'Jane generation' want to 'force feminism's legs apart like a rude lover, liberating her from the beige suit of political correctness' (2). She is keen to emphasise that the group of sexual mavericks writing for her anthology engage in a series of playful sexual expressions that indicate bravery and progress: 'Our writing *is* play, but it is play *despite* and *in resistance to* a context of danger and prohibition, *not* a result of imagining there is none' (2; emphasis in original).

Advocates of this late twentieth-century sexualised feminist culture call for a vision of the future that is a continuation of the freedoms of the sexual revolution coupled with an awareness of sexual oppression activated by the feminist movement. For example, contemporary young women's magazines like *BUST* and *Bitch*, which both debuted in the 1990s, herald the right to be sexual while also demanding a revolution in representation that allows new configurations of sexuality/femininity to emerge. As the editors of *BUST*'s 'Sex Issue' assert, '[w]e want the freedom to be a top, a bottom, or a middle. The freedom to say "maybe" and mean it. The freedom to wear spike heels one day and Birkenstocks the next' (Stoller and Karp 2). What characterises these magazines is not only a sexy kind of feminism but also an implicit acceptance of the fact that this sexualised feminist stance is necessarily embedded in popular culture. As such, a founding principle and subject matter of *Bitch* magazine are a critical examination and celebration of popular representations of women and girls. As the magazine's full title – *Bitch: Feminist Response to Pop Culture* – suggests, feminist 'revolution' is conceived mainly in the realm of representation and in the creative re-articulation of femininity and sexuality. These young women writers and activists thus articulate their desire for feminist continuity/conflict in the controversial gap between sexual objectification and liberation, giving rise to a 'politics of ambiguity' that goes beyond 'the black-and-white binaristic thinking' of previous feminist waves (Siegel, *Sisterhood, Interrupted* 140, 142).

Critics take issue with both the sexual and popular focus of this new feminist culture, arguing that it leads to an embrace of populism as well as a simplistic equation of sex with power. They are concerned that the media plays up a fashionable form of feminism – variously referred to as 'do-me feminism' or 'bimbo feminism' – that acts as an anachronistic throwback to an earlier time (Siegel, *Sisterhood, Interrupted* 10). The notion of sexual/feminine empowerment is criticised as 'a new arrangement of an old song' that mobilises women's sexuality and femininity in service of a patriarchal agenda and status quo (Helford 297). The do-me feminist draws a sense of power and liberation from her sexual difference and thus can be said to propagate the 'old-fashioned' idea that 'women get what they want by getting men through their feminine wiles' (Kim 325). Moreover, by rejecting the concept of group oppression and subjugation, the do-me feminist favours individual effort, and as such, she has been discussed as an individualistic figure who 'tips her hat to past feminist gains but now considers them unnecessary and excessive' (Helford 299). As Charlotte Brunsdon writes, the do-me feminist can be 'accommodated within familiar . . . western narratives of individual success', supplanting the analysis of sexual politics with the notion of personal choice (86). In Janet Lee's eyes, this newly empowered feminine/sexy woman can be understood as a media persona constructed to be in unison with patriarchy:

> bored by feminism and its unglamorous connotations . . . the media . . . [has] decided that we've *done* feminism and it's time to move on. We can call ourselves 'girls', wear sexy underwear and short skirts; because feminism taught us that we're equal to men, we don't need to prove it anymore. (168; emphasis in original)

According to this glamorised, all-achieving, stress- and problem-free media invention, women's economic progress and social position are dependent on personal initiative and do not require continued feminist action and solidarity. In this sense, the do-me feminist has been dismissed by critics as a token opportunist whose progress and choices are no longer obstructed by structural oppressions but result from her own will and self-determination. Critics are adamant that the do-me feminist's emphasis on sexual and individualist achievement undermines and denies feminism's ongoing fight for greater change on a societal level. The 'me'-based feminism of the twenty-first century is said to flatten the dynamics of the feminist movement into one-dimensional characters that are nothing more than cartoons – or in Ruth Shalit's words, 'Gilliganesque caricature[s]' and 'brilliant iteration[s] of Jessica Rabbit' (32). Nowhere is the do-me feminist stance more contentious than in the mainstream of popular culture, where feminism has come to be associated with sexually aggressive behaviour, glamorous styling and provocative posturing.

CASE STUDY: *SEX AND THE CITY* (1998–2004)

When in 2004 the final credits of HBO's *Sex and the City* rolled, a media frenzy of tributes and commentaries on the show ensued, testifying to its importance to many viewers. Based on Candace Bushnell's 1996 novel – which itself developed from a weekly newspaper column in the *New York Observer* between 1994 and 1996 – the series chronicles the lives and loves of four Manhattan-based single professional women in their thirties and forties. The narrative is structured around the musings of writer Carrie Bradshaw (Sarah Jessica Parker), whose column for the fictional *New York Star* provides the thematic framework by setting a different question to be resolved in each episode. Questions in the first few seasons include: are relationships the religion of the nineties? Is secret sex the ultimate form of intimacy? Is it better to fake it than to be alone? In order to explore these issues, the series depicts the experiences of Carrie and her close female friends – public relations expert Samantha Jones (Kim Cattrall), art dealer Charlotte York (Kirsten Davies) and attorney Miranda Hobbes (Cynthia Nixon) – as they navigate their privileged urban lives defined by sexual freedom, professional independence, consumerism, romance and friendship. The show proved to be a worldwide success with over 11 million viewers in the United States alone, and won an Emmy award for outstanding comedy series in 2001, as well as being made into a feature-length film in 2008 (Gill, *Gender and the Media* 241).

Sex and the City has often been lauded for its innovative representation of female friendship and sexuality. As Jane Gerhard explains, the series is structured by two major and overlapping themes: the homosocial bonds between the four main protagonists and the explicitness with which their multiple sexual encounters are portrayed and recounted (43). While the individual characters spend much of their time in the pursuit of heterosexual enjoyment and satisfaction, their perspectives and experiences are always presented and debated within a female world of friendship. In effect, they come to resolutions about their problems or questions – mostly related to their single lives and dating habits – within the network and through the support of the other women. For example, Miranda's decision to go through with her pregnancy is met by Charlotte's joyful announcement to the others that 'we're having a baby!' Rosalind Gill suggests that one of the pleasures offered by the show is its 'feminine address' and 'potential for feminine identification': '*Sex and the City* is about being "one of the girls"; it opens up a world of female bonding' as 'the primary relations the women have are those with each other' (*Gender and the Media* 243–4). The friendship that unites the characters offers them an emotional alternative and family structure to the world of boyfriends and potential husbands – a bond so strong that it sees them through not only their unavoidable break-ups with characteristically marriage-shy New York men but also, as the show progresses, cancer, divorce and religious conversion.

As its title emphasises, another important thematic that characterises the show is its sexual explicitness – both in the way in which the characters are shown having sex with multiple partners throughout the series and in the frank language they use to describe their various sexual encounters. As Deborah Siegel notes, 'The *Sex and the City* four have been hailed as proto-types for the new sexually empowered woman' (*Sisterhood, Interrupted* 154). Without doubt, Carrie and her friends are beneficiaries of the sexual revolution, as they are able to fulfil their desires without censure. The character of Samantha has been particularly notable as a portrayal of a sexually assertive woman in her forties who is demonstrably uninhibited: she is not afraid to display her body – tellingly, she appears nude in most episodes – and articulate her sexuality outspokenly and confidently. Samantha's libertine attitude towards sexuality governs her perception of herself and her life as a single woman in Manhattan – as she tells her friends in an early episode, 'You can bang your head against the wall and try and find a relationship or you can say *screw it* and go out and have sex like a man' (quoted in Levy 170). In an interview, actress Kim Cattrall highlights the progressive and liberating aspects of her screen persona's candid attitude towards sexuality: 'I don't think there's ever been a woman who has expressed so much sexual joy [on television] without her being punished. I never tire of women coming up and saying, "You've affected my life"' (quoted in Gauntlett 61). Jane Gerhard proposes that the explicit sex talk that makes up many of the protagonists' conversations is as intimate as the sexual acts themselves and has a number of significant effects: the talk works 'in the same way that consciousness-raising sessions did for second wave feminists', providing an account of the '"dissonance" the characters experience between ideas about heterosexual romance and their experience of straight sex' (45). Equally, the talk also foregrounds the gratifications of heterosexual sex for women, the pleasures they take in sex and in narrating their encounters to each other. In Gerhard's eyes, this should be seen as an important contribution that the show makes – 'these women are the subjects of heterosexual sex, not its object' (45).

Other commentators have been less optimistic about *Sex and the City*'s promise of sexual freedom and egalitarianism. In *Gender and the Media* (2007), Rosalind Gill points out that, while the show is clearly informed by second wave feminism – featuring independent and successful working women – it contains a number of backlash elements that reveal its ambivalent attitude towards feminism. For example, in Gill's eyes, the bold and sophisticated voices of Carrie Bradshaw and her family of female friends only 'mask their very ordinary, traditional feminine desires' as the four women expend most of their energy looking for Mr Right – or in Carrie's case, the elusive and symbolically named Mr Big (242). Even tough-talking Samantha proves to be vulnerable to these feminine urges: when she falls ill with the flu in one episode, she discovers that none of her lovers will come and nurse her, leaving her to doubt her single lifestyle. Feverish and miserable, Samantha tells Carrie, who eventually comes to give her medicine, 'I should have gotten married' and 'if you don't have a guy who cares about you, it all means shit' – these fears are intensified later in the series when Samantha is diagnosed with breast cancer (quoted in Negra 7). Samantha's emotional collapse is dismissed at the end of the episode as a 'delirium', but it provides a glimpse of a less glamorous version of single female life. Moreover, critics have also taken issue with the show's frank sexual banter, which offers 'a nod to equality' but ends up supporting a heterosexual script (quoted in Gill, *Gender and the Media* 243). As Angela McRobbie and Ariel Levy have argued, in these circumstances the notions of choice and entitlement have to be interrogated, as the characters use their 'feminist' freedom to choose to re-embrace traditional femininity and engage in hedonistic acts of consumption that focus as much on 'Manolo Blahniks and Birkin bags' as on sexual liberation and emancipation ('Notes on Postfeminism'; Levy 172). Ultimately, *Sex and the City* can be said to walk a fine line between exploring women's independence and sexual autonomy and reinforcing a patriarchal vision that revolves around heterosexual attractiveness and romance. Notwithstanding the disagreements over the series' messages and meanings, what goes uncontested is the fact that the show has been influential in its representation of women, inspiring a number of women-centred narratives such as *The L Word* and *Desperate Housewives*.

RAUNCH CULTURE

More generally, the emergence of do-me feminism can also be situated within the context of an increasing sexualisation of late twentieth-century culture that finds its expression in the propagation of discourses about and representations of sex and sexuality across a range of media forms (Gill,

Gender and the Media). A 1999 article in the *New York Times* noted 'the continuing push towards more explicit sexuality in advertisements, movies and on network television', particularly 'the appropriation of the conventions of pornography . . . by the mainstream entertainment industry, the fashion and fine arts worlds' (quoted in McNair, *Striptease Culture* 61). Attwood as well refers to the contemporary 'preoccupation with sexual values, practices and identities; the public shift to more permissive sexual attitudes; the proliferation of sexual texts' and 'the emergence of new forms of sexual experience' (Attwood 78). From the star image of Paris Hilton to Madame Tussaud's wax modelling of porn star Jenna Jameson, texts citing highly sexualised and pornographic styles and aesthetics have become common features of popular media culture in Western societies. A number of critics have sought to diagnose this phenomenon as, variously, 'pornographication' or the mainstreaming of pornography (McNair, *Mediated Sex*), the 'pornofication' of desire (Paasonen et al.), porno chic (McNair, *Striptease Culture*) and the rise of raunch culture (Levy). The expansion of what Brian McNair calls the 'pornosphere' has been interpreted by some as a release from stifling mores and principles and a democratisation of desire that includes diverse sexualities and sexual practices. As McNair suggests, the accelerating flows of sexual information – aided by new communication technologies – have led to a 'less regulated, more commercialised, and more pluralistic sexual culture (in terms of the variety of sexualities which it can accommodate)' (*Striptease Culture* 11). Other critics have pointed instead to uneven gender effects of this mainstreaming of pornography and to the resexualisation and commoditisation of women's bodies in the wake of feminist critiques that worked to neutralise representations of female sexual objectification (Gill, *Gender and the Media*). These commentators have highlighted that women in particular have to be wary of the notion of 'porno chic' that involves depictions of pornography in non-pornographic contexts, and risks providing these sexualised images with a sense of respectability and, indeed, autonomy and freedom.

A specific point of contention has been the use of irony in sexualised imagery coupled with the idea that contemporary women are active sexual subjects rather than passive sexual objects. Discussing 'laddish' men's magazines like *FHM* and *Loaded* – well known for their racy front covers, regular features like 'High Street Honeys' (ordinary women posturing in their lingerie) and competitions like '100 Sexiest' lists and 'Britain's Best Bum' – David Gauntlett argues that these representations of women are motivated by 'genuine' irony rather than sexism (168). Gauntlett maintains that these magazines are fully aware that 'women are as good as men, or better' and that 'the put-downs of women . . . are knowingly ridiculous, based on the assumption that it's silly to be sexist (and therefore is funny, in a silly way), and that men are usually just as rubbish as women' (168). Irony provides a 'protective layer' between lifestyle information and the readers while the 'humour' of the articles implies that they can be read 'for a laugh' (168). While Gauntlett is convinced that contemporary uses of irony do not provide a 'get-out clause' against criticism (168), other commentators have stressed that this is a 'catch-all device' that means 'never having to say you are sorry' (Gill, *Gender and the Media* 110). As Nick Stevenson, Peter Jackson and Kate Brooks argue, irony allows someone to express 'an unpalatable truth in a disguised form, while claiming it is not what they actually meant' (quoted in Gill, *Gender and the Media* 40). Criticism can be forestalled in this way and critics are rendered speechless, as '[a]ny objections we might feel are set up as contradictory because we are supposed to "know" that this is ironic and therefore not exploitative' (Whelehan, *Overloaded* 147). The ironic pornographic discourses prevalent in contemporary cultural texts are particularly damaging and treacherous, as they present women as knowingly and willingly engaging in their own sexualisation. Potentially sexist depictions of women can thus be played down as an ironic 'joke' shared by women and men alike, and critics who object to these portrayals do not have to be taken seriously because they just 'don't get it' and are not sophisticated enough to read through the irony (Gauntlett 168).

Another important characteristic that defines the pornographication of the mainstream and complicates the work of contemporary cultural/feminist critics is the idea that women now adopt a sexualised stance as an expression of positive female autonomy rather than objectification. In her examination of gender representations in the media, Rosalind Gill argues that nowadays women have undergone a 'shift from sexual objectification to sexual subjectification', whereby they are not 'straightforwardly objectified but are presented as active, desiring sexual subjects who choose to present themselves in a seemingly objectified manner because it suits their liberated interests to do so' (*Gender and the Media* 258). Gill notes that contemporary femininity is now predominantly seen as a bodily property (rather than a social structural or psychological one), whereby the possession of a 'sexy body' is presented as women's key source of identity (255). This modernisation of femininity includes a 'new "technology of sexiness" in which sexual knowledge and sexual practice are central' (258). Gill is sceptical about the liberating potential of sexual subjecthood, warning that 'subjectification' might just be 'how we "do" objectification today' (111). She suggests that the shift from sexual object to desiring sexual subject represents a move to 'a new "higher" form of exploitation': 'a shift from an external, male judging gaze to a self-policing narcissistic gaze' (90, 258). The focus on femininity/sexuality as an avenue to agency is seen to be representative of a neo-liberal society that constructs individuals as self-determining and free (Gill and Arthurs, 'New Femininities?').

In *Female Chauvinist Pigs* (2006), Ariel Levy also rejects the notion of sexual subjecthood, insisting that what some are calling 'the new feminism' is really 'the old objectification', disguised in stilettos (81). She blames a phenomenon she dubs 'raunch culture' – the 'glossy, overheated thumping of sexuality' exemplified by programmes such as *Girls Gone Wild* and *Sex and the City* (31) – for co-opting the ideals of sex radicalism and feminism by equating sexually provocative behaviour with freedom. As Levy writes, '[r]aunch culture isn't about opening our minds to the possibilities and mysteries of sexuality. It's about endlessly reiterating one particular – and particularly commercial – shorthand for sexiness' (30). The women who adopt this kind of raunchy 'trash culture' are dismissed unceremoniously as 'FCPs' – 'Female Chauvinist Pigs' or 'women who make sex objects of other women and of themselves' (44, 4). Levy draws a direct link between raunch culture and postfeminism by describing the Female Chauvinist Pig as a 'post-feminist' who surrounds herself with 'caricatures of female hotness' and acts 'like a cartoon woman' who has 'big cartoon breasts, wears little cartoon outfits, and can only express her sexuality by spinning around a pole' (in so-called 'Cardio Striptease' classes that are offered in many gyms and perpetuate the idea that 'Stripping equals sex!') (93, 198, 107, 20). For Levy, the archetypal FCP is Paris Hilton, the 'breathing embodiment of our current, prurient, collective fixations – blondeness, hotness, richness, anti-intellectualism' (30).

CASE STUDY: PARIS HILTON

Paris Hilton – heiress to the Hilton hotel chain – came into the limelight when a home sex video featuring Hilton and former boyfriend Rick Salomon found its way into Internet distribution in 2003, weeks prior to her reality television debut in *The Simple Life*. The Hilton sex tape – widely circulated online under the title *One Night in Paris* – became a staple on Internet porn sites, leading to instant celebrity, complete with journalistic coverage and magazine photo shoots. Since her adventures in amateur pornography, Hilton has become one of the most recognisable and marketable female celebrities in the US, warranting a range of endorsement deals: there is a Hilton jewellery line, perfumes, a modelling contract for Guess jeans, a bestselling book (*Confessions of an Heiress*) and CD. Hilton's brand-name product lines sell best in Japan, where *Vanity Fair* describes her as 'as big, if not bigger than, any movie star' (Smith, 'The Inescapable Paris' 280).

As Ariel Levy has argued, Hilton's case is noteworthy because it exemplifies the repurposing of pornography and the proliferation of porno chic

across contemporary media. Compared with previous examples of famous
figures managing the exposure of pornographic images – Levy cites Vanessa
Williams, who was stripped of her Miss America crown in 1983 after nude
photos of her appeared in *Penthouse*, and who years later recreated herself as
an actress and singer – Hilton has made good use of her exposure to turn
herself into a profitable brand. As Levy comments, 'then, being exposed in
porn was something you needed to come back from. Now, being in porn is
itself a comeback' (27). In Levy's account, Hilton is presented as 'the perfect
sexual celebrity for this moment', as she arouses the public's interest not in the
existence of sexual pleasure itself but in 'the appearance of sexiness' (30). For
example, in her television series *The Simple Life* – which follows Hilton and
fellow socialite Nicole Richie as they struggle to do manual, low-paid jobs
such as cleaning and farm work – Hilton plays the role of the clued-up teenager, telling girls and boys alike how they can look 'hot'. In effect, as Levy
points out, 'hotness has become our cultural currency, and a lot of people
spend a lot of time and a lot of regular, green currency trying to acquire it'
(31). Hotness in this case does not just refer to sexual attractiveness but is also
closely related to saleability and commercial appeal. As Naomi Wolf puts it,
Hilton can be described as 'an empty signifier' that 'you can project absolutely
anything onto' (quoted in Smith, 'The Inescapable Paris' 280). Media experts
and producers have lined up to re-invent her as an actress, a pop singer, a
model and author, making the 'Paris Hilton' trademark highly profitable and
earning Hilton a sizeable fortune, with an approximate yearly income of $7
million in 2005–6 (*Forbes* magazine). While Hilton herself maintains that
she is a canny businesswoman who is proud of her independence – as she
emphasises in a number of interviews, she 'loves to work' and 'it feels good
that I don't have to depend on a man or my family for anything' (Hattenstone
18) – critics have largely dismissed her as an example of mainstreamed porno
chic that draws on conventionally heteronormative imageries. As Susanna
Paasonen et al. maintain, '[t]here is indeed little to be considered transgressive in the public/pubic acts of . . . Paris Hilton' (12).

SEXUAL SUBJECTIVATION

While it would be convenient to conclude that sexual subjecthood is a commercial media ploy that is exploited by a few cartoonish women, we also want
to draw attention to the potential for resignification that is lodged within
the re-articulations of sexuality. Stéphanie Genz has recently argued that it
might be useful to adopt a 'postfeminine' framework to discuss contemporary
expressions of sexuality and femininity (*Postfemininities* 31). In an effort to
produce a more nuanced reading of twenty-first-century sexual and feminine

identities, Genz suggests that 'we have to open ourselves up to new modes of critique, subjectivity and agency that might not fit our pre-existing models and frameworks' (96). In order to explore the paradoxes of a postfeminist femininity/sexuality, she proposes that we adopt a non-dualistic model of subject formation that breaks down well-established dichotomies between feminist and feminine identities; subject and object; victim and perpetrator; complicity and critique. The '"pink-packaged" power of sexual subjecthood' is described as entailing 'a simultaneous objectification', as 'postfeminin-ity is at its core a paradoxical construction that effects a double movement of empowerment and subordination' (31). Drawing on the Foucauldian concept of *assujetissement* (or 'subjectivation'), Genz proposes that '[t]his doubled process may help us to comprehend and explore the paradoxes of a postfeminist femininity that can work in empowering and subordinating ways'. Critiques such as these highlight the complex identity positions that women take up in contemporary society, as both a conscious and unconscious 'choice'. In Ien Ang's words, many women of the new millennium can be said to reside in a strangely unsettled in-between space where they are 'free and yet bounded', inhabiting a contradictory site that is simultaneously con-straining and liberating, productive and oppressive (165). What makes this contemporary critical site so thought-provoking and contentious is precisely the varying degrees of 'freedom' and 'boundedness', with critics vigorously debating as to where this precarious balance lies.

RECOMMENDED FURTHER READING

Genz, Stéphanie. *Postfemininities in Popular Culture.* Basingstoke: Palgrave Macmillan, 2009.

Gerhard, Jane. '*Sex and the City*: Carrie Bradshaw's Queer Postfeminism.' *Feminist Media Studies* 5.1 (2005): 37–49.

Gill, Rosalind. 'From Sexual Objectification to Sexual Subjectification: The Resexualisation of Women's Bodies in the Media.' *Feminist Media Studies* 3.1 (2003): 100–6.

Levy, Ariel. *Female Chauvinist Pigs: Women and the Rise of Raunch Culture.* London: Pocket Books, 2006.

5

Postmodern (Post)Feminism

OVERVIEW

This chapter addresses the contentions surrounding the problematic meeting of feminism and postmodernism and explores the theoretical and practical implications of a postmodern feminism. As will be demonstrated, such a conjunctive relationship is fraught with complexities, as 'it is clear to anyone engaged in these enterprises that neither feminism nor postmodernism operates as one big happy family' (Singer 471). There is no unified postmodern theory, or even a coherent set of positions, just as there is no one feminist outlook or critical perspective. Instead, one is struck by the plurality of postmodern and feminist positions and the diverse theories lumped together under these headings. There is a variety of different links between feminist and postmodern theory, with the proposals of conjunction ranging from a strategic corporate merger, to the suggestion of various postmodern and feminist versions varying in strength, to the downright rejection of a postmodern feminism. These calls for (non-)alliance often draw upon a reductive conceptualisation and simplification of the two entities and propose a facile distinction between feminism's political engagement and postmodernism's theoretical self-absorption. In the following, we resist such dualistic responses, which do not account for the wide range of relationships between feminist and postmodern enterprises, and we maintain that there is no shorthand way to characterise the differences and conjunctions between these two multifaceted discourses or movements.

Prevalent in academic circles, theoretical strands of postfeminism are informed by both postmodern and feminist analyses – as well as the complexities inherent in 'postmodern feminism'. This understanding of postfeminism highlights its pluralistic and anti-foundationalist tendencies, whereby it rejects the notion of a universal and singular conception of 'Woman' and instead foregrounds the individual differences between women. This emphasis on difference and individualism links postmodern postfeminism to its more popular manifestations. We will explore the debates surrounding postmodern feminism, centring on the problem of subjectivity as the point of contention and division (what Susan Hekman calls the distinction between the *constituting* self of the humanist/modern tradition and its *constituted* postmodern counterpart). In so doing, we consider various manifestations of postmodern (post) feminism, including postcolonial and hip-hop feminism. We will discuss the pop icon Madonna, the French performance artist Orlan and the hip-hop star Lil'Kim as representatives of a postmodern (post)feminist stance. These female performers have been credited with re-inventing their identities and re-appropriating feminine/female iconography and fashion (most famously exemplified by Madonna's conically breasted Gaultier corset). This self-fashioning will be examined in relationship to Linda Hutcheon's theory of *complicitous critique* (a paradoxical postmodern form of critique that is bound up with its own complicity with domination).

THE POSTMODERN SUBJECT

The notion of the 'subject' has been accorded a vital importance in postmodern theories that cast doubt on the idea of the autonomous and free agent – often identified as an integral component of modernity – and articulate a self that is always within power structures and subjected to multiple discursive formations. As a conceptual category, the postmodern subject is fluid rather than stable, constructed rather than fixed, contested rather than secure, multiple rather than uniform, deconstructed rather than whole. In effect, postmodern (or post-structuralist) thinking problematises the concept of the *constituting* subject of the Cartesian tradition, along with the notions of agency, creativity and resistance, and instead stresses the discursive construction and the *constituted* nature of the individual (Hekman). Following Fredric Jameson, this deconstructive attack can be referred to as 'the death of the subject' or 'the end of the autonomous bourgeois *monad*', whereby the spontaneous and rational self developed by Enlightenment thinkers is radically decentred and dismissed ('Postmodernism, or The Cultural Logic of Late Capitalism' 71–2).

The postmodern dispersal of the subject has been reinforced by feminist scholars as this deconstructive notion seems to further their attempts to open up the subject category to women. The contemporary feminist movement is informed by postmodernism's questioning of the major tenets of the subject-centred epistemology of modernity as it realises its potential to advance a cultural politics of diversity. Feminists reject the philosophical notion of a transcendent subject, a self thematised as universal and free from any contingencies of difference. The feminist critique is based on a distrust of modern theory and politics that, it is argued, have devalued women's subject positions and neglected their vital concerns. As Best and Kellner maintain, feminists 'have quite rightly been suspicious of modernity . . . because the oppression of women has been sustained and legitimated through the philosophical underpinnings of modern theory and its essentialism, foundationalism and universalism' (206). The principal thrust of the feminist argument is that the subject has been conceived as inherently masculine, and thus, it has been a significant factor in maintaining the inferior status of women. In its gendered conceptualisation of the subject category, the humanist discourse of 'Man' covertly supports and justifies male domination of women as it constructs a binary opposition between the sexes, exemplified by two antithetical sets of characteristics that position Man as the voice of reason and objectivity while enslaving Woman in domestic activities and excluding her from public life. Accordingly, as Susan Hekman points out, 'efforts to open up, reform, or reconstitute the masculine subject have been a central aspect of the feminist movement for several decades', and she notes that, unless the subject is reconstructed, 'the subjection of women that it fosters will necessarily continue' (45).

In this way, there are profound similarities and affinities between postmodern and feminist attacks on universalism, foundationalism and dichotomous thinking, and on this level, postmodern theory is 'of use to feminism and other social movements, providing new philosophical support and ammunition for feminist critique and programmes' (Best and Kellner 207). As Best and Kellner point out, 'the postmodern emphasis on plurality, difference and heterogeneity has had immense appeal to those who have found themselves marginalized and excluded from the voice of Reason, Truth and Objectivity' (207). As critiques of modernity, feminism and postmodernism are suspicious of the imperial claims of Enlightenment philosophy revolving around concepts of knowledge, subjectivity and forms of social domination. In fact, 'feminism encourages postmodern theory to articulate the critique of the humanist universal "Man" as a discourse of male domination', thereby producing a more differentiated analysis of the production of subjects in terms of gender identities (207).

POST–THEORY

As we mentioned in the introduction, postfeminism can be discussed as an inherent part of a post-theoretical tendency that articulates 'the deconstruction of current hegemonic systems' and entails a convergence of theories emanating from diverse fields and disciplines (de Toro 16, 10). While we welcome post-theory's rejection of epistemological purity in favour of a pluralistic conception of theory, we also contend that such a mixing of disciplines and evocation of difference cannot be adopted unquestioningly, as is evidenced in the case of postmodern feminism. According to advocates of post-theory, the amalgamation of different epistemologies can be imagined as a mutually beneficial coalition, proceeding from a recognition of the diversity of the two entities to be combined and without the expectation and safeguard of some unifying principle. In this optimistic formulation, 'the prospect of a merger . . . is undertaken as a way of intensifying and enhancing the value of each entity taken separately' (Singer 472). Contrastingly, we maintain that the intersection of feminism and postmodernism cannot be conceptualised as a romantic and uncomplicated communion and blending of diverse epistemological fields, but has to be described as an open and intense confrontation of two multifaceted and contradictory contexts. Feminism and postmodernism operate as forms for social production and exchange, and in both contexts there is little agreement amongst practitioners with regard to that which they may be said to have in common. These internal specificities further complicate the question of articulating a proposal of convergence that does justice to the diversity of feminist and postmodern viewpoints.

We argue that post-theory's seemingly unproblematic alliance of postmodernism and feminism threatens to elide both movements' inherent complexities. Rather than embracing epistemological plurality for its own sake, one has to interrogate the nature of the linkage and analyse the conceptual use and strategic function of the post-theoretical 'and'. In this chapter, we will consider various theoretical and practical attempts to define a postmodern feminism and/or postfeminism, and we assert that a large number of these calls for conjunction rely on a binary structure whereby postmodernism's ontological uncertainty is opposed to a feminist politics and working model which depend on a Cartesian notion of subjectivity, agency and creativity. The critical juncture of feminism and postmodernism has been theorised employing a falsely dualistic formulation, whereby feminism is based on the notion of an autonomous and self-reflexive female subject whereas postmodernism is defined as a theoretical/philosophical perspective, debilitating for feminist agency and politics. Following these conceptualisations, postmodern theory is seen to undermine women's/feminists' sense of selfhood and their capacity for criticism and resistance. Postmodernism is interpreted as a political threat for feminism, as its primary motivation is philosophical while feminism's primary motivation is political. We suggest that the intersections of feminism and postmodernism cannot be conceived as a harmonious union, nor can they be mapped onto a simplistic dualism that opposes feminist practice to postmodern theory. Instead, postmodernism and feminism are engaged in a multivalent and contradictory dialogue, forging a postmodern feminism and/or postfeminism that exceeds binary logic.

In fact, the rift between postmodernism and feminism is seen to be the result of two tendencies proceeding from opposite directions towards the same objective: to debunk traditional/patriarchal philosophy. Postmodernists and feminists both criticise Western concepts of Man, history and metaphysics, but their criticisms do not necessarily converge. In this way, feminism is described as 'a call to action' that 'can never be simply a belief system' as 'without action, feminism is merely empty rhetoric which cancels itself out' (Alice 12). Diametrically opposed to this activist stance, the postmodern discourse is characterised by an inherent relativism and declares itself concerned not with the question of establishing meanings, but with the challenge of any univalent structure and concept. As Nancy Hartsock deplores, 'postmodernism . . . at best manages to criticize these theories [of enlightened modernity] without putting anything in their place', concluding that 'for those of us who want to understand the world systematically in order to change it, postmodern theories at their best give little guidance' (159).

According to these views, the effect of postmodernism has been a limitation of political and critical intervention as its introspective and deconstructive sensitivity turns into tongue-tying anxiety and quietism. Within postmodernism, the category of intention is seen to be overdetermined to the extent that subjectivity is little more than a construct grounded on discourses, beyond individual control. Myra Macdonald reveals that women in particular are questioning whether 'we have the right to offer criticism as "women", when "women" may be an essentialist, patriarchal category that denies difference within it' (38). Applied to feminism's own identity as representing the interests of women, postmodernism's fracturing of the subject poses a potential threat to feminist theory and politics as it forecloses the possibility of a sovereign feminist selfhood. Postmodernism represents a political liability for feminism, in so far as it challenges a unified conception of the feminist movement. The encounter of feminism and postmodernism is fraught with conceptual and practical dilemmas for, as Nancy Fraser and Linda Nicholson ask, 'how can we combine a postmodernist incredulity toward metanarratives with the social-critical power of feminism?' (34).

The key questions raised by feminist critics focus on the issues of agency and subjectivity and are concerned with the specific nature of the political action that feminists can design and pursue in the absence of a systematic, general and theoretical account of the condition of women. Feminist critics maintain that postmodern deconstructionism gives little sense of how to justify generalisations about women and ultimately dissolves the foundations of the feminist movement. Consequently, fears mount up that the postmodern critique 'may not only eliminate the specificity of feminist theory but place in question the very emancipatory ideals of the women's movement' (Benhabib 78). As Moi asserts, 'the price for giving in to [this] powerful discourse is nothing less than the depoliticisation of feminism [as] it will be quite impossible to argue that women under patriarchy constitute an oppressed group, let alone develop a theory of their liberation' (95). It is suggested that, for feminism, postmodernism's invocation of difference and its dismissal of the *constituting* agent of modernity translate into a self-destructive pluralism and abstract individualism. Diversified beyond the possibility of union, critics are concerned that the feminist movement will become fractured and fragmented to such an extent that it cannot be said to represent and politically advance the interests of women, as a structurally disadvantaged category relative to men. The outcome is a depoliticised and personalised feminism that makes individuation of its members a principal goal but cannot be employed as a politics of resistance or a programme for change.

Thought through to its logical conclusion, postmodern theory may even result in a nihilistic stance that dismantles and dismisses the subject category altogether as a fiction or construct. As Patricia Waugh notes, postmodernism 'may even situate itself at a point where there is no "subject" and no history in the old sense at all. . . . "Identity" is simply the illusion produced through the manipulation of irreconcilable and contradictory language games' (*Feminine Fictions* 7). This view is encapsulated by Jean Baudrillard's pessimistic position, which assumes that 'the postmodern world is devoid of meaning; it is a universe of nihilism where theories float in a void, unanchored in any secure harbour' (quoted in Best and Kellner 127). According to Baudrillard, the postmodern is 'characteristic of a universe where there are no more definitions possible. . . . It has all been done. The extreme limit of these possibilities has been reached. It has destroyed itself. It has deconstructed its entire universe' (24).

Postmodernists' theoretical deconstructionism, critics fear, can turn into stagnation and quietism as they refuse to offer any declarations of faith or meaning. By deconstructing subjectivity, postmodernism is seen to abolish those ideals of autonomy and accountability that are necessary for the idea of historical change. Seyla Benhabib voices her concerns that a complete rejection of the concepts of selfhood and agency debilitates the possibility of critical theory. Benhabib notes that postmodern views of subjectivity are incompatible with feminist politics, as they 'undermine the very possibility of feminism as the theoretical articulation of the emancipatory aspirations of women' (29). She is adamant that such utopian thinking is 'a practical-moral imperative', as 'without such a regulative principle of hope, not only morality but also radical transformation is unthinkable' (20). As she notes, 'social criticism without some form of philosophy is not possible, and without social criticism the project of a feminist theory which is at once committed to knowledge and to the emancipatory interests of women is inconceivable' (90).

Following postmodern theorists, feminist efforts must be directed towards dismantling all totalising and essentialist patterns of thought, including its own unifying myths and grounding assumptions. The category 'Woman' can no longer be embraced as a collective identity whereby women can bond and express their relative lack of power vis-à-vis men in society. As a consequence, the feminist movement has to interrogate its own foundation, forged as an inclusive, women-centred basis for social thought and political action. Some critics are anxious that this might result not only in the depoliticisation of feminism but also in its eradication as a social movement: 'Nominalism threatens to wipe out feminism itself' for 'if the concept of woman is a fiction, then the very concept of women's oppression is obsolete and feminism's raison d'être disappears' (Alcoff 419; Brooks 23). The dilemma facing feminist theorists is that their very self-definition is grounded in a concept that they must also de-essentialise in all of its aspects, which ultimately leads to the 'nagging question [of] whether the uncertain promise of a political linkage between feminism and postmodernism is worth the attendant potential risks' (di Stefano 77).

In the most pessimistic formulations of the postmodern/feminist synthesis, feminism is absorbed by postmodern theory, and its specificity and politics are negated. Paradoxically, while the decentred space of the postmodern is adorned with ciphers of heterogeneity and multiplicity, it can also be seen as a neutralising realm, subsuming differences into the meta-category of the 'undifferentiated' where all singularities become indistinguishable and interchangeable in a new economy of 'sameness'. As Nancy Hartsock notes, despite postmodernists' 'desire to avoid universal claims and despite their stated opposition to these claims, some universalistic assumptions creep back into their work' (159).

Feminist theorists have been wary of this gesture of inclusion that arrogates feminism into postmodernism, suggesting that the postmodern condition should not be mistaken for a structural *fait accompli*, a one-dimensional phenomenon that impacts upon everyone in the same way. As Ien Ang reveals, such totalising accounts assume that there is 'a linear, universal and radical historical transformation of the world from "modernity" to "postmodernity"' (2). Ang asserts that one has to go beyond the many sweeping generalisations and platitudes enunciated about postmodernism and concentrate on its signification as a break with modernity, 'the very dispersal of taken for granted universalist and progressivist assumptions of the modern' (2). The underlying thread of these remarks is that postmodernism must question its own globalising narratives and reject a description of itself as embodying a set of timeless ideals. As Nicholson points out, postmodernism 'must insist on being recognized as a set of viewpoints of a time, justifiable only within its own time' ('Introduction' 11). Postmodern theorising and its invocation of difference must be historical, following from the demands of specific contexts and attuned to the cultural specificity of different societies and periods.

As Patricia Waugh notes, women can only 'begin to problematize and to deconstruct the socially constructed subject positions available to them' once they have 'experienced themselves as "subjects"' (*Feminine Fictions* 25). Starting from the position of fragmented subjectivity, women's 'dreams of becoming "whole"' cannot be dismissed and rejected as 'the reactionary move it might constitute in the writings of a representative of hegemony', since they are 'far less likely to mistake themselves for the universal "man" anyway' (Koenen 134). Feminism has provided its own critique of essentialist and foundationalist assumptions that is not interchangeable or synonymous with the postmodern deconstructive position. Postmodernism is criticised for its gender-blindness, whereby it assumes and then rejects relationships that women have never experienced as subjects in their own right. Furthermore, even if women were to adopt postmodern deconstructionism, 'the luxury of female anti-essentialism' could still only be accorded to the privileged, as 'non-white, non-heterosexual, non-bourgeois women are still finding political impetus in summoning up womanhood as identity and femininity as a construct which excludes and punishes them most painfully of all' (Whelehan, *Modern Feminist Thought* 211). The majority of women are not in a position to make choices and reject the politically enabling category of 'Woman', and thus, they might not be willing to yield the ground on which to make a stand against their oppression.

Consequently, suspicions arise in some feminist quarters that postmodernism is a 'remasculinizing' strategy and an anti-feminist appropriative scheme, whereby feminism is subsumed 'into the postmodernist critique of "the tyranny of the signifier"' and it is reduced to 'simply another of the "voices of the conquered"' . . . that challenge the West's desire for ever-greater domination and control' (Jones, '"Post-Feminism": A Remasculinization' 9, 14). According to this view, feminism is negated and its political theory is appropriated and defused as merely one postmodernist strategy among many to criticise modernist ideologies. Postmodernism's questioning of subjectivity and its scepticism regarding the possibilities of a general theory are interpreted as patriarchal ploys to silence the confrontational voices of feminism and to divert feminists from 'tasks more pressing than deciding about the appropriateness of the label "feminist"' (Modleski 6). In this context, postmodernism and by extension postfeminism appear as a Trojan horse pretending to expand the feminist debate but, in effect, allowing male critics to enter and take over feminism. Tania Modleski is one of the key proponents of this pessimistic and defensive appraisal of the postmodern/feminist synthesis whereby 'men ultimately deal with the threat of female power by incorporating it' (7). She entitles her book *Feminism without Women* (1991), and she employs this phrase to suggest the triumph either of a male feminist perspective that excludes women or of a feminist anti-essentialism so radical that every use of the term 'Woman', however provisional, is disallowed. Modleski is concerned that, in its extreme interpretations, anti-essentialism has inaugurated a postfeminist stance that is not only without 'Woman' but also without the possibility of 'women'. She concludes that the postmodern and postfeminist 'play with gender in which differences are elided can easily lead us back into our "pregendered" past where there was only the universal subject – man' (163).

Accordingly, it is suggested that 'if feminism can learn from postmodernism it has finally to resist the logic of its arguments' and reject 'its more extreme nihilistic' implications (Waugh, 'Introduction' 189, 190). It is argued that feminism must posit some belief in 'the notion of effective human agency, the necessity for historical continuity in formulating identity and a belief in historical progress' (195). The underlying assumption is that feminism has to articulate a core belief in a self that, despite being produced through discursive and ideological formations, nevertheless has a material existence and history in human relationships. This view presupposes that, no matter how constituted by discourse, the subject retains a certain ability and agency, as without such a regulative ideal, the very project of female emancipation becomes unimaginable. Feminist critics are adamant that, in order to be effective as a politics of liberation, the feminist movement must maintain a distance and autonomy from postmodern theories that valorise free play of meaning, even as it sees the potential that these theoretical positions offer in disrupting hierarchies of power once taken for granted.

In other words, feminist politics and action can only be formulated if they maintain the modern idea of a creative and autonomous self. Feminism has to take into account its own epistemological anchorage in the theories and ideas of enlightened modernity. The very discourse of emancipation is 'a modern discourse', as 'modern categories such as human rights, equality, and democratic freedoms and power are used by feminists to criticize and fight against gender domination' (Best and Kellner 208). Consequently, Patricia Waugh argues that 'feminism cannot sustain itself as an emancipatory movement unless it acknowledges its foundations in the discourses of modernity' ('Introduction' 190). Moreover, feminist critics maintain that, even if feminism draws upon postmodern forms of disruption, it cannot repudiate entirely the framework of enlightened modernity without perhaps fatally undermining itself as an emancipatory politics.

Yet, as we have already discussed, feminists are also involved in a critical project designed to attack the totalising claims of modern philosophy, to expose its limitations and highlight their own exclusion from the humanist discourse of Man. In this sense at least, feminism can be seen to be an intrinsically 'postmodern' discourse. We suggest that feminism has to be cognizant regarding its own ambiguous positioning between modernity and postmodernity, as it tries to advance the idea of a self that eschews the sexism of the Cartesian subject while simultaneously retaining the notion of agency and autonomy. The feminist movement cannot unproblematically embrace an unreconstructed modern subject or postmodernism's decentred self, as it is engaged in a struggle to reconcile context-specific difference with universal political claims. Feminism has to negotiate its position in the problem space between essentialism and anti-essentialism, in which neither interminable deconstruction nor uncritical reification of the category 'Woman' is adequate to its demands. As a conceptual category, feminism has to recognise a central contradiction in its attempt to define an epistemological base, as women seek equality and recognition of a gendered identity that has been constructed by cultural formations that feminism simultaneously seeks to challenge and dismantle. By conjuring up the category 'Woman' as their common, political denominator, feminists are in danger of reproducing the essential constructions of gender that they also set out to contest. In many ways, one could argue that feminism is suspended between its desire to posit an autonomous female/feminist self and the necessity of having to deconstruct the modern discourse of subjectivity.

POST(MODERN)FEMINISM

As we have already noted, the feminist debate over subjectivity is structured by the strained relation between the *constituting* self of the humanist/modern tradition and the *constituted* subject of postmodernity. According to Susan Hekman, there is a sharp opposition between these two conceptions: the constituting subject is 'transcendent, rational, and autonomous' whereas 'that which is constituted (which cannot be labelled a "subject" at all) is determined and unfree – a social dupe' (47). Feminist theorists have sought to reformulate the postmodern dismissal and decentring of subjectivity and articulate a new approach to the subject. They have tried to alter the parameters of the controversy surrounding the concept of subjectivity and redefine the relationship between the constituted and constituting selves. Specifically, they have posed the questions of how agency can be defined and attributed to a non-Cartesian subject and how resistance can be posited for this subject.

Various critical attempts have been made to reconcile feminism's modern and postmodern, essentialist and anti-essentialist components, as feminist theorists are engaged in the process of forging a postmodern feminism that integrates both contexts' 'respective strengths while eliminating their respective weaknesses' (Fraser and Nicholson 20). This 'postmodern, unbounded feminism' unifies 'coalitionally rather than foundationally' in such a way that postmodernism and feminism operate like 'those fictive entities known as corporations, under whose auspices a wide range of enterprises are organized and collected' without assuming any essential relationship between them (Schwichtenberg 132; Singer 472). As Linda Singer suggests, the postmodern/feminist meeting should be interpreted as a 'corporate merger' that is not undertaken as 'a romantic project of desire nor out of the need for some form of mystical communion', but as a strategic union 'born out of an interest in consolidating competition, diversifying one's assets, or operating from a greater position of strength and viability' (472). This model of conjunction assumes and proceeds from a recognition of the diversity and difference of the two entities to be combined without the expectation of unification or resolution. For example, Nancy Fraser and Linda Nicholson suggest that we can reconcile political (feminist) commitments with their theoretical (postmodern) sympathies by substituting pragmatism for the hyper-theoretical claims of postmodernism. In order to mediate between philosophical adequacy and political efficacy, feminism has to adopt a pragmatic approach that does not shift concerns about difference to theoretical questions but remains focused on practical considerations. Other feminist critics have followed similar lines of thought, arguing that 'we need to be pragmatic, not theoretically pure' if we want to preserve the possibility of 'project[ing] utopian hopes, envision[ing] emancipatory alternatives, and infus[ing] all our work with a normative critique of domination and injustice' (Bordo 242; Fraser et al. 159).

Seyla Benhabib provides an example of this pragmatic union of feminism and postmodernism in her conceptualisation of a postmodern scale that offers variously intense versions of postmodern theses that are distinguished in terms of their compatibility with feminism. Benhabib notes that the complex interaction of postmodernism and feminism around the notion of identity 'cannot be captured by bombastic proclamations of the "Death of the Subject"' (83). She suggests a way out of the subject-centred dilemma by advocating a 'weak' version of this theory that situates the subject in relation to social, cultural and discursive surroundings. Contrastingly, a 'strong' version of the same thesis undermines all concepts of intentionality, accountability, self-reflexivity and autonomy. Benhabib maintains that only the 'weak' version is compatible with feminism, as it stresses variability and diversity, while the strong/radical version is counterproductive for feminist theory, politics and practice, reducing the subject to an endless state of flux. Any attempt to link feminism with a 'strong' postmodernism can only engender incoherence and self-contradictoriness, undermining all efforts at effective theorising and leading feminism to a passive stance from which it is reticent to formulate a feminist concept of autonomy for fear of lapsing into essentialism.

Benhabib's proposition relies on a rejection of an extreme postmodern theory that provides no basis for a politics of alliance, as it is one-sided, excessively prohibitive and politically disabling. Instead, she draws on a 'weak' postmodernism as a method of feminist pluralisation and a strategy of disruption that 'can teach us the theoretical and political traps of why utopias and foundational thinking can go wrong' (30). In this mediating attempt, 'pure' postmodern theory is injected with a dose of feminism's political concreteness while feminism is diversified in its exchange with postmodern anti-essentialism. Benhabib endeavours to criticise 'the metaphysical presuppositions of identity politics' and challenge 'the supremacy of heterosexist positions in the women's movement', without completely debunking the notions of selfhood and agency (81). In our eyes, this delineation of the postmodern/feminist junction retains the idea of a modern agent who drives towards autonomy in order to avoid a conception of the subject as wholly determined. Benhabib does not ascribe to a complete deconstruction of the Cartesian self, but rather seeks to incorporate some of its key elements. Her analysis rests on a modern definition of agency imported from the Cartesian subject and rooted in a dichotomised understanding of the *constituting* self of modernity and its *constituted* postmodern counterpart. Benhabib's account of the postmodern/feminist meeting results in a predominantly modern feminism infused with a postmodern strain to create a more diverse politics for the contemporary age.

Contrastingly, we maintain that feminism's intersection with postmodern theory and the emergence of postfeminism cannot be comprehended by having recourse to a modern epistemology of subjectivity. The postmodern/feminist link needs to displace the opposition between the *constituted* and *constituting* selves and formulate concepts of agency from within the constructivist constraints. In this way, liberal fantasies of a rational agent have to be abandoned in favour of a subject who is firmly located within a network of power/discourse. This entails a contentious redefinition of agency and intentionality as the products of discourse, implicated in and conditioned by the very relations of power they seek to rival. In our understanding, political action and selfhood cannot be presented as emanating from an untainted inner space that is opposed to the outer world of external determination; rather they are part of an inherently multiple, dynamic and contradictory discursive field that depolarises and blurs the binary distinctions between the Cartesian self and the postmodern non-self. It is important to question the notion of a neutral realm of feminist politics and assert that there is no outside position from which feminism's connection with postmodernism can be evaluated. We adopt a view of postmodernism as a politically ambivalent, but none the less political, discourse whose directionality is not fixed as it provides a double movement of subversion and reinforcement. In this sense, as we elaborate in the final chapter of this book, we resist contemporary critiques that assume that postmodernism/postfeminism is disqualified from political involvement and postulate that the postmodern/postfeminist discourse offers a paradoxical critique that works within the very systems it attempts to undermine. Additionally, we suggest that the proliferation of difference – precipitated by postmodern theory – not only complicates the perception of (feminist) political agency but also becomes entangled with economic considerations of a late capitalist society that recognises the commercial appeal of signifiers of 'diversity'. This holds true for political identities linked to both race and gender that have been appropriated in dominant culture through 'the brand identity of the urban and postfeminism' (Banet-Weiser 215). As Banet-Weiser notes, one has to acknowledge the mediated forms of both race and gender that 'come to us in the contemporary context as a commodity' (204). This adds another layer to the postmodern/feminist problematic and highlights the fact that 'agency' and 'diversity' are now consumer-driven marketing tools.

CASE STUDY: MADONNA

As Madonna turned fifty in 2008, her ability to keep redefining the parameters of her identity did not abate. Whether it is as a woman, mother, pop icon or fifty year old, the American singer challenges our preconceptions of who 'Madonna' is and, more broadly, what these identity categories mean within a postmodern context. Madonna can be said to represent the archetypal postmodern (post)feminist woman, constantly contesting and reworking her identity. In part, the key to her identity is that it cannot be fixed, and as she explains in an interview on her documentary *Truth or Dare* (1991) – or, as it was known in Europe, *In Bed with Madonna* – we can never have access to the 'real' Madonna: 'I wanted to see that my life isn't so easy, and one step further than that is the movie's not completely me. You could watch it and say, I still don't know Madonna, and good. Because you will never know the real me. Ever' (quoted in Kaplan 149).

Madonna's postmodern characteristics pose a problem for some feminists, who 'view her multiple personae as a threat to women's socialization, which entails the necessary integration of female identity' (Schwichtenberg 130). As Schwichtenberg proposes, Madonna 'uses simulation strategically in ways that challenge the stable notion of gender as the edifice of sexual difference' (130). In particular, the singer's hyperfeminine/sexualised performances in her music videos and films (such as the sexually provocative *Body of Evidence* [1993]) have been the subject of critical debates that interrogate Madonna's use

and manipulation of gender conventions and styles. In her flaunting of feminine characteristics and female body parts – most (in)famously exemplified
by the cone-breasted Gaultier corset she wore for her 1990 'Blond Ambition'
tour – Madonna lays bare 'the devices of femininity, thereby asserting that
femininity is a device. Madonna takes simulation to its limit in a deconstructive maneuver that plays femininity off against itself – a metafemininity that
reduces gender to the overplay of style' (134). Madonna's postfeminist reworking of her identity – using femininity as a vehicle to empowerment in what
could be described as a 'feminine masquerade' (Schwichtenberg) – provides a
commentary on the artifice of gender. For example, her performance in the
music video of 'Material Girl' shows how the gaze can be realigned through
the use of the hyperfeminine. In 'Material Girl' Madonna replays the iconic
femininity of Marilyn Monroe in order to deconstruct femininity through
the act of appropriating Monroe's feminine look. Madonna also challenges
moral and sexual boundaries in the video of 'Justify My Love', with depictions of bisexuality, sadomasochism and group sex. In these videos, Madonna
negotiates the postfeminist double bind – or, in Linda Hutcheon's words, a
complicitous critique – that does not shy away from using femininity as a means
to its undoing and resignification. As Hutcheon explains, 'this is a strange
kind of critique, one bound up . . . with its own complicity with power
and domination, one that acknowledges that it cannot escape implication in
that which it nevertheless still wants to analyze and maybe even undermine'
(*Politics of Postmodernism* 4). While exposing femininity for what it is – a device
– Madonna employs it as an excessive performance to parody gender in 'a dou-
bling back on femininity in a masculinity that is feminized' (Schwichtenberg
135). In this way, Madonna encourages the viewer to 'reread her body as the
intersection of converging differences' (135).

CASE STUDY: ORLAN

On 30 May 1987 the French performance artist Orlan began a series of
surgical procedures to transform her body through a project entitled 'The
Reincarnation of Saint Orlan'. Her objective was to remodel her body using
aesthetic ideals taken from Western art. From the lips of Gustave Moreau's
Europa to the nose of Jean-Léon Gérôme's *Psyche*, Orlan deployed cosmetic/
plastic surgery as 'a path towards self-determination' (Davis 174). As Orlan
explains: 'I am the first artist to use surgery as a medium and to alter the
purpose of cosmetic surgery: to look better, to look young. "I is an other."
I am at the forefront of confrontation' (quoted in McCorquodale 91). Here
Orlan explores not only a reworking of the body, but also a re-imagining of
the self – an altercation with the Other that demands a complete change of

identity. In fact, 'she desires to "pass" as a new person with a new character and a new history' (Gilman 323).

According to Davis, Orlan's 'project represents the postmodern celebration of identity as fragmented, multiple and – above all – fluctuating and her performances resonate with the radical social construction of Butler . . . and her celebration of the transgressive potential of such performativity' (174). Orlan exposes how femininity and 'beauty' are culturally constructed, historically specific and, by extension, open to resignification. In so doing, she demonstrates how femininity itself can be mobilised as a tool against patriarchy and the male gaze, as the feminine body becomes 'a site for action and protest rather than . . . an object of discipline and normalization' (177). Walking the tightrope of postfeminist identity, Orlan also demonstrates how technology – in this case cosmetic surgery – can be used by women for feminist objectives. Orlan's surgical performances provide an example of how women can work against the grain of femininity in a postfeminist move that attempts to wrest back control of their bodies. As Orlan keenly asserts, she is 'the creator not just the creation; the one who decides and not the passive object of another's decision' (175).

POSTCOLONIAL (POST)FEMINISM

Intimately linked to the notion of postmodern postfeminism is the idea that postfeminism emerges from the contribution of minority feminists who demand a diversification of the feminist movement and a non-ethnocentric and non-heterosexist feminism. This understanding of postfeminism aligns the postmodern concern for difference and feminist concepts of freedom and equality with postcolonial interests that see racial, class and ethnic oppressions at the bottom of women's marginalisation. Here postfeminism has been interpreted as 'a product of the interventions of women of color into the feminist debate' (Koenen 132). Within this context, 'postfeminism, diverging from earlier essentialist and monolithic concepts of "woman", embraces the idea of gender as a performative rather than a biological category, the deconstruction of the unified subject, and the concepts of difference/fragmentation' (131–2). As a 'post' discourse, postfeminism is seen to deconstruct the homogenising effects of feminism's conception of 'Woman' as a universal sign involved in a common struggle. At face value, postfeminism would seem to offer rich theoretical possibilities for women of colour to resignify white middle-class Western feminism. However, it is also important to acknowledge the tension between these postfeminist theories and their use by women of colour. As Koenen argues, '[w]hite postfeminism elevated the traditional center of "male, pale, and Yale" over the periphery of black and female, thus unwittingly duplicating a much-criticized hegemonic strategy of studying and canonizing white male master texts' (132). In this sense, the relationship between postfeminist and postcolonial discourses is burdened with the dilemma of definitional ambiguity that – as we have highlighted throughout – marks postfeminism as a doubly coded phenomenon.

Developing in the 1980s, postcolonial feminism sought to critique Western feminism's failure to acknowledge and represent the diversity of women adequately. In fact, '[p]ostcolonial feminisms seek to disrupt the power to name, represent and theorize by challenging western arrogance and ethnocentrism, and incorporating the choices of marginalized peoples' (McEwan 100). This question of power within feminism becomes increasingly crucial as feminism is challenged from the inside by previously unheard voices of marginalised, colonised and indigenous women who object to feminist theories that fail to address their needs. As a social and political movement that claims to embrace women's interests beneath the umbrella term of 'sisterhood', feminism is criticised for developing a methodology that uses as its paradigm white, heterosexual and middle-class female experience. Imelda Whelehan recognises a dominant feminist stream of 'white, heterosexual and bourgeois thought' that embodies the possible meanings and definitions ascribed to feminism, accompanied by a marked reluctance on the part of such 'feminists to address the degrees of social acceptance and privilege that they' enjoy 'at the expense of others' (*Modern Feminist Thought* 107, 108). This '"mainstream" feminist analysis of female oppression' is denounced as 'flawed and narrow in its focus' as it does not take into account that 'a patriarchal ideology also supports a racist and heterosexist one' (110, 120). Black and lesbian feminists actively counter and reject these methodological boundaries of feminist discourse, refusing to be silenced by a '"hegemonic" feminism with its roots clearly located in the Anglo-American influences so powerful in the conceptualization of second wave feminism' (Brooks 4). Their critique of the racist, ethnocentric and heterosexist assumptions of a largely white, middle-class and heterosexual feminism is seen to result in a breakdown of feminist consensus, a collapse from the inside, and its replacement by a pluralistic postfeminist stance.

In this way, historically speaking, the postfeminist phenomenon could be interpreted as a product of the interventions of women of colour and lesbian theorists into the feminist debate, as it takes into account the demands of marginalised and colonised cultures for a non-ethnocentric and non-heterosexist feminism. In this sense, postfeminism can be seen to address the notion of power within feminism, insisting that one has to 'rethink the feminist project in ways that do not oversimplify either the nature of power in general, or questions of power relations among women and among feminists' (Elam 67, 58). Claims of victimisation are problematised, as concepts such as 'oppression', 'patriarchy', 'identity' and 'difference' as used by white middle-class feminists are challenged by black and lesbian feminists, fighting for visibility within mainstream feminism. Their demands for a diversification of the feminist movement are epitomised and illustrated by Michelene Wandor's insistence that 'the political – and personal – struggle now needs a larger, more diverse "we", who will combine in resistance to all the overlapping oppressions' (quoted in Thornham 42).

In fact, one cannot pose a clear distinction between the pressures from inside and outside feminism, as postmodernism/poststructuralism are embraced by non-mainstream feminists as adequate frames to theorise the multivalent, contradictory and conflicting voices and demands of contemporary women. These marginalised feminist voices reinforce the postmodern belief that no singular explanation for relations of power will suffice and no monolithic interpretation or alteration of praxis will in itself effect social change. As Linda Nicholson points out, postmodernism 'provides a basis for avoiding the tendency to construct theory that generalizes from the experiences of Western, white, middle-class women' and 'offers feminism some useful ideas about method, particularly a wariness toward generalizations which transcend the boundaries of culture and region' ('Introduction' 5).

CASE STUDY: LIL'KIM AND HIP-HOP FEMINISM

In recent years, the growing popular proliferation of hip-hop has marked it out as part of the ongoing commoditisation of race, which has seen hip-hop deployed widely in commercials for major brands like Coca-Cola and Burger King. Hip-hop has been transformed 'from being the symbolic anathema of the dominant commercial apparatus to serving as one of its most strategically effective symbolic instruments' (Smith, quoted in Tasker and Negra 205). Hip-hop's adoption by marketing executives and the media in general as a powerful selling device has been matched by a diversification of its influence into the unlikely area of feminist theory. With the publication in 1999 of Joan Morgan's book *When Chickenheads Come Home to Roost: My Life as a Hip-Hop Feminist*, the concept of 'hip-hop feminism' was born. For Morgan, 'hip-hop feminism' designates a contemporary feminist stance that engages with ambiguity and difference, or as she puts it, it is a 'feminism brave enough to fuck with the grays' (quoted in Siegel, *Sisterhood, Interrupted* 142). As Morgan implies, this is a controversial form of feminism that is happy to court contradiction – playing with the tools of women's exploitation – on the path to female empowerment. Morgan touches upon these inevitable incongruities of 'hip-hop feminism', arguing that women are often complicit in their representation within rap and hip-hop culture, as 'many of the ways in which men exploit our [women's] image and sexuality in hip-hop is done with our permission and cooperation' (78). For many feminists, this is very dangerous ground, as it seems to support a patriarchal script that justifies the suppression and subordination of women on the basis that they are in part to blame. However, Morgan's argument gives voice to the ongoing dilemma that many African-American and Latina-American women and girls confront in their enjoyment and consumption of hip-hop culture and music without being offended and debased. In fact, as Pough argues, the 'sexually explicit lyrics of these rappers offer black women . . . a chance to be proud of – and indeed flaunt – their sexuality' (quoted in Neal 2). Although many female hip-hop artists would not associate themselves with feminism – as for many black women it is still a label restricted to white, middle-class women – Morgan's category of 'hip-hop feminism' demonstrates how feminism can be resignified for new and minority groups of women.

Such a contentious form of feminism can be readily aligned with the notorious, Grammy Award-winning rapper Kimberly Denise Jones – otherwise know as Lil'Kim. A native of Brooklyn, New York, Lil'Kim combines hardcore rap with explicit – and at times pornographic – sexuality. With song titles like 'Suck My D**k', 'Queen Bitch' and 'Don't Mess with Me', Lil'Kim is not afraid to take up the sexist language of male rappers and hip-hop artists, as a riposte to misogynistic ideas and practices. In her music, Lil'Kim celebrates the 'sex object' role assigned to women by male rappers, transforming it into a position of power by using female sexuality and hardcore rap. She literally sings back the lyrics of oppression to male rappers, reminding them – as she does in 'Don't Mess with Me' – that 'I'm that Bitch!' In this way, Lil'Kim's brand of 'hip-hop feminism' takes what could be described as a postfeminist turn, as femininity and sexuality are used for self-definition and self-gain.

RECOMMENDED FURTHER READING

Benhabib, Seyla. 'Feminism and Postmodernism: An Uneasy Alliance.' In *Feminist Contentions: A Philosophical Exchange.* Seyla Benhabib, Judith Butler, Drucilla Cornell and Nancy Fraser. New York and London: Routledge, 1995. 17–34.

Fraser, Nancy, and Linda J. Nicholson. 'Social Criticism without Philosophy: An Encounter between Feminism and Postmodernism.' In *Feminism/Postmodernism.* Ed. Linda J. Nicholson. London and New York: Routledge, 1990. 19–38.

Hekman, Susan. 'Reconstituting the Subject: Feminism, Modernism and Postmodernism.' *Hypatia* 6.2 (1991): 44–63.

Schwichtenberg, Cathy. 'Madonna's Postmodern Feminism: Bringing the Margins to the Center.' In *The Madonna Connection: Representational Politics, Subcultural Identities, and Cultural Theory.* Ed. Cathy Schwichtenberg. Oxford: Westview Press, 1993. 129–45.

6

Queer (Post)Feminism

The relationship between feminism and queer theory is not a straightforward one. At face value, they seem a likely pairing as both at some level attempt to deconstruct identity categories and register difference. Yet queer theory has been challenged by some feminist critics because it seems to neglect political theories in favour of a focus on gender and sexual transgression. This said, there are many fruitful intersections between feminism and queer theory, perhaps most strikingly in the work of Judith Butler – whose theories we will explore in more detail later in this chapter.

Developing out of the radical movements of the 1960s, queer theories have their roots outside academia. In particular, the Gay Liberation Movement of the late 1960s and 1970s – which can be traced to the Stonewall Riots in New York in 1969 – marks a seminal moment in the development of rhetoric and political doctrine to challenge the 'heterosexism' of mainstream society. The primary objective of queer politics during this period was to increase public visibility. As Geltmaker asserts: 'Our refusal to live in a closet is one way of "just saying no" to a world, a nation, and a regional culture intent on closing borders to those who are "different"' (650). The objective here is the breaking down of barriers through an acknowledgement of diversity. By the 1990s, queer theory marked a radical reconfiguration of the intersection of sexuality, representation and subjectivity. Foregrounding the politics of difference, queer theory disrupted binary configurations of the subject by advancing a destabilisation of identity.

In this chapter we address this destabilisation and 'queering' of the hetero-sexual and heterosexist norm as theorised by gay and lesbian critics. Queer theory takes up the postmodern/poststructuralist concern with breaking down essentialist notions of gender and sexual identity and replacing them with contingent and multiple identities. As a deconstructive strategy, queer theory aims to 'denaturalise heteronormative understandings of sex, gender, sexuality, sociality, and the relations between them' (Sullivan 81). Popular culture as well has witnessed the increasing popularity and mainstreaming of gay and bisexual characters and narratives that do not centre on heterosexuality, from the successful television series *Will & Grace* (1998–2006) and *The L Word* (2004–9) to the critically acclaimed *Boys Don't Cry* (1999). Yet the developing frequency of representations of gays and lesbians within the media is, as Rosalind Gill warns, part of a 'queer chic' aesthetic that signifies homosexuality 'through highly specific and highly sexualized codes' (*Gender and the Media* 103). Homosexuality – like race and ethnicity (see Chapter 5) – has thus become a commodity. Within this context, we begin by examining Judith Butler's theory of gender performativity, in particular her discussion of drag performances of gender that disrupt the seemingly natural continuity of heterosexuality. From here, we analyse Judith Halberstam's notion of 'female masculinity' (1998) and 'transgender bodies' (2005) – in relationship to the film *Boys Don't Cry* – which argues for a more flexible taxonomy of masculinity.

GENDER PERFORMATIVITY

Judith Butler has been instrumental in the formulation and theorisation of gender *performativity*, whereby femininity and masculinity come into being when a body performs or 'does gender' in a stylised reiteration of conventions that eventually become naturalised and consolidated. As Butler notes, gender is 'an identity tenuously constituted in time' and 'instituted through the stylisation of the body' ('Performative Acts' 402). The gendered body is performative in the sense that it has 'no ontological status apart from the various acts which constitute its reality', and thus, gender 'can be neither true nor false, neither real nor apparent, neither original nor derived' (*Gender Trouble* 136, 141). Instead, 'gender is always a doing', a 'performance that relies on a certain practice of repetition' that retroactively produces the effect of identity and the illusion that there is an inner gender core (*Gender Trouble* 25; 'Lana's "Imitation"' 2). Hence, 'all gendering is a kind of impersonation and approximation', an 'imitation for which there is no original' but rather the idea of an imaginary or fantasised origin ('Imitation and Gender Insubordination' 313).

While the everyday performativity of gender resides in unacknowledged acts of citation that produce the female body as feminine, Butler's particular interest lies in disrupting this appearance of natural continuity and making 'gender trouble'. For Butler, drag in particular acts as a subversive practice that challenges gender identity, because '*in imitating gender, drag implicitly reveals the imitative structure of gender itself – as well as its contingency*' (*Gender Trouble* 137; emphasis in original). Drag marks a conflict between gender and performance, as 'the so-called sex of the performer is not the same as the gender being performed' (Sullivan 86). By exposing gender as a reiterative mechanism and a performative achievement, Butler explores the potential of an unfaithful and critical repetition that might displace the very constructs by which it is mobilised. As she writes:

> if the ground of gender is the stylised repetition of acts through time, and not a seemingly seamless identity, then the possibilities of gender transformation are to be found in the arbitrary relation between such acts, in the possibility of a different sort of repeating, in the breaking or subversive repetition of that style. ('Performative Acts' 402)

In other words, femininity and masculinity become available for a deconstructive practice and/or politics that use and resignify simulation in ways that challenge the stable notion of gender as the edifice of sexual difference. Rather than being a mono-logical and homogeneous structure, the gender template is opened up to integrate a more complex set of signposts that refashion the body and allow the subject to disengage from the roles of an apparently naturalised femininity/masculinity. Yet, at the same time as asserting that gender can 'be rendered thoroughly and radically *incredible*', Butler is also aware that this form of parodic imitation cannot be confused with a voluntarist stance whereby subjects choose their various identities much as they would select their clothes (*Gender Trouble* 141). Butler insists that 'gender performativity is not a question of instrumentally deploying a "masquerade"', for such a construal of performativity presupposes an intentional subject *behind* the deed ('For a Careful Reading' 136). On the contrary, gender is an involuntary and imposed production within a culturally restricted space, and it is always put on under constraint as a compulsory performance that is in line with heterosexual conventions. In this way, femininity is 'not the product of a choice, but the forcible citation of a norm, one whose complex historicity is indissociable from relations of discipline, regulation, punishment' (*Bodies that Matter* 232).

With this in mind, performativity can simultaneously be theorised in terms of subversion and normativity, whereby it both empowers and constrains the subject. As Butler admits, 'there is no guarantee that exposing the naturalized status of heterosexuality will lead to its subversion', as the gender meanings taken up in these parodic styles remain 'part of hegemonic, misogynist culture' (*Bodies that Matter* 231; *Gender Trouble* 138). Butler's notion of gender parody is characterised by an undeterminable disruptive and revolutionary potential that cannot be summed up by a dualistic logic as *either* a powerful and self-conscious protest *or* a disempowering and unconscious placation. In relation to postfeminism, the importance of the concept of gender parody lies in its transgressive doubleness, whereby it both undermines and reinforces normative representations of gender, blurring the opposition between activity and passivity, subject and object.

CASE STUDY: *WILL & GRACE* (1998–2006)

Will & Grace provided a seminal moment in TV sitcom history as the first network television series to showcase a gay man as the principal character. Telling the story of Will Truman – a gay New York lawyer – and his relationship with Grace Adler – a straight Jewish woman who runs her own interior design firm – along with their friendship with Jack McFarland – a struggling gay actor and sometime student nurse – and Karen Walker – the alcoholic wife of wealthy businessman Stan Walker – the series charted new territory with its comic portrayal of the relationship trials and tribulations of Will and Grace. Garnering widespread popular acclaim and substantial viewing figures, with over 17 million viewers tuning in at the height of its popularity in the US in 2001 – making it the fourth highest rated programme in March of that year – the series marked what Gauntlett describes as 'a growing acceptance of gay characters' (85). In fact, by its third series *Will & Grace* was 'one of 22 shows that portrayed gay or lesbian characters in lead, supporting or recurring roles' (Battles and Hilton-Morrow 87).

However, the series' popularity amongst the viewing public was not matched by critics' appraisals, as they criticised it for stereotyping gay characters and reifying a heterosexual matrix. In addition, critics attacked the series' representation of the gay community as narrow, singular and homogeneous. More broadly, what we witness in *Will & Grace* is part of a developing commoditisation of gay and lesbian culture, where glamour is sexualised and deployed to sell 'queer chic' to the 'hetero-masses'. As Rosalind Gill argues, queer chic taps into the 'pink economy' – the expanding market for gay and lesbian identities – and 'can seem to add "edge", risk and sexiness to products that are often associated with straight men and traditional sexism' (*Gender and the Media* 103). Although the characters of Will and Jack offer two very different and celebrated representations of the gay man and – within the context of the lack of leading and supporting gay characters on network TV in the late 1990s – could be seen as progressive, they are still 'positioned within a narrative space that relies on familiar comedic conventions for addressing homosexuality – equating gayness with a lack of masculinity' (Battles and

Hilton-Morrow 89). Jack's camp performances fit directly into the historic association within the media of the gay man as 'queen'. In this way, Jack's excessive displays of his 'gayness' are represented as non-threatening and comedic – illustrated, for example, by Will's response to Jack's assertion that not many people know that he is gay when they meet him: 'Jack, blind and deaf people know you're gay. Dead people know you're gay.' Will also conforms to the media stereotype of the well-groomed gay man who adopts a commercial form of masculinity that 'is in no way different from the same image being sold to heterosexual men' (90).

This conservative narrative frame seemingly contains any subversive possibilities that *Will & Grace* poses to the American mainstream media, offering the wider viewing public a safe peek into a world that many would not be familiar with and at the same time providing a gay audience with 'a space for identification and self-construction' (Battles and Hilton-Morrow 102). Here, as with many postfeminist texts, the danger of ultimately reinforcing heterosexual and heteronormative structures, while in this case attempting to resignfy gay characters to a mass audience, is a domain of risk that must be entered.

CASE STUDY: *THE L WORD* (2004–9)

First aired in January 2004, *The L Word* was the first primetime drama to explore lesbian and bisexual relationships and identities. Representing the 'queer' lifestyles of a group of well-dressed lesbian and bisexual women from West Hollywood, the series has been both praised for breaking new ground and criticised for offering what has been described as 'soft-core girl-on-girl pornography aimed at heterosexual men or couples' (Sedgwick, 'Foreword' xix). For Tasker and Negra, this is indicative of a conservative postfeminism that 'absolutely rejects lesbianism in all but its most guy-friendly forms, that is, divested of potentially feminist associations' (21). Marketed as a lesbian version of *Sex and the City* – dubbed by some 'Sex and the Clittie' – and as such censured for its white, femme bias, *The L Word* offers a 'visible world in which lesbians exist, go on existing, exist in forms beyond the solitary and the couple, sustain and develop relations among themselves of difference and commonality' (Sedgwick, '*The L Word*' B10). Yet for some critics this visibility is still governed by a heterosexual frame, as 'lesbian lives are simultaneously fetishised and celebrated, mediated through a curious heterosexual gaze that is marked as both male and female' (Tasker and Negra 21). In many ways, this is where the conflict of representation resides in *The L Word* – in the tension between making lesbian identities visible and the demands of the mainstream (heteronormative) media.

This tension is well expressed in episode nine ('Late, Later, Latent') of the second season when Mark's financial backers for his film on lesbian life emphatically respond to his pitch by telling him that 'red-blooded men don't give a fuck about this anthropological bullshit . . . They want hot lesbian sex and they want it now.' Within this context, Samuel Chambers argues that '*The L Word* is a heternormative show about homosexuals' that deploys a narrative structure that 'often serves to perpetuate, preserve and sustain the normativity of heterosexuality' ('Heteronormativity' 82). For Chambers:

> the implicit message that lesbians are sexy, attractive objects of desire, even for straight men, crop up repeatedly, whether in the form of the straight man observing lesbian sex ('Lawfully', 1:6) or in the representation of lesbians in/as the pornographic model . . . ('Losing It', 1:3). These reminders . . . help to blunt any challenge that lesbian sex might pose to the preservation and exaltation of heteronormativity. ('Heteronormativity' 91)

While at one level Chambers is correct in his appraisal of *The L Word*'s failure to undo the heteronormative matrix, the show does nevertheless engage with and at times trouble this frame of reference. In part, this troubling of heternormativity could be described as a postfeminist lesbian approach to sexuality that re-appropriates the symbols of heterosexual femininity for a homosexual identity. By walking the postfeminist tightrope, *The L Word* replaces the historic media stereotypes of lesbians as ugly, unfashionable bra-burners with chic, well-dressed, sexy West Hollywood women, and in so doing mobilises the markers of heterosexual femininity for lesbians and bisexuals. Although open to criticism as just 'lipstick lesbianism' – which often represents two conventional, feminine, young women embracing and seems aimed at a heterosexual male audience and gaze – glamour, according to Jennifer Vanasco, 'equals power, and the more perceived power television lesbians have . . . the better chance we have to gain that power' (183). In this sense, *The L Word* deploys glamour in a postfeminist turn that celebrates queer chic as a means to empower lesbian and bisexual women.

CASE STUDY: *BOYS DON'T CRY* (1999)

The independent film *Boys Don't Cry* – starring Hilary Swank as Brandon Teena and Chloë Sevigny as Brandon's girlfriend Lana Tisdel – is based on the real-life story of a female-to-male transsexual who was murdered on 31 December 1993. A week prior to her death, Brandon was kidnapped and raped by John Lotter and Marvin Thomas Nissen – two ex-convicts that Brandon had befriended – who were later convicted of the murder. The film portrays the unconditional love between Brandon and Lana and the ultimate threat that Lotter and Nissen feel that Brandon poses to their masculinity. For film-maker Kimberly Pierce, *Boys Don't Cry* was not simply a matter of telling Brandon's story, but an attempt to recuperate his identity in the face of the lurid glare of the press and media. According to Pierce, press coverage was 'focused almost exclusively on the spectacle of a girl passing as a boy, without any understanding of why a girl would want to pass' (quoted in Leigh 18). 'Passing' for many transsexuals involves being accepted as the gender you present yourself as, without 'being denied a job, laughed at, beaten up, or even killed because one is "weird"' (Sullivan 106). According to Hale, the crisis in identity that Brandon experienced was the central focus of media reports at the time: 'a state of crisis over identity, sexual and otherwise, characterises not only "Brandon's" brief life but also the media attention devoted to this murdered youth. Much of this crisis finds its focal point in the necessity of being named' (312). Brandon's name – born as Teena Brandon, he later inverted the name to Brandon Teena – provided the semantic focus for this process of definition as Brandon was 'named' as 'he', 'she' and even 'it' by the press and authorities. The attempt to position Brandon within one gender identity category amounted to 'a refusal to acknowledge that this person was a *border zone dweller*: someone whose embodied self existed in a netherworld constituted by the margins of multiple overlapping identity categories' (Hale 318; emphasis in original).

Brandon Teena's story demonstrates the dilemmas surrounding the expression of a 'trans' identity within contemporary culture and the strictly policed borders of gender identity. Although *Boys Don't Cry* received widespread critical acclaim, with Hilary Swank picking up a Best Actress Academy Award, Brandon's story reveals how difficult it is to rewrite bodily identity, to 'rewrite the cultural fiction that divides a sex from a transex, a gender from a transgender' (Halberstam, 'F2M' 226). Within this context, queer theory can function to destabilise binary distinctions and dissolve divisions. For Judith Halberstam, the existence of the distinct category of the masculine woman 'urges us to reconsider our most basic assumptions about the functions, forms, and representations of masculinity and forces us to ask why the bond between men and masculinity has remained relatively secure despite the continuous assaults made by feminists, gays, lesbians, and gender-queers on the naturalness of gender' (*Female Masculinity* 45). In *Female Masculinity* (1998), Halberstam argues that 'female masculinity is a specific gender with its own cultural history rather than simply a derivative of male masculinity' (77). The case of Brandon Teena exemplifies the fact that the bastion of masculinity, which has historically been seen as a stronghold of male identity, is not unassailable but becomes available for an alternative construction that undermines static gender norms. As Halberstam suggests, 'many bodies are gender strange to some degree or another, and it is time to complicate on the one hand the transsexual models . . . and on the other hand the heteronormative models' (153–4). In this sense, *Boys Don't Cry* serves as a challenge to our assumptions about where the distinctions between genders are drawn, queering the relationship between subject and object.

RECOMMENDED FURTHER READING

Berlant, Lauren, and Michael Warner. 'What Does Queer Theory Teach Us about X?' *PMLA* 110.3 (1995): 343–9.

Butler, Judith. *Gender Trouble: Feminism and the Subversion of Identity*. London and New York: Routledge, 1990.

Chambers, Samuel A. 'Heteronormativity and *The L Word*: From a Politics of Representation to a Politics of Norms.' In *Reading The L Word: Outing Contemporary Television*. Eds Kim Akass and Janet McCabe. London and New York: I. B. Tauris, 2006. 81–98.

Halberstam, Judith. *Female Masculinity*. Durham, NC, and London: Duke University Press, 1998.

7

Men and Postfeminism

In this chapter, we examine the relationship between men and (post) feminism, discussing the emergence of the men's movement as a result of women's social enfranchisement and the cultural influence of feminist ideas and policies. The questioning of the term 'Woman' by feminism and the interest in gender relations produce a variety of responses by men who endeavour to redefine masculinity and understand their place within/alongside feminism. Initially, we chart what has been described as an ongoing crisis in masculinity which reached its pinnacle in the popular press in the USA and UK in 2000 (Beynon). Considering the transforming political, social, economic and cultural landscape between the late 1960s and the present day, we identify important developments within these areas that have impacted upon our understanding and representation of masculinity and male identity – such as the economic shift from Fordism to post-Fordism, neo-liberal philosophies and 9/11. In so doing, we pick up on recent developments within masculinity studies that have analysed men as a politically gendered category (bounded by specific masculine cultural forms) that can no longer be ascribed a normative location as transparent, neutral and disembodied. From here, we focus in detail on three versions of masculinity that have evolved since the 1980s – the 'new man', the 'metrosexual' and the 'new lad' – in order to advance and define a fourth, new category of masculinity for the twenty-first century – the 'postfeminist man'. Through the use of topical case studies on representative cultural icons (such as David Beckham as the epitome of the 'metrosexual'), fiction and film (*Fight Club* [1996; 1999]), we show men's responses to the shifting terrain of masculinity since the early 1980s.

MASCULINITY IN CRISIS

> Crisis is . . . a condition of masculinity itself. Masculine gender identity is never stable; its terms are continually being re-defined and re-negotiated, the gender performance continually re-staged. Certain themes and tropes inevitably re-appear with regularity, but each era experiences itself in different ways. (Mangan 4)

Crisis, as Mangan highlights, is not a new condition of masculinity, nor, it is argued by some critics, is it confined to the last decades of the twentieth century and the early twenty-first (Kimmel; Ferrebe; Beynon). In fact, Kimmel argues that the last two hundred years have witnessed male concerns and anxieties over the intrusion of the 'feminine' into 'masculine' spheres of influence. Often these crises in masculinity are aligned by critics with war. For example, Ferrebe identifies a crisis in masculinity in Britain post-Second World War, as thousands of soldiers returned to civilian life. The country that these soldiers returned to had been transformed by the need to function without them. Their heroic displays of masculinity upon the battlefields of Europe and beyond, as they fought to protect British sovereignty, were now redundant within the new social structures and economies of postwar Britain. The traditional spheres of influence (women/home, men/workplace) had been redefined by the exodus of women from the home to the factory in support of the war effort. In fact, as Ferrebe argues, 'the older generation felt itself to be disinherited from the public sphere, just as the country they had remembered seemed increasingly diminished in importance' (11).

It could be argued that this postwar condition of masculinity provides us with a paradigm for understanding the complex relationship between masculinity and conflict in general – as redundancy often leads to backlash from within the newly conceived structures of economic, social and political power. More recently, for example, the transformative effects of conflict are seen in British and American fiction, film and television series post-9/11. *Jarhead* (2003; 2006), *Outlaw* (2006), *House M.D.* (2005–) and *Grey's Anatomy* (2006–) provide us with versions of masculinity that are coming to terms with being displaced and/or wounded (more often than not literally). This results in the 'postfeminist man' who frequently relies upon a prosthetic appendage to his masculinity (for example, House's walking stick), in order to disguise the fact that he is no longer whole and hegemonic. In these examples, phallic aggression and hegemonic masculinity become misdirected and undermined as new blended characteristics of masculinity ('old man', 'new man', 'new lad' and 'metrosexual') congeal from these failed or defunct masculinities into postfeminist subject positions.

Another way of approaching the relationship between masculinity and crisis is through the distinct shift in the 'politics of looking' that came about in the 1980s. As various commentators have suggested, the expanding commercialisation of masculinity in the 1950s, 1960s and 1970s culminated in the 'male on male' gaze of the 1980s. Whereas previously the female body had been the exclusive site of sexualised and voyeuristic representations by the media, the 1980s witnessed 'the commercial exploitation of men-as-sex-object' (Beynon 103). This version of commercial masculinity transformed the male body into an 'objectified commodity' that saw the rise of retail clothing outlets for men, new visual representations of masculinity on television and in the media, and the growth of men's lifestyle magazines. The results of this commercialisation of masculinity were witnessed at all levels of society. For instance, according to Ross, '[t]he football fan of the early Eighties was no longer a rattle-waving, scarf-wearing wally or a toothless skinhead grunt, but a mass of label-wearing, style-coded casual wear freaks' (29). Yet it would be incorrect to assume that no man was left behind by these changes. The economic pressures exerted on masculinity to transform during this period excluded tens of thousands of working-class men. In fact, the accompanying shift from the mass production of Fordism to the niche production of post-Fordism further sidelined the 'old industrial man', as downsizing and outsourcing led to unstable work patterns for the working classes. Many men were not able to adjust to the new shape of masculinity and 'were experiencing their work changes, this so-called feminization of labour . . . like a smack in the eye' (Coward 51). Commercial masculinity demanded wealth and good looks if men were to engage fully with the 'new man' of the 1980s.

As Edwards argues, these developments set the course for masculinity as:

> wealthy, good-looking and well-located young men [were] increasingly socially valorised over older, uglier or poorer men . . . Those with the looks, the income and the time on their side have never had it so good in terms of the opportunities which the expansion of men's style and fashion have to offer them . . . But those without the luck, the looks or the time have never had it so bad. (*Men in the Mirror* 133–4)

Within this context, masculinity is bound by social, cultural and economic practices. The male body (particularly the young, 'good-looking' male body) is (re-)inscribed as the site of opportunity and power, not because of physical prowess and economic value linked to labour, but as a signifying surface for commercialised masculinity.

CONTEMPORARY MASCULINITIES

Since the early 1980s we have been bombarded by the popular media and academics alike with numerous varieties of male identity which have been aligned with various types of masculinity. From the 'soft lad' to the 'new boy'; the 'modern romantic' to the 'new father'; the 'new man' to the 'new lad', via the 'metrosexual'; male identity and masculinity have become unstable, readily contestable, increasingly transferable, open to (re-)appropriation and constantly in motion (Chapman; Mort; Edwards; Simpson). Masculinity, or the more commonly discussed 'hegemonic masculinity' – which, as Connell notes in his seminal text *Masculinities* (1995), 'refers to the cultural dynamic by which a group claims and sustains a leading position in social life' – has become a 'historically mobile relation' and is 'no longer a position from which to judge others but a puzzling condition in its own right' (Connell 77; Coward 94). Some critics argue that men are becoming redundant in a biological, social and economic way as the historic roles of 'heroic masculinity', 'old industrial man' or simply 'old man' have been phased out by ongoing technological, social and political change since the late 1960s. In fact, 'women are asserting that they can conceive and rear children on their own. They don't need men to father their children . . . women can do without them in the workplace' (Clare 100).

This rhetoric of redundancy encouraged men in some quarters to counter this perceived threat to their masculinity and position of power upon their patriarchal pedestals. Fearful that their response to the transforming gender roles of the 1970s and 1980s, which saw them adopt the guise of the 'new man' – pro-feminist, nurturing and sexually ambivalent – had made them go 'soft', men's concerns and interests soon conglomerated into a recognisable men's movement. Loosely divided between pro-feminist and masculinist groups – such as Seidler's contributions in the UK to the magazine *Spare Rib* (supporting the women's movement), the Canadian White Ribbon Campaign (working against male violence directed at women) and Robert Bly's 'Iron John' movement (reawakening the 'deep masculine') – men reacted in a variety of ways to the questions posed and advances gained by second wave feminism.

At the most notorious end of this spectrum of responses, Bly's much-debated search for an authentic 'masculine self' in his text *Iron John* (1990) could be described as the legacy of the rapidly dissolving and vilified 'old man' as portrayed by, for example, Sylvester Stallone in the *Rambo* series of films. Described by Chapman as 'bare-chested and alone, wading through the Vietcong swamp with not even a tube of insect repellent for comfort', these men were represented as seemingly in touch with their masculinity – in this case a throwback to an aggressive, phallic masculinity (227). As the tide of the popular imagination ebbed away from the macho body of these angry men towards the protective father-figure in the early 1990s (Gauntlett), Bly's intervention called upon men to reclaim their true manhood. According to Bly, it was conceived not as a counterattack on the women's movement, but instead an attempt to get men back in touch with their 'deep masculine' selves. Seen by feminist critics as part of an anti-feminist backlash, Bly's 'New Age masculinist community' claimed the hearts, heads and dollars of many mainstream Americans (Faludi; Brabon).

Beyond the backlash sentiments of Bly's 'Iron John' movement, it demonstrated the contested location of masculinity in the USA and UK in the late 1980s and 1990s as the pro-feminist 'new man' was evolving into the retro-sexism of the 'new lad'. As we will explore later in this chapter, this transition was not smooth or seamless and it would be wrong to assume that the characteristics that defined the 'new man' simply evaporated in the 1990s. Although it can be argued that the 1980s was the decade of the 'new man' and the 1990s that of the 'new lad', what is significant in the 1990s is that we begin to see a process of seepage between the categories or types of men as they try to come to terms with the shifting social and economic environment and grapple with conflicting varieties of masculinity (Gill, 'Power and the Production of Subjects'). In what could be described as an opening up of postfeminist possibilities and subject positions, we witness the uneasy and problematic 'subjectivation' – 'both the becoming of a subject and the process of subjection' (Butler, *Psychic Life of Power* 83) – of men as simultaneously and seemingly irreconcilably pro- and anti-feminist in their (re)turn to 'masculine' pursuits. Contrary to Tim Edwards' assertion that 'the reconstruction of masculinity . . . demonstrate[s] very few signs of post-feminist consciousness' – which relies upon a limited reading of postfeminism – we embrace the ambiguities and incongruities of the 'post' prefix when applied to feminism which harbours pro-feminist and backlash identities (*Men in the Mirror* 51).

Masculinity in the late twentieth and twenty-first centuries has assumed a variety of shapes, forms and subject positions. Many of these new manifestations have been derived in part from the commercialisation of masculinity witnessed from the 1980s to the present day, as new masculinities have become part of selling lifestyle choices to men across the social spectrum. In fact, as Edwards maintains, these new men are a 'crystallisation of consequences – economic, marketing, political ideology, demography and, most widely, consumer society in the 1980s' (*Men in the Mirror* 39–40). The product of this 'crystallisation of consequences' for men in the twenty-first century is what Mort describes (within the context of the 1980s 'new man') as a 'hybrid character' (15). This amalgamated nature of contemporary masculinity has developed out of a series of – at times competing – 'hybrid scripts' that have become enmeshed to form conflicting and conflicted subject positions. As we will go on to discuss later in this chapter, the most recent manifestation of this hybridity is the 'postfeminist man' – the epitome of 'bricolage masculinity' that has developed as we '"channel hop" across versions of the "masculine"' (Beynon 6). However, before analysing the 'postfeminist man', it is important to have a sense of three preceding versions of masculinity – the 'new man', the 'metrosexual' and the 'new lad' – whose characteristics compete and congeal into the 'hybrid' form of the 'postfeminist man'.

NEW MAN

The 'new man' has been described conflictingly as pro-feminist, narcissistic, anti-sexist, self-absorbed and sexually ambivalent. He is often seen within the context of a response to feminism, as 'a potent symbol for men and women searching for new images and visions of masculinity in the wake of feminism and the men's movement' (Chapman 226). Originating in the early 1970s, the 'new man' was conceived as a 'nurturing' figure seemingly in tune with the demands of feminism and women in general. In this 1970s version, he is 'attempting to put his "caring and sharing" beliefs into practice in his daily life' (Beynon 164). Contrastingly, in the 1980s the 'new man' developed a more hedonistic and narcissistic edge, embracing consumer culture as advertising executives transformed the male body into a lifestyle billboard that was no longer selling just products but also a way of life. This potentially more sinister version has been attacked as 'nothing less than the advertising industry's dramatization of its own self-image and driven primarily by commercial greed' (Beynon 115). Here the 'new man' is criticised for being exclusively Western, white, middle-class and elitist – a distant and alien representation of masculinity, decidedly 'other' from the day-to-day lives of the majority of 'real' men.

These changing meanings and characteristics of the image of the 'new man' from the 1970s to 1980s are witnessed in the evolving critical descriptions of the 'newness' of the 'new man'. For example, in *Male Order: Unwrapping Masculinity* (1988), Chapman acknowledges that while the 'new man' can be recognised as a response to feminism, the category is

ambiguous, at times negative and ultimately (in its most positive manifestations) an impossibility:

> The 'new man' is many things – a humanist ideal, a triumph of style
> over content, a legitimation of consumption, a ruse to persuade those
> that called for change that it has already occurred . . . [W]hile the 'new
> man' may well have provided some useful role models for those redefin-
> ing their masculinity . . . [he] is an ideal that even the most liberated
> man would never lay claim to. (226, 228, 247)

Within this context, there is very little 'new' about the 'new man'. In this
formulation, he is the misleading and unobtainable by-product of a consumer
society obsessed with new lifestyle choices. While the now infamous 1980s
images of men holding babies – supposedly displaying their sensitive side –
marked a shift in the range of subject positions available to men, it would
be incorrect to assume that the 'new man' signalled a clear break from older
versions of masculinity and patriarchy. A more fruitful understanding of the
'new man' is provided by positioning him as a response to the transformative
influences of postmodernity on the male subject. As Mort highlights, multiple subject positions lead to multiple (and conflicting) masculinities:

> I am not arguing that the 1980s 'new man' is totally new. But nor
> am I saying that nothing has changed . . . For we are not just talking
> images here: images are underscored by the economics and cultures
> of consumption . . . The 1980s [saw] an intensification of that process
> and proliferation of individualities – of the number of 'you's' on offer.
> (207, 208)

This plurality of identity provided a 'new' framework in which male
identities and masculinities were reconceived. A variety of new subject
positions was available to men as the category of 'man' and (hegemonic)
'masculinity' grew – in the process redefining the location of those 'bodies
that matter' (Butler). Thus, the 'new man' was not 'new'; rather he was a
re-invention or rebranding of masculinity – expanding the boundaries of
hegemonic masculinity – that spread out of the shift in the politics of looking
and the pressures of consumer culture in the 1980s. At his worst, the 'new
man' was 'a patriarchal mutation, a redefinition of masculinity in men's
favour, a reinforcement of the gender order, representing an expansion of
the concept of legitimate masculinity and thus an extension of its power over
women and deviant men' (Chapman 247). As such, the 'new man' paved
the way for the ongoing commercialisation of masculinity that continued
unabated into the 1990s, reaching its apotheosis in 1994 with the arrival of
the 'metrosexual'.

METROSEXUAL

The term 'metrosexual' was coined in 1994 by Mark Simpson to describe 'a young man with money to spend, living in or within easy reach of the metropolis . . . He might be officially gay, straight or bisexual, but this is utterly immaterial because he has clearly taken himself as his own love object and pleasure as his sexual preference' (quoted in Simpson, 'Metrosexual' 1). Epitomised by David Beckham, the 'metrosexual' extends the narcissistic and self-absorbed characteristics of the 'new man', revelling in the consumerist heaven that is the modern-day metropolis. Sexually ambivalent, the 'metrosexual' embraces gay culture but only as a product of late capitalism. The 'metrosexual' puts his body on display, parading what Simpson describes as the 'essence of masculinity: the desired male body' and adopting techniques that have 'long been understood by advertisers in the gay press who have often employed photos of headless idealized male bodies' (*Male Impersonators* 107).

Here, the boundaries between the 'metrosexual' and the 'new man' become blurred – as do those between homosexual and heterosexual masculinities – as narcissism and the commoditisation of masculinity become the organising features of both forms. In fact, 'in discussing metrosexuality we are on remarkably similar territory to the New Man and . . . indeed the New Lad' (Edwards, *Cultures of Masculinity* 43). These similarities mark a growing trend in the shifting shape of masculinity throughout the twentieth century (and beyond) to adopt increasingly 'hybrid' and enmeshed subject positions. The 'metrosexual' sits uneasily in the middle of a sliding scale – as an excessive display of stylised heterosexual masculinity that is ultimately camp in its excess – that has the 'new man' and the 'new lad' on either side. More groomed than the 'new man' and not as sexist (or ironic) as the 'new lad', the 'metrosexual' is 'less certain of his identity and much more interested in his image . . . because that's the only way . . . you can be certain to exist' (Simpson, 'Metrosexual' 2). The metrosexual's projection of a seemingly assured male identity (as a caring narcissist and/or a family man who is brand-conscious) masks a more general (and expanding) instability at the heart of contemporary masculinity – one that has come to be embodied in the first decade of the twenty-first century by the 'postfeminist man'.

Since the early 2000s there have been a number of calls to mark the passing of the 'metrosexual'. Recently Marian Salzman has argued that he has been superseded by the 'übersexual' male, 'who mixes old-fashioned honour with good conversation' (quoted in Hoggard 1). The 'übersexual' is, according to Salzman, less narcissistic than the 'metrosexual' – 'He thinks positively of women but he doesn't go out of his way to seek their acceptance and approval.

Because he's not bitter or boxed in, he can cope with living in a world increasingly dominated by femininity' (quoted in Hoggard 1). Although Salzman is perhaps overstating the importance of femininity within contemporary culture – especially outside of Western Europe and North America – it becomes apparent that 'new' masculinities are increasingly bound up in men's lifestyle choices that find their expression within the neo-liberal political and economic arenas of the West. At the same time, Salzman's 'übersexual' male seems to resurrect 'backlash' scripts that are regressive and exclusive. The appeal and impact of 'metrosexual' figures like David Beckham may be trans-social and trans-global, but the associated lifestyle choices are limited and limiting, and often only accessible to a small number of affluent individuals who can buy into an identity whose foundations are commoditised masculinity. The 'metrosexual' of the mid-nineties illustrates the precariousness of masculinity in the twentieth century, as 'new' and 'old', homosexual and heterosexual masculinities compound and evolve in increasingly 'hybrid' forms. In this way, the 'metrosexual' – who begins to make over 'masculinity from a postfeminist perspective' (Cohan 182) – moves masculinity one step closer to the 'postfeminist man'.

CASE STUDY: DAVID BECKHAM

According to Mark Simpson, David Beckham is the 'ultimate manifestation' of the metrosexual man ('Metrosexual' 1). Aware of the marketability of his metrosexual identity and fully embracing commoditised masculinity, Beckham provides an excellent example of the 'hybrid' nature of masculinity in the twenty-first century (Cashmore). Yet 'Beckham is not so much a new form of masculinity as a brand selling everything from Dolce & Gabbana to Gillette shaving products' (Edwards, *Cultures of Masculinity* 43). As Beckham's official website makes clear, he has multiple identities – footballer, style icon, ambassador, actor – that coalesce to form 'David Beckham' and, at the same time, open up numerous identity pathways and subject positions that have traditionally seemed incompatible. Beckham's attraction is in part delineated by the ability of his identity to cross boundaries – social, racial, economic, sexual, national. As Ellis Cashmore observes, 'Beckham captivates a global audience that includes young females who have no obvious interest in sport, gay men for whom Beckham has acquired almost fetishist properties . . . working-class kids who proclaim their nationalism through their champion' (6).

At once the epitome of heterosexual masculinity and a gay icon – not least because he is married to the former pop star and now fashion designer Victoria (or Posh Spice) – Beckham's broad appeal is defined by the numerous identities that can be projected onto his body. After all, '[w]e, his public . . . make Beckham *Beckham*' (Cashmore 3). In fact, as Cashmore suggests, we are all implicated in the construction of the figure that is David Beckham. As a metrosexual man, his identity is malleable, transferable and at times uncertain. However, in contrast to the malleability of his identity, his image is instantly recognisable to millions of people across the globe, and as such it is fixed. He can be an inspirational figure for the working-class British man; reflect a way of life that connects with successful black American hip-hop artists; and at the same time seemingly undermine these strong assertions of traditional heterosexual masculinity through his use of nail varnish, sarongs and plucked eyebrows. Although Beckham has been heralded as a style guru for the homosexual man, the metrosexual 'is of course not necessarily homosexual at all but rather homosocial, centred on men looking at other men, competing with other men' (Edwards, *Cultures of Masculinity* 43). As a representative example of the commoditisation of masculinity, Beckham's image – and the products he endorses – presents new lifestyle choices, showing men what they can be. The metrosexual's fluid identity and contradictory – even conflicting – associations find their zenith in popular and marketable representations of David Beckham. Here – in its most positive manifestations – metrosexual masculinity is broad and inclusive, defying ideological and sexual roles, and as such, it provides the foundations for the postfeminist man.

NEW LAD

> New Man and New Lad, apparently antagonistic phenomena, were in fact intimately related – both were the offspring of glossy magazine culture. Both were also about a kind of commodified masculine self-consciousness that stemmed from insecurity and rootlessness – though, ironically, New Lad was much more successful in selling men fashion and vanity products than New Man. (Simpson, 'Metrosexual' 3)

The relationship between the 'new man' and the 'new lad' identified by Mark Simpson hides the 'backlash' scenarios underpinning the development of the 'new lad'. If the 'new man' was a product of the 1980s, then the 'new lad' is most definitely a product of the 1990s and should be recognised as a reaction against both the 'new man' and (to a lesser degree) the 'metrosexual'. Also arriving in 1994, with the launch of *Loaded* magazine, the 'new lad' embraced 'laddish' behaviour – revelling in naked images of 'girls', games, 'footie' and booze. In fact, according to Beynon, the '"new lad" is defensive about fashion, ambivalent in his attitude towards women (he has pornographic notions of them rather than relationships with them) and he believes life should be one huge alcohol and drug-induced party' (118). Whereas the 'new man' was pro-feminist, the 'new lad' is pre-feminist, displaying retro-sexism in what can be described as 'a nostalgic revival of old patriarchy; a direct challenge to feminism's call for social transformation, by reaffirming – albeit ironically – the unchanging nature of gender relations and sexual roles' (Whelehan, *Overloaded* 5).

Yet while revisiting the domain of the 'old man', the 'new lad' is eager to throw off the constraints of traditional, patriarchal representations of masculinity. According to Gill, 'the "new lad" offers a refuge from the constraints and demands of marriage and nuclear family. He opened up a space of fun, consumption and sexual freedom for men, unfettered by traditional adult male responsibilities' ('Power and the Production of Subjects' 27). In this sense, the new lad's appeal was broader than that of the 'new man', as it spoke directly to working-class masculinities that were excluded by the 'upmarket' and commoditised representation of the 'new man'. As Edwards notes, 'the New Lad has succeeded so well where previous invocations of consumerist masculinity failed precisely because it reconciled, at least artificially, the tension between the playboy and the narcissist or, to put it more simply, it reconstructed personal consumption and grooming as acceptable parts of working-class masculinities' (*Cultures of Masculinity* 42). This said, recent statistics illustrate these marketing successes still have a long way to go, with British men spending only £57 million on skincare – an average of less than £2.50 per man, per year – compared to £602 million spent by women (Sandison). Although the roots of the 'new lad' may be bound up with those of the 'new man', the new lad's characteristics are more closely aligned with those of the 'old man' – the main distinction being the embrace of postmodern irony to justify certain ways of behaving.

In particular, it is apparent that the 'new lad' mobilises irony as a defence against accusations of sexism and misogyny. According to Gill, it is important to recognise that '[n]ew stereotypes have not necessarily displaced older ones but may coexist alongside these, or perhaps merely influence their style' and that '[s]exy "babes" are still selling cars' (111, 112). In this way, the 'new lad' wants it both ways, jettisoning the responsibilities of patriarchy while maintaining its privileges.

TOWARDS THE POSTFEMINIST MAN

Since the beginning of the new millennium masculinity has undergone another transformation. The result of this ongoing conglomeration of at times contradictory and conflicting masculinities is what we describe as the 'postfeminist man' – which captures the current state of masculinity in the

West. The 'postfeminist man' displays a compound identity, revealing the fact that numerous representations of masculinity may coexist in new, hybrid forms. As Brabon argues, 'the postfeminist man is not the signifier for the re-masculinisation of contemporary culture – a straightforward rejection of second-wave feminism that can easily be identified as part of the backlash – but, in contrast, an unstable and troubled subject position that is doubly encoded' (57). On the one hand, the 'postfeminist man' accommodates backlash scripts – drawing upon characteristics of the 'new lad'. On the other hand, he is more self-aware, displaying anxiety and concern for his identity while re-embracing patriarchal responsibilities which the 'new lad' defiantly threw off. In many ways, the 'postfeminist man' could be described as the 'new lad' grown up or a less sensitive 'new man'. Moreover, although the 'postfeminist man' is heterosexual, he is style- and brand-conscious, while being slightly bitter about the 'wounded' status of his masculinity, which has been affected by second wave feminism. He is a melting pot of masculinities, blending a variety of contested subject positions, as well as a chameleon figure still negotiating the ongoing impact of feminism on his identity. In short, the 'postfeminist man' is defined by his problematic relationship with the ghost of hegemonic masculinity as he tries to reconcile the threat he poses to himself and the social systems he tries to uphold.

CASE STUDY: *FIGHT CLUB* (1996; 1999)

David Fincher's 1999 film *Fight Club* – based on Chuck Palahniuk's 1996 novel of the same name – provides a critique of masculinity and male sub-jectivity in the late twentieth century. Following the life of the nameless insomniac narrator, Jack (Edward Norton), and his alter ego, Tyler Durden (Brad Pitt), the film recounts the creation of 'fight club' – an underground male sparring club. As the bond between men develops through the act of unarmed combat, 'fight club' evolves into an anti-capitalist group that goes by the name 'Project Mayhem'. *Fight Club* shows how, through the physical act of fighting and the collective action of 'Project Mayhem', men try to make connections with each other and give meaning to their lives in a seemingly empty postmodern world where only physical pain can confer a sense of purpose and identity.

At the heart of this urban Gothic tale is the fear that men's lives have become nothing more than 'by-products of a lifestyle obsession'. In effect, *Fight Club* negotiates the dilemmas facing the 'postfeminist man'. Tyler – Jack's violent Other – defines this trauma of contemporary masculinity in almost Baudrillardian terms, noting that 'everything's a copy of a copy of a copy'. While *Fight Club* can be read as a backlash text – 'what you see at fight club is a generation of men raised by women' (Palahniuk 50) – a more productive path of analysis is provided by the issues of self-image explored in the novel and the film as men confront the possibility that they are merely a product of 'ornamental culture' (Faludi, *Stiffed* 35). For example, Jack's uncertainty about what a 'real' man looks like – as he gestures towards a Calvin Klein underwear advertisement, asking Tyler, 'Is that what men look like?' – confirms that signifier and signified have become disconnected. Here masculinity is unstable and uncertain, its form contested and undermined.

Fight Club must be read within the context of the recession of the early 1990s, which according to Susan Faludi had a significant impact on the shape of masculinity as men lost their sense of economic authority (*Stiffed*). Yet, as Faludi notes, economic recovery did not signal a straightforward recovery of male authority and power. Far from it: men could no longer rest assured that masculinity would provide the economic rewards historically associated with male identity. As Brabon suggests, the 'bleak inefficacy of men in the postmodern era provides a backdrop to Jack's troubled negotiation of his own masculinity through his encounters with his schizophrenic alter ego, Tyler Durden. Tyler offers Jack multiple personalities and subject positions, being, as Tyler says, "all the ways in which you could be – that's me"' (64). While the excessive violence witnessed in *Fight Club* can be interpreted as a response to this inefficacy as men search for an identity, both the attempted reclamation and deconstruction of masculinity represented in the book and film are not straightforward reactions to second wave feminism or a backlash against women. On the contrary, as Brabon writes, 'the men in *Fight Club* are defined by the absent father and the alienating images of male identity in contemporary culture' (65). What *Fight Club* reveals is a masculinity which is aware of its 'wounded' status, self-consciously struggling with the legacy of the 'old man', 'new man', 'metrosexual' and 'new lad'.

RECOMMENDED FURTHER READING

Beynon, John. *Masculinities and Culture*. Buckingham and Philadelphia: Open University Press, 2002.

Brabon, Benjamin A. 'The Spectral Phallus: Re-Membering the Postfeminist Man.' In *Postfeminist Gothic: Critical Interventions in Contemporary Culture*. Eds Benjamin A. Brabon and Stéphanie Genz. Basingstoke: Palgrave Macmillan, 2007. 56–67.

Connell, R. W. *Masculinities*. Cambridge: Polity, 1995.

Faludi, Susan. *Stiffed: The Betrayal of the American Man*. New York: William Morrow, 1999.

8

Cyber-Postfeminism

OVERVIEW

In this chapter, we analyse the multiple intersections of technology and feminism that have been the focus of cyberfeminism. Beginning with a consideration of the relationship between the cyborg and feminism, we revisit Haraway's influential work on the cyborg. Teasing out the utopian feminist potential of her thesis – alongside the work of Plant, Balsamo and Braidotti – we argue that the paradoxical figuration of the cyborg (as a site for both liberation and conservative backlash scenarios) fruitfully intersects with the politics of postfeminism in the late twentieth and early twenty-first centuries. From here, we explore how cyborg technologies are being used by women (and men) in a postfeminist era to rescript heteronormative categories through micro-political actions. We introduce the category of the postfeminist cyborg as a figure that moves along the border between conformity and transgression, complicity and critique. In conclusion, we consider the relationship between the posthuman and feminism, as new postgender locations open up that attempt to take us beyond dualistic configurations of the subject. We examine diverse variations of the cyberfeminist project by referring to the cyberpunk classic *Neuromancer* (1984) as well as providing case studies on the series of *Alien* films (1979, 1986, 1992, 1997) and the computer-game persona Lara Croft.

FEMINISM AND CYBORGS

Cyberspace provides a terrain of possibilities and challenges for (post) feminism. Loosely positioned along a spectrum of pro- and anti-cyberspace

feminists – from the pro-cyberspace, utopian feminism of Sadie Plant to
the more techno-wary criticism of Nicola Nixon – 'cyberfeminisms can
be differentiated by their political stances in relation to . . . technology and
how its effects on gender and identity are understood' (Chatterjee 200). Yet
it is important to recognise that 'there is a marked ambivalence in cyberfeminism as to how cyberspace can be understood in relation to the feminist
political project' (200). On the one hand, cyberspace is full of potential
as critical issues centring on female embodiment seemingly dissolve in a
virtual, postgender world. For its advocates and supporters, cyberspace offers
a locus where gender and sexual identities can be questioned and problematised in a fluid exchange that does not (necessarily) privilege a patriarchal
form of femininity and female subjectivity (Halberstam and Livingstone).
In its most positive manifestations it is 'the matrix not as absence, void, the
whole womb, but perhaps even the place of woman's affirmation' (Plant,
'The Future Looms' 60). Instrumental in this debate are Donna Haraway's
seminal texts 'A Manifesto for Cyborgs' (1985) and *Simians, Cyborgs and
Women* (1991), which provide a productive critical account of the interface
between technology, gender and sexuality. Central to Haraway's work is
the idea that technology is generating a new ontology – the very possibilities of new ways of being. As she points out, 'the cyborg is a creature in a
post-gender world: it has no truck with bisexuality . . . or other seductions
to organic wholeness through a final appropriation of all powers of the
parts into a higher unity' (*Simians* 150–1). This opens up the possibility for
'gender bending' and 'postgenderism', which, as George Dvorsky notes, is a
diverse social, political and cultural movement whose adherents affirm the
elimination of gender through the application of advanced biotechnology
and reproductive technologies.

Yet on the other hand, some critics find this flexible and 'plastic' manifestation of the postmodern self disingenuous and misleading. In particular, the figure of the cyborg – as witnessed in a number of contemporary
popular manifestations, such as Seven of Nine in the *Star Trek: Voyager* series
(1995–2001) – is problematic, often reinstating a traditional, sexualised and
hyperfeminine female body. In Gillis' eyes, 'the transgressive promise of
the cyborg and the posthuman has not always been evident', as 'the cyborg
as metaphor is fraught with difficulties precisely because it is already such a
ubiquitous image in popular culture, an image that, unfortunately, replicates
traditional ways of thinking about gender' (Gillis, 'Cyberspace, Feminism
and Technology' 216; Booth and Flanagan 15).

A more productive pathway that takes us beyond debates on the bodily
limitations/possibilities of Haraway's cyborg is offered by an expanding critical focus on the posthuman. In an attempt to transcend the Cartesian dualism

of the subject, critics like Halberstam ('Automating Gender') and Hayles have attempted to integrate and redefine our understanding of the relationship between the body and machine in a posthuman context. For Hayles, 'there are no essential differences or absolute demarcations between bodily existence and computer simulation, cybernetic mechanism and biological organism, robot teleology and human goals' (3). In other words, cyberspace becomes a location where the distinction between the subject and the object, the self and the other, dissolves. Accordingly, 'the posthuman contests old categories of identity formation that function to essentialise and exclude women and replaces them with a more complex range of subject positions' (Toffoletti 115). Within this context, cyberspace offers a particularly liberating site for women as it has the potential to sever their links with the female body.

The metaphor of the cyborg provides rich opportunities for (post)feminism. The cyborg does not simply mount a riposte to the Cartesian subject, eroding its inherent dualism, but also challenges us to question how we define the (female) body and its relationship to technology. In other words, the cyborg raises fundamental questions about human identity. According to Balsamo:

> Cyborgs are hybrid entities that are neither wholly technological nor completely organic, which means that the cyborg has the potential not only to disrupt persistent dualisms that set the natural body in opposition to the technologically recrafted body, but also to refashion our thinking about the theoretical construction of the body as both a material and a discursive process. (11)

Within this context, the cyborg as a 'feminist boundary rider' has been particularly useful for the cyberfeminist's critique of the female subject (Toffoletti 21). Addressing the historically and culturally constructed connections between men and technology – a relationship that more broadly excludes women from full subjecthood – critics like Haraway, Wajcman and Plant have sought to redress these limiting and artificial links. As Wajcman reminds us, the 'very definition of technology . . . has a male bias. This emphasis on technologies dominated by men conspires in turn to diminish the significance of women's technologies, such as horticulture, cooking and childcare, and so reproduces the stereotype of women as technologically ignorant and incapable' (137).

In effect, women have historically been 'othered' from technology and it is this history of technology's gendered bias towards men that Donna Haraway rethinks in her 1985 article 'A Manifesto for Cyborgs'. The influence of Haraway's work on cybertheory, postmodern and feminist theories is of such importance because, as Gillis suggests, 'it provides a useful way of critiquing Enlightenment ideas, and offers an opportunity to think about the body without the boundaries of gender' ('Cyberspace, Feminism and Technology' 208). Haraway calls for an attempt 'to build an ironic political myth faithful to feminism, socialism and materialism' (7). In so doing, she confronts the imposition of boundaries and definitions on the female body by patriarchy and asserts that there is 'nothing about being "female" that naturally binds women. There is not even such a state as "being" female, itself a highly complex category constructed in contested sexual scientific discourses and other social practices' (14). In accordance with other postmodern theories, Haraway dismantles the gendered category of 'female', illuminating its con-structedness and the lack of 'essential' unity between feminists and women in general. Identifying the conflicting/conflicted power of patriarchy, colonialism and capitalism as the forces that have worked to fragment and divide women's/feminism's political identity, she argues that 'white women, including socialist feminists, [have] discovered . . . the non-innocence of the category of "woman"' (16). Here 'woman' is a loaded term, saturated with numerous ideologies that have served both to homogenise and to fragment a collective sense of womanhood.

In order to work against the disintegrating effects of a phallocentric society – where the categories of 'female' and 'woman' are tainted by patri-archal ideologies – Haraway maintains that cyberfeminists 'have to argue that "we" do not want any more natural matrix of unity and that no con-struction is whole' (16). Within this context, the metaphor of the cyborg provides a valuable alternative model of subjectivity that it is not bound by Western/patriarchal scripts that define gender identities and the origins of civilisation (12). For Haraway, cyborg writing is concerned with 'the power to survive, not on the basis of original innocence, but on the basis of seizing the tools to mark the world that marked them as other. . . . Feminist cyborg stories have the task of recoding communication and intelligence to subvert command and control' (33). Cyborg writing is involved in the re-appropriation of the symbols of oppression by rescripting gender identi-ties and subverting the language of patriarchal domination. The power of the cyborg metaphor and its subversive potential – as a form that counters the homogenising effects of the grand narratives of Western culture – are worked through at the level of the text, as 'writing is pre-eminently the technology of cyborgs, etched surfaces of the late twentieth century. Cyborg politics is the struggle for language and the struggle against perfect com-munication, against the one code that translates all meaning perfectly, the central dogma of phallogocentrism' (34).

Building upon Haraway's provocative analysis, Judith Halberstam outlines the full impact of the cyborg as a device that not only liberates possible asso-ciations between femininity, femaleness and feminism – in what could be described as a thoroughly postfeminist articulation of the female/feminist/feminine self – but also covers up (by dissolving) any distinctions between gender and its various representations:

> The female cyborg becomes a terrifying cultural icon because it hints at the radical potential of a fusion of femininity and intelligence . . . A female cyborg would be artificial in both mind and flesh, as much woman as machine, as close to science as to nature . . . As a metaphor, she challenges the correspondences such as maternity and femininity or female and emotion. As a metonym, she embodies the impossibility of distinguishing between gender and its representation. ('Automating Gender' 454)

We must tread with care, however, as the metaphor of the cyborg is just that – a metaphor – and as Stacy Gillis has argued recently, popular representations of the cyborg often fail to move beyond the patriarchal script of femininity/female identity as they walk the tightrope of transgression and conformity. William Gibson's cyberpunk classic *Neuromancer* (1984) – which introduced the concept of cyberspace – provides a good example of how postfeminist attempts to transcend patriarchal scripts are often problematic and at times seemingly regressive. As Gillis maintains, figures like Molly Millions in Gibson's novel cannot move beyond the limitations of the hypersexualised female body. While Millions embraces the image of the ass-kicking techno-babe, she is still restricted by her sexualised femininity: she is 'contained by the language of sexuality. Her nails may conceal a weapon but they are coloured burgundy and serve to lengthen her fingers' ('(Post)Feminist Politics of Cyberpunk' 12). 'Ultimately,' writes Gillis, 'the cyborgic female body is modified only so as to accentuate or enact sexual promise' (15). In this way, just as cyberspace is in many ways inherently conservative, the cyborg encompasses backlash scripts and retro-sexism in its display of feminine excess. Yet there is no denying that increasingly, outside the fictional world, we are starting to live cyborg lives: 'Cyborgs actually exist. About 10 percent of the current US population are estimated to be cyborgs in the technical sense, including people with electronic pacemakers, artificial joints, drug-implant systems, implanted corneal lenses, and artificial skin' (Hayles 115). Here the metaphor of the cyborg becomes 'real' as technology increasingly plays its part in modifying and 'enhancing' the human body.

POSTFEMINIST CYBORGS

Whereas the cyborgic male is limited in its representations of the excesses of masculinity – as the muscular body of Arnold Schwarzenegger's Terminator from the *Terminator* trilogy of films (1984; 1991; 2003) highlights – the female cyborg's identity is more malleable and dexterous. The cyborgic male's identity can only revolve around displays of masculine aggression, attempts to become more human and/or a protecting father-figure. Contrastingly, the female cyborg blends sexuality with assertiveness, hyperfeminine characteristics with tough-girl strength, allowing her to transcend the patriarchal limits of female identity/femininity.

Taking into account the paradoxical and at times conflicting images of the cyborg, it seems to readily align itself with the postfeminist woman, who (in her most positive manifestations) conforms to *and* reworks patriarchal scripts from behind the mask of heteronormative, sexualised femininity. It would be incorrect to assume that such a pairing is straightforwardly predicated on Haraway's conception of the cyborg, but the strands of her cyborg politics (albeit corrupted by a return to the corporeal and the normative) permeate contemporary culture through the new cyborgs of the twenty-first century.

One manifestation of this new cyborg identity is witnessed through the rapidly expanding extreme makeover phenomenon, which deploys the new technology of cosmetic surgery to reconstruct the body in order to shape a 'better' self. Becoming part of the everyday fabric of women's lives, cosmetic surgery and the extreme makeover open up new possibilities for women to harness what could be described as cyborg technologies. As we watch numerous transformations of women in programmes such as *Extreme Makeover* (first aired on ABC in 2002) and *The Swan* (aired on Fox in 2004), we behold the arrival of the postfeminist cyborg woman who has turned to cosmetic surgery to enhance her heteronormative sense of self. More and more women (and men) in Western Europe and the United States in particular are choosing to embrace cosmetic surgery to augment their organic matter in what could be described as the metaphor of the cyborg made flesh. However, whereas Haraway's configuration of the cyborg is emancipatory and transgressive, these postfeminist cyborg women seek normative ideals as they attempt to contain and improve their 'transgressive' bodies. Perhaps somewhat ironically, these women harness cyborg technologies (such as breast augmentation – the most popular procedure in the UK with 28,921 performed in 2006) in order to conform to patriarchal scripts, but in so doing – as their exuberant responses to the 'makeover reveal' expose – they discover a revitalised self that has been unshackled from their bodily inadequacies. Here one of the paradoxes of postfeminism is revealed – a contradiction that can be explained by the subject's relationship to power.

As Foucault reminds us in *Discipline and Punish* (1977), the process of subject formation involves a double bind, as the 'power of the norm'

functions in two ways: 'In a sense,' he notes, 'the power of normalization imposes homogeneity, but it [also] individualizes' (184). In this way,
the postfeminist cyborg woman is involved in working with and against
the power structures inherent within subjectivity as she becomes object
(of the heterosexual male gaze) and subject (to a 'new' self). As we have
already mentioned, this dialectic is also implicit in Foucault's discussion
of subject formation, which has been developed by Judith Butler among
others. According to Butler, subjection is understood not only as subordination but also as 'a securing and maintaining, a putting into place of a
subject' (*Psychic Life of Power* 90–1). For us, postfeminism and the postfeminist woman must be understood within this context of the double bind
of subjectivity. This concept of normalisation can be employed to explain
the paradoxical position of the postfeminist woman's use of the technology of cosmetic surgery. Within this context, the extreme makeover series
Brand New You (aired in the UK on Channel 5 in 2005) offers an obvious
example of the homogenising aspects of normalisation as the participants'
bodies are measured for their deviation from the norms of heterosexual
desirability. As Heyes points out, 'normalization is obscured . . . by avidly
proffered alternative narratives that stress identity over beauty, and taking
one's life into one's hands to become a better person' (23). As one *Brand
New You* contestant asserts, she is 'finding it much easier to look in the
mirror' and her transformation 'will allow [her] to lead a more normal life'
(*Brand New You* 12 June 2007).

Kathryn Morgan voices concerns about the makeover process, noting that
'while the technology of cosmetic surgery could clearly be used to create and
celebrate idiosyncrasy, eccentricity, and uniqueness, it is obvious that this is
not how it is presently being used' (35). Indeed, 'choice' could be nothing
more than 'necessity', whereby 'elective cosmetic surgery . . . *is becoming the
norm*' and those 'women who contemplate *not using* cosmetic surgery will
increasingly be stigmatized and seen as deviant' (26; emphasis in original).
This is one of the contradictions of the rhetoric of choice that the postfeminist woman grapples with: what looks like individual empowerment, agency
and self-determination can also signal conformity and docility. Rosemary
Gillespie refers to this as 'the paradox of choice': 'The decision whether or
not to undergo cosmetic surgery clearly involves individual choice, yet the
concept of choice is itself enmeshed in social and cultural norms' (79). The
postfeminist cyborg must navigate the pitfalls of this 'paradox of choice',
struggling with the patriarchal framework that dictates potentially sexist
configurations of the female body as hypersexualised, in order to rescript the
body for the world of cyberspace in such a way that femininity and feminism
are not competing discourses (Genz, *Postfemininities in Popular Culture*).

POSTHUMAN FEMINISMS

The challenge that faces us in a posthuman world centres not only on dismantling the dualism of the Cartesian subject, but also on jettisoning our internalised sense of the 'normal' body. The posthuman possibilities that technology offers pose a new set of questions that, as Rosi Braidotti notes, demand that we scrutinise the very condition and meaning of 'human': 'What counts as human in this posthuman world? How do we rethink the unity of the human subject, without reference to humanistic beliefs, without dualistic oppositions, linking instead body and mind in a new flux of self?' (179). The questions Braidotti asks identify how the limits of the human are evolving within a posthuman context.

As Toffoletti states, the posthuman 'cannot simply be explained by the transcendence, extension or penetration of the human body via technologies. Rather, it is the bodily transformations and augmentations that come about through our engagements with technology that complicate the idea of a "human essence"' (13). Critics like Braidotti and Toffoletti argue that this complicating or troubling of the category of human by the intervention of technology creates a new politics of identity, which, we suggest, can be positively deployed by (post)feminism. For Toffoletti, the posthuman opens up a range of subject positions beyond dichotomous relationships between men and women. Embracing what could be described as a postfeminist directionality or 'line of flight', the posthuman becomes 'a figuration that exceeds signification; in Baudrillard's terms it "disappears" in the process of transforming into something else beyond the effects of technology as affirmative or negative for women' (Deleuze and Parnet 36; Toffoletti 26). Here the posthuman marks a point where boundaries dissolve and the relationship between the signifier and referent is brought into question in such a way that terms like 'human' and 'woman' are (potentially) no longer tainted by biological and ideological preconceptions.

This does not mean, however, that the posthuman – or, for that matter, postfeminism – is apolitical. On the contrary, as Braidotti notes, the 'hyperreality of the posthuman predicament . . . does not wipe out politics or the need for political resistance' (12). Posthuman (and postfeminist) politics turn on the individual – at the point where the individual is called into question, where the body is deconstructed and 're-formed'. For postfeminism, it is micro-politics that is the new framework of action and resistance, moving from collective to individual expressions of identity politics. As already discussed, for an increasing number of people (particularly women), technology is involved in helping them to navigate the 'paradox of choice', moving them beyond the limits of the human in both

normalising and liberating directions. Here micro-politics is a hybrid politics for a hybrid identity – a neo-liberal ideology of the self that assimilates
the objects of technologies into the redefined parameters of the individual,
dissolving the ever-thinning line between self and other. In this sense,
both posthuman and postfeminism are impure discourses that blend and
bind the forms that they 'post' – reifying and rewriting the categories of
human, feminism, woman.

CASE STUDY: *ALIEN*

Released in 1979, the first of the four *Alien* films (*Alien* [1979]; *Aliens* [1986];
Alien 3 [1992]; *Alien Resurrection* [1997]) introduces us to Sigourney Weaver's
feisty character, Lieutenant Ellen Ripley, and the perilous journey of the
spaceship *Nostromo* as it investigates a distress signal. Over the course of the
four films, we witness Ripley's various and ultimately deadly alien encounters as she is killed and reborn as a clone. According to Judith Newton, *Alien*
is 'seemingly feminist' (84) – as Ripley/Weaver takes centre stage, single-
handedly repelling the alien – but feminist theorists' responses to Ripley
display an unease over her status as an action heroine. Carol Clover, for
example, criticises reviews of *Aliens* that cast it as 'a feminist development'
as 'a particularly grotesque expression of wishful thinking' (117). In part,
criticism is directed at Ripley for adopting the role of the male hero while
embodying 'traditionally feminine qualities' (Newton 87). Importantly, it
would be incorrect to assume that because she adopts the traditional position
of the male hero, she is simply imitating men. Ripley 'presents audiences
with an image of a female character who is *both* victim and her own rescuer:
a character which breaks down the hierarchical division of active-male/
passive-female' (Hills 43). In this sense, Ripley's femininity and in-between
status can be analysed productively within a postfeminist context. She is
perhaps best described as a 'post-*Woman* woman' – blurring and collapsing the
binary distinctions between the genders (Braidotti 169). Ripley displays the
multiple subject positions of the postfeminist woman – a spectrum of identity
that does not deny conflicting and seemingly irreconcilable 'selves'.

As the films develop from *Alien* to *Alien Resurrection*, Ripley's 'monstrous
corporeality' is reconceived through the technology of cloning – as sleeping
beauty or 'Snow White' (as one of the marines labels her in *Aliens*) evolves
from worker to warrior, mother to champion, woman to alien–human
hybrid (Hills 47). In fact, as Fred Botting has recently argued, '[t]he logic
of a particular version of the "post" – post-human and postfeminist – seems
fully realised in *Alien Resurrection*: the categories of human and gender appear
obsolete, along with all the ideological bases – nature, bodies, feelings, ideals

– that support them' (181). Dissolving dualistic configurations of the subject and dismantling hierarchical structures, Ripley's hybrid identity marks her out as a postfeminist figure who challenges our expectations of what it means to be a woman in a posthuman era.

CASE STUDY: LARA CROFT

Created in 1996 by Eidos Interactive for the *Tomb Raider* video-game series, Lara Croft has divided and split feminist critics. Lauded as the greatest 'cyberbabe' in the *Guinness Book of World Records* – with more than 1,000 Internet fan sites and appearances on over 200 magazine covers (including *Time* and *Newsweek*) – Lara Croft is a hybrid figure, an action heroine who displays hyperfeminine bodily characteristics. Tapping into the 1990s Girl Power phenomenon, Croft and *Tomb Raider* rework the male-dominated action-adventure genre epitomised by *Indiana Jones* by putting centre stage a feminine, hot-pants-wearing fighting machine. The game goes to some lengths to give Lara a fictional biography, whereby she is portrayed as simultaneously an English aristocrat, daughter of Lord Henshingly and educated at Wimbledon High School for girls; a tomb-raiding adventurer and martial arts expert; and sex symbol for the gamer – who, it must be acknowledged, has ultimate control over Lara's movements and actions. In this way, Croft is a postfeminist boundary rider who provides women (and men) with a new female/feminine figure of identification, deploying physical prowess to battle with men and monsters. She has, as Helen Kennedy notes, a 'bimodal' appeal for young men and women as both an object of sexual desire and an emancipated, strong woman.

The inherent threat to masculinity embodied by the action heroine's empowered status is short-circuited, however, for, as critics emphasise, Lara is 'a *girl*, not a woman. From the tip of her schoolgirl plait to her army boots, she is a luscious tomboy' (Stables 20). At the same time, through her heroic actions and physical prowess, Lara also manipulates and subverts gender roles, reinforcing and undermining the way we are expected to read the hyperfeminine script of her body. Her potential is defined by the way identities (both male and female) can be projected onto her bodily surface in cyberspace: 'She is an abstraction, an animated conglomeration of sexual and attitudinal signs (breasts, hotpants, shades, thigh holsters) whose very blankness encourages the (male and female) player's psychological projection' (Poole quoted in Stables 19). Lara Croft captures a number of postfeminist possibilities, opening up subject positions that seem – at the level of the female body – irreconcilable. She is thus a postfeminist figure par excellence – conventional in her stylised and accentuated femininity and innovative in her active heroine status (Tasker, *Action and Adventure Cinema*).

RECOMMENDED FURTHER READING

Balsamo, Anne. *Technologies of the Gendered Body: Reading Cyborg Women.* Durham, NC, and London: Duke University Press, 1996.

Gillis, Stacy. 'The (Post)Feminist Politics of Cyberpunk.' *Gothic Studies* 9.2 (2007): 7–19.

Halberstam, Judith. 'Automating Gender: Postmodern Feminism in the Age of the Intelligent Machine.' *Feminist Review* 17.3 (1991): 439–60.

Haraway, Donna J. *Simians, Cyborgs and Women: The Reinvention of Nature.* New York and London: Routledge, 1991.

9

Third Wave Feminism

OVERVIEW

In this chapter we examine the notion of 'third wave feminism', which emerged in the 1990s and has often been described by its advocates in antithesis to postfeminism. According to third wave feminists, postfeminism can be understood in terms of a conservative/patriarchal discourse that seeks to criticise and undermine second wave feminism. By contrast, third wave feminism defines itself as a budding political movement with strong affiliations to second wave feminist theory and activism – the conflict between third wavers and postfeminists often being exemplified by the supposed dichotomy between the politically informed Riot Grrrls and the mainstream, fashionable Spice Girls. Third wave feminism speaks to a generation of younger feminists – born in the 1960s and 1970s – who see their work founded on second wave principles, yet distinguished by a number of political and cultural differences. Third wave feminists embrace contradiction and diversity as inherent components of late twentieth-century and twenty-first-century women's (and men's) lives, and they envision a new model of feminist thinking and practice that goes 'beyond black or white' and situates itself within popular culture in an effort to bridge the gap between consumption and critique (Siegel, *Sisterhood, Interrupted* 142). We suggest that the adoption of a binary logic to conceptualise the relationship between third wave feminism and postfeminism is misleading in many cases as it does not account for the slippage between the two terms and often rests on an overly simplistic view of postfeminism as defeatism. We analyse the rifts and overlaps between the third wave and postfeminism through an examination of the television series *Buffy the Vampire Slayer*.

THIRD WAVE FEMINISM

The mid-1990s saw a number of largely non-academic publications by a younger generation of women who were keen to debate the meanings and relevance of feminism for their late twentieth-century lives. Anthologies and edited collections such as *Listen Up: Voices From the Next Feminist Generation* (1995, ed. Barbara Findlen), *To Be Real: Telling the Truth and Changing the Face of Feminism* (1995, ed. Rebecca Walker) and *Manifesta: Young Women, Feminism, and the Future* (2000, Jennifer Baumgardner and Amy Richards) provide personal accounts of feminist awakenings and are meant as guides to feminism for a mainstream audience. These writings announced the advent of and set the tone for a new, 'third wave' of feminism, marked by a desire to renew feminist commitment as well as distinguish itself from its second wave precursor. As Barbara Findlen, a former editor of *Ms.* magazine, writes about the young feminist contributors to *Listen Up*, '[w]e're here, and we have a lot to say about our ideas and hopes and struggles and our place within feminism. We haven't had many opportunities to tell our stories, but more of us are finding our voices and the tools to make them heard' (xvi). The term 'third wave' was popularised by Rebecca Walker in a 1995 article in which she encouraged young women to join their (second wave) mothers and embrace feminism ('Becoming the Third Wave') – previous usages include a 1987 essay in which Deborah Rosenfelt and Judith Stacey reflect on the ebbs and flows of feminism throughout the 1970s and 1980s, proposing that 'what some are calling a third wave of feminism [is] already taking shape' (359).

An underlying concern of many of these studies outlining the third wave is to establish and demarcate its parameters as well as characterise its proponents: For Jennifer Baumgardner and Amy Richards, for example, the third wave consists of 'women who were reared in the wake of the women's liberation movement of the seventies' (15), while for Leslie Heywood and Jennifer Drake, it is the generation 'whose birth dates fall between 1963 and 1974' ('Introduction' 4). A less precise delineation is favoured by Rory Dicker and Alison Piepmeier, who maintain that 'we want to render problematic an easy understanding of what the third wave is' (5).

By adopting the 'wave' metaphor, the third wave clearly situates itself within what Deborah Siegel calls 'the oceanography of feminist movement' – a chronology that comprises the surge of feminist activism in the nineteenth and early twentieth centuries – commonly referred to as the 'first wave' of feminism, which culminated around the campaign for women's suffrage in the 1920s – and the 'second wave' resurgence of feminist organising in the 1960s ('The Legacy' 52). As Gillis, Howie and Munford note in their introduction to *Third Wave Feminism* (2004), '[t]o speak about a "third wave" of feminism . . . is to name a moment in feminist theory and practice' (1). The very invocation of 'third wave feminism' and the mobilisation of the adjective 'third' indicate a desire to establish a link with previous feminist waves and ensure a continuation of feminist principles and ideas. The self-declared third wavers Leslie Heywood and Jennifer Drake emphasise that 'to us the second and third waves of feminism are neither incompatible nor opposed' (3). In Deborah Siegel's eyes, one should think of the third wave as 'overlapping both temporally and spatially with the waves that preceded it' – 'just as the same water reforms itself into ever new waves, so the second wave circulates in the third, reproducing itself through a cyclical movement' ('The Legacy' 60–1). Mimicking the nomenclature of its predecessors, third wave feminism acknowledges that it stands on the shoulders of other, earlier feminist movements and in this sense acts as a stance of resistance to popular pronouncements of a moratorium on feminism and feminists.

While the third wave is inextricably linked to the second, it is also defined in large part by how it differs from it. Gillis and Munford state categorically that 'we are no longer in a second wave of feminism' and now need to delineate 'a feminism which could no longer, in any way, be identified as "victim feminism"', a feminism that does not 'hurt itself with . . . simplistic stereotyping and ideological policing' ('Harvesting' 2, 4). The third wavers' orientation to feminism is different because, among other reasons, they have grown up with it. Baumgardner and Richards, for instance, propose that 'for anyone born after the early 1960s, the presence of feminism in our lives is taken for granted. For our generation, feminism is like fluoride . . . it's simply in the water' (17).

Third wave writers and activists insist that feminism cannot be based on 'anachronistic insularity' and separatism but has to adopt a 'politics of ambiguity' that embraces tolerance, diversity and difference (Gillis and Munford, 'Harvesting' 2; Siegel, *Sisterhood, Interrupted* 140). As Baumgardner and Richards explain, 'most young women don't get together to talk about "Feminism" with a capital F. We don't use terms like "the politics of housework" or "the gender gap" as much as we simply describe our lives and our expectations' (48). The third wave is keen to 'make things "messier"' by using second wave critique as a central definitional thread while emphasising ways that 'desires and pleasures subject to critique can be used to rethink and enliven activist work' (Heywood and Drake, 'Introduction' 7). According to the third wave's agenda, 'there is no one right way to be: no role, no model' – instead 'contradiction . . . marks the desires and strategies of third wave feminists' who 'have trouble formulating and perpetuating theories that compartmentalize and divide according to race and gender and all the other signifiers' (Reed 124; Heywood and Drake, 'Introduction' 2; Walker,

'Being Real' xxxiii). The third wave subject is always in process and accommodating multiple positionalities, 'including more than excluding, exploring more than defining, searching more than arriving' (Walker, 'Being Real' xxxiii). Third wave feminism thus seeks to make room for 'the differences and conflicts *between* people as well as *within* them' and 'to figure out how to use [these] differences dynamically' (Reed 124; emphasis in original).

Third wave feminism is clearly informed by postmodern theorising as well as a multiculturalist sensibility, arguing for the political possibilities that the postmodern present makes available. The third wave functions as a 'political ideology currently under construction', welcoming pluralism and describing itself as a postidentity movement that engages with the postmodern challenge to a unified subjectivity (Pender, 'Kicking Ass' 165). As Rebecca Walker suggests in an interview entitled 'Feminism Only Seems to Be Fading: It's Changing', 'the next phase in feminism's evolution will entail a politics of ambiguity, not identity' (quoted in Siegel, 'The Legacy' 53–4).

Third wave feminism addresses the subject's experience of having fragmented and conflicting selves that do not constitute a seamless and coherent whole. In this way, 'with no utopic vision of the perfectly egalitarian society or the fully realized individual', third wave feminists 'work with the fragmentation of existing identities and institutions', creating a new theoretical/ political space that 'complicates female identity rather than defining it' (Reed 124). Simultaneously, the third wave is committed to political action, asserting that 'breaking free of identity politics has not resulted in political apathy' but rather has provided 'an awareness of the complexity and ambiguity of the world we have inherited' (Senna 20). In effect, third wave theory and practice consider anti-essentialism and political engagement as indispensably allied. The movement sees itself as 'a political stance and a critical practice', thriving on the contradictions that ensue from postmodernism's questioning of the identity category (Siegel, 'The Legacy' 54, 59).

Further to being a theoretically informed movement, the third wave also locates itself within popular culture and understands a critical engagement with the latter as the key to political struggle. This is in marked contrast to second wave feminism, which, for the most part, took a 'hard line', anti-media approach, favouring separatism over the 'spin game' (Whelehan, *Feminist Bestseller* 138). As Heywood and Drake put it, 'we're pop–culture babies; we want some pleasure with our critical analysis' (51). They highlight that 'it is this edge, where critique and participation meet, that third wave activists must work to further contentious public dialogue' (52). The third wave thus contests a politics of purity that separates political activism from cultural production, 'ask[ing] us . . . to re-imagine the disparate spaces constructed as "inside" and "outside" the academy . . . as mutually informing and intersecting spheres of theory and practice' (Siegel, 'The Legacy' 70). Many third wavers critically engage with popular cultural forms – television, music, computer games, film and fiction – and position these within a broader interrogation of what 'feminism' means in a late twentieth- and twenty-first-century context. They concentrate on the proliferation of media images of strong female characters to interpret consumer culture as a place of empower-ment and differentiate themselves from second wave feminists who had been critical of the misogyny of the popular realm.

One of the most prominent and public icons of the third wave is Courtney Love, lead singer of the Riot Grrrl band Hole and wife of the late Kurt Cobain. For Heywood and Drake, Love personifies the third wave and its politics of ambiguity:

> She combines the individualism, combativeness, and star power that are the legacy of second wave gains in opportunities for women . . . with second wave critiques of the cult of beauty and male dominance . . . Glamorous and grunge, girl and boy, mothering and selfish, put together and taken apart, beautiful and ugly, strong and weak, respon-sible and rebellious, Love bridges the irreconcilability of individuality and femininity within dominant culture, combining the cultural cri-tique of an earlier generation of feminists with the backlash against it by the next generation of women. ('Introduction' 4–5)

While the third wave's bond with its second wave forerunner is marked by continuity and change – illustrating the third wave's 'central drama' of 'wanting to belong but being inherently different' (Siegel, *Sisterhood, Interrupted* 140) – its relationship with postfeminism is far less ambiguous. Many third wavers understand their position as an act of strategic defi-ance and a response to the cultural dominance of postfeminism. From its initiation, the third wave has resolutely defined itself against postfeminism: in fact, third wave pioneers Rebecca Walker and Shannon Liss were keen to establish an ideological and political split between the two, pronouncing '[w]e are not postfeminist feminists. We are the third wave!' (quoted in Siegel, *Sisterhood, Interrupted* 128). Heywood and Drake also emphasise that, within the context of the third wave, '"postfeminist" characterises a group of young, conservative feminists who explicitly define themselves against and criticise feminists of the second wave' – among these 'young' feminists are included Katie Roiphe and Rene Denfeld, who reject notions of 'victim feminism' (1). The effect of these announcements is both to link third wave feminists to their second wave mothers and to distinguish them from their alienated postfeminist sisters who supposedly discard older feminists' strategies. Second and third waves of feminism are thus united in their condemnation of an exceedingly popular and retrograde postfeminism that is seen to be in line with the economic, political and cultural forces governing the market and mainstream media.

A pertinent example of this rift is the often-cited distinction between popular Girl Power discourse and the underground Riot Grrrl movement (see Chapter 3). Some critics insist that the Riot Grrrl's 'angry rebellion' against the patriarchal structures of the music scene is in opposition to the media-friendly 'absurdity' of Girl Power, which amounts to 'a very persuasive and pervasive form of hegemonic patriarchal power' (Gillis and Munford, 'Genealogies' 174; Harris, 'From Suffragist' 94). While Girl Power (promoted by the Spice Girls) is at best no more than 'a bit of promotional fun', the Riot Grrrls can be placed within feminism's radical and activist history, taking 'cultural production and sexual politics as key sites of struggle' (Coward 122; Heywood and Drake, 'Introduction' 4). Ultimately, these critics claim, third wave feminism should be acknowledged as an emerging political ideology and 'forms of feminist activism', while postfeminism 'shuts down ongoing efforts to work toward change on the level of both theory and practice' (Heywood and Drake, 'It's All About the Benjamins' 7; Sanders 52).

As we have suggested already in Chapter 3, this rhetoric of antagonism is sometimes misleading, as it does not account for the overlap between the third wave and postfeminism, nor does it allow for a politicised reading of the latter. We have argued throughout for a more nuanced and productive interpretation of the prefix 'post' and its relations to feminism, whereby the compound 'postfeminism' is understood as a junction between a number of often competing discourses and interests. This expanded understanding goes beyond a limited interpretation of postfeminism as anti-feminist backlash and encourages an active rethinking that captures the multiplicity and complexity of twenty-first-century feminisms.

There are of course a number of important differences between postfeminism and the third wave, significantly at the level of foundation and political alignment; yet there are also a range of similarities, as the third wave and postfeminism both posit a challenge to second wave feminism's anti-popular and anti-feminine agenda. Sarah Banet-Weiser maintains that postfeminism is 'a different political dynamic than third wave feminism', with the latter defining itself more overtly as a kind of feminist politics that extends the historical trajectory of previous feminist waves to assess contemporary consumer culture (206). Postfeminism, on the other hand, does not exist as a budding political movement and its origins are much more impure, emerging from within mainstream culture, rather than underground subculture – in Tasker's and Negra's eyes, postfeminism can be seen as a 'popular idiom' while third wave feminism is 'a more scholarly category' and 'self-identification' (19). Moreover, unlike the third wave, postfeminism is not motivated by a desire for continuity and a need to prove its feminist credentials – what Diane Elam terms the 'Dutiful Daughter Complex' or Baumgardner and Richards describe as a 'scrambling to be better feminists and frantically letting these women [second wave feminists] know how much we look up to them' (85).

This unwillingness or rather indifference to position itself in the generational wave narrative, however, need not imply that postfeminism is apolitical and anti-feminist. On the contrary, in the following chapter, we will analyse the notions of a postfeminist politics and/or a political postfeminism that – while not identical to other, particularly feminist, strategies of resistance – adopt a more flexible model of agency that is doubly coded in political terms and combines backlash and innovation, complicity and critique. We also need to remind ourselves that there is a potential overlap between third wave feminism and postfeminism that should not be interpreted, as some critics propose, as a 'dangerous and deceptive slippage' but rather an unavoidable consequence of contradiction-prone contemporary Western societies and cultures (Munford 150). In effect, the third wave is the target of similar objections that have been raised in connection with postfeminism, mainly related to its resolutely popular and consumerist dimensions. Discussing Courtney Love's 'postmodern feminism', Gillis and Munford, for example, question whether the politics of Girl culture can be reconciled with her 'bad girl philosophy' ('Genealogies' 173). While Love clearly confounds the dichotomisation of 'Madonna and Whore', her reliance on brand culture and her embrace of feminine paraphernalia – exemplified by her provocative statement that 'we like our dark Nars lipstick and La Perla panties, but we hate sexism, even if we do fuck your husbands/boyfriends' – propel a debate as to 'what extent . . . this commodification neutralise[s] feminist politics' (173). The third wave and postfeminism thus occupy a common ground between consumption and critique, engaging with feminine/sexual and individual forms of agency. Both third wave feminism and postfeminism have drawn on popular culture to interrogate and explore twenty-first-century configurations of female empowerment and re-examine the meanings of feminism in the present context as a politics of contradiction and ambivalence.

CASE STUDY: *BUFFY THE VAMPIRE SLAYER* (1997–2003)

In their introduction to the edited collection *Fighting the Forces* (2002), Rhonda Wilcox and David Lavery note that 'good television' – in opposition to 'bad television' that is simply 'predictable, commercial, exploitative' – is characterised by its ability to resist the pressures of social and artistic expectations and the conventions of the business, 'even while it partakes in [these forces] as part of its nature' (xvii). *Buffy the Vampire Slayer* is identified as such a case of 'good television', not only confounding the laws of the horror genre but also offering a new kind of female protagonist that disrupts any clear set of distinctions between 'passivity, femininity and women on the one hand and activity, masculinity and men on the other' (Tasker, *Spectacular Bodies* 77). Joss Whedon, the creator of the series, has often been quoted as saying that *Buffy the Vampire Slayer* was explicitly conceived as a reworking of horror films in which 'bubbleheaded blondes wandered into dark alleys and got murdered by some creature' (quoted in Fudge 1). As he notes, 'the idea of Buffy was to . . . create someone who was a hero where she had always been a victim. That element of surprise, that element of genre busting is very much at the heart of . . . the series' (quoted in Thompson 4). Whedon is determined to 'take that character and expect more from her', deconstructing the label of blonde (i.e. dumb) femininity and linking it with notions of power and strength (quoted in Lippert 25).

Buffy the Vampire Slayer enacts in its title the foundational myth and the premise of the entire series, centring on an ex-cheerleading, demon-hunting heroine who tries to combine being a girl with her vampire-slaying mission. From its US premiere in 1997 to its primetime finale in 2003, the series followed the fortunes of Buffy Summers (Sarah Michelle Gellar) as she struggled through the 'hell' that is high school, a freshman year at U.C. Sunnydale, and the ongoing challenge of balancing the demands of family, friends and relationships with her work as the 'Slayer' whose duty is to fight all evil (Pender, 'Kicking Ass' 165). The 'joke' of the cheerleading demon hunter is not a 'one-line throwaway gag' but encapsulates Buffy's ongoing battle with her composite character as the 'Chosen One' – who, as the voiceover to the show's opening credits relates, 'alone will stand against the vampires, the demons and the forces of darkness' – and as a sixteen-year-old teenager who wants to do 'girlie stuff' (Pender, *'I'm Buffy'* 42).

Blending elements of action, drama, comedy, romance, horror and occasionally musical, the series has been lauded as a reinterpretation of established cinematic and generic concepts and identities. With her long blonde hair and thin, petite frame, Buffy is visibly coded by the conventional signifiers of attractive, helpless and (to some extent) unintelligent femininity. The show foils both viewers' and characters' expectations by portraying this cute cheerleader not as a victim but a 'supremely confident kicker of evil butt' (quoted in Krimmer and Raval 157). According to Whedon, Buffy is intended both to be a feminist role model and to subvert the non-feminine image of the 'ironclad hero – "I am woman, hear me *constantly* roar"' (quoted in Harts 88). Buffy has been celebrated as a 'radical reimagining of what a girl (and a woman) can do and be' and a 'prototypical girly feminist activist' (quoted in

Pender, 'Kickin Ass' 165). In particular, Buffy has been embraced as 'the new poster girl for third wave feminist popular culture', continuing the second wave's fight against misogynist violence – variously represented as types of monsters and demons – and articulating new 'modes of oppositional praxis, of resistant femininity and, in its final season, of collective feminist activism that are unparalleled in mainstream television' (Pender, 'Kicking Ass' 164).

The climax of season 7 is specifically noteworthy as it sees Buffy – with the help of the 'Scooby gang', her friends Willow (Alyson Hannigan) and Xander (Nicholas Brendon) – redistribute her Slayer power and 'change the rule' that was made by 'a bunch of men who died thousands of years ago' and prescribes that 'in every generation, one Slayer is born' ('Chosen'). Buffy's Slayer strength is magically diffused and displaced onto 'every girl who could have the power', so that 'from now on, every girl in the world who might be a Slayer, will be a Slayer'. In transferring power from the privileged, white Californian teenager to a heterogeneous group of women, *Buffy the Vampire Slayer* can be said to address the 'issue of cultural diversity that has been at the forefront of third wave feminist theorising' (Pender, 'Kicking Ass' 170). Buffy's final description of herself as unbaked 'cookie dough' has also been highlighted by critics as exemplifying the third wave's politics of ambiguity, its deliberate indeterminacy and 'inability to be categorized' ('Chosen'; Gilmore 218). Despite the end of the series in 2003, *Buffy* has had an active afterlife, giving rise to an online journal (*Slayage*) and several conferences and anthologies devoted to the burgeoning field of 'Buffy studies'.

Other commentators have been more sceptical about the series (and its conclusion) and Buffy's suitability as a feminist role model. They draw attention to the show's 'mixed messages about feminism and femininity', upholding a dualistic rationale that defines 'Buffy's form and Buffy's content' as 'distinct and incompatible categories' (Fudge 1; Pender, '*I'm Buffy*' 43). For example, Anne Millard Daughtery condemns the Slayer's feminine exterior on the grounds that 'for all the efforts taken to negate the traditional male gaze, Buffy's physical attractiveness is, in itself, objectifying' (151). Buffy's 'girl power' is seen as 'a diluted imitation of female empowerment' that promotes 'style over substance' and ultimately lacks a political agenda (Fudge 3). She is censured for being a 'hard candy-coated feminist heroine for the girl-power era' whose 'pastel veneer' and 'over-the-top girliness in the end compromise her feminist potential'. This polarised viewpoint defines action heroines by their adoption or refusal of femininity and is forced to conclude that 'Buffy cannot be a feminist because she has a cleavage' (Pender, '*I'm Buffy*' 43).

Following this line of argument, *Buffy the Vampire Slayer* has been discussed as a contemporary version of the 1970s 'pseudo-tough', 'wanna be' action heroines exemplified by Wonder Woman and Charlie's Angels. As Sherrie

Inness explains, femininity was used in this context as a way to allay the heroine's toughness, tone down and compensate for her assertiveness and display of strength (*Tough Girls*). Contrastingly, we maintain that such an attempt to create a dichotomy between feminism and femininity – and in a similar manner, postfeminism and the third wave, girl and grrrl – is disadvantageous for a number of reasons, not only leading to a reification of masculine power/feminine weakness but also negating the transgressive potential of the action-adventure heroine who occupies an empowered and heroic position. We contend that Buffy's feminine and feminist, girl and grrrl components should not be separated, and we interpret her as a liminal contemporary character who transcends binary formulations and subverts gender frameworks that underlie the concepts of masculine activity and feminine passivity. It is in this gap between dualities that the postfeminist possibilities for more complex and diverse understandings of modern-day womanhood, feminism and femininity are revealed.

RECOMMENDED FURTHER READING

Genz, Stéphanie. *Postfemininities in Popular Culture*. Basingstoke: Palgrave Macmillan, 2009.

Gillis, Stacy, and Rebecca Munford. 'Genealogies and Generations: The Politics and Praxis of Third Wave Feminism.' *Women's History Review* 13.2 (2004): 165–82.

Heywood, Leslie, and Jennifer Drake, eds. *Third Wave Agenda: Being Feminist Doing Feminism*. Minneapolis and London: University of Minnesota Press, 1997.

Siegel, Deborah L. 'The Legacy of the Personal: Generating Theory in Feminism's Third Wave.' *Hypatia* 12.3 (1997): 46–75.

10

Micro-Politics and Enterprise Culture

OVERVIEW

In this final chapter, we advance the notion of a politicised postfeminism and/or a postfeminist politics, problematising in this way critical perceptions of postfeminism as a depoliticised and anti-feminist backlash. This not only implies a reconsideration of postfeminism but also involves a rethinking of the political sphere and the concept of the individual. We suggest that postfeminism is doubly coded in political terms and is part of a neo-liberal political economy that relies on the image of an 'enterprising self' characterised by initiative, ambition and personal responsibility (Rose). The modern-day 'enterprise culture' invites individuals to forge their identity as part of what Anthony Giddens refers to as 'the reflexive project of the self' – that is, in late modernity individuals increasingly reflect upon and negotiate a range of diverse lifestyle choices in constructing a self-identity (*Modernity and Self-Identity*).

Following Patricia Mann, we argue that the vocabulary of political actions has to be expanded, and we examine the notion of postfeminist 'micro-politics', which takes into account the multiple agency positions of individuals today (160). Micro-politics differs from previous models of oppositional politics (including second wave feminist politics) in the sense that it privileges the individual and the micro-level of everyday practices. Postfeminist micro-politics is situated between two political frameworks, incorporating both emancipatory themes and ones more explicitly concerned with individual choices (Budgeon, 'Emergent Feminist (?) Identities'). We will discuss micro-politics by referring to postfeminist sexual agents who use their body as a commodity to achieve autonomy and agency. This stance is illustrated by the

American designer/writer/women's rights activist Periel Aschenbrand, whose provocative T-shirt campaigns politicise fashion by exploiting sexuality to sell feminism to a new generation of women.

INDIVIDUALISATION AND ENTERPRISE CULTURE

As we have indicated on a number of occasions, postfeminism has been conceived (and criticised) by many commentators as a purely individualistic phenomenon that is disqualified from political action. Postfeminism has been defined as a depoliticisation of feminism, inherently opposed to activist and collective feminist politics. The notions of a postfeminist politics and/or a political postfeminism have been seen as futile, if not oxymoronic. The post-feminist subject – in particular, the fashionable and marketable 'girl' of Girl Power discourse – has been described in antithesis to second wave activists who publicly and collectively campaigned for feminist goals of female emancipation and equality. Critics have argued that postfeminism at best is simply apathetic and indifferent to politics while at worst it amounts to a 'proudly backward' counterassault on women's rights (Faludi, *Backlash* 12). Postfeminism is condemned not just for being apolitical but for producing, through its lack of an organised politics, a retrogressive and reactionary conservatism.

In this chapter, we want to complicate the perception of postfeminism as a depoliticised and/or anti-feminist backlash that acts as a ruse of patriarchy to spread false consciousness among women. We propose that a more productive interpretation of postfeminism situates it as part of a changing political and cultural climate that responds to, among other issues, the destabilisation of gender relationships, a diversification and mainstreaming of feminist ideas and an increased emphasis on 'choice' and 'self-empowerment' in neo-liberal rhetoric. As Patricia Mann observes, in the current era, in which fewer people are willing to connect ideologically with any political movement, feminism should be regarded as a 'theoretical and psychological resource rather than an identifying political uniform' (100). The existence of feminism as a kind of 'common sense' has been noted by various commentators who examine the shifting conditions of being feminist and doing feminist work in the twenty-first century (Gill, *Gender and the Media*; McRobbie, 'Mothers and Fathers'). Feminism's increasingly mediated and non-collective/activist status has a number of important consequences, both for the role of the feminist cultural critic – who engages with more diverse and contradictory fields of enquiry – and more generally for our conception of political power and agency. With the certainty of a stable and secure feminist perspective and politics slipping away, different understandings of political engagement and feminist activity – as well as of the relationship between feminism and its subject – have to be explored that acknowledge this shift to feminism as an individualistic media discourse.

A key place to start this process of rethinking is the concept of the individual itself, which has gained a lot of attention in discussions of postfeminism and contemporary politics. While the individual has always been at the heart of feminist activism and politics – exemplified by the well-known second wave slogan 'the personal is political' – it was largely envisaged as a catalyst and step towards collective action and organised protest. For example, second wave strategies like consciousness-raising might have started in the private sphere where women shared personal experiences of sexual and material subjugation, but these individual grievances were soon related to a broader context of social injustice affecting all women. Consciousness-raising directly drew on women's victimisation in their everyday lives to politicise their personal outlooks and pave the way for a wider politics of engagement. In this sense, there was a clearly defined and structured link between individual women and the feminist sisterhood, personal expression and political action, single awareness and collective consciousness. The individual was seen as a springboard from which to look beyond the private space traditionally designated for women into the public worlds of education, profession and social opportunity. Agency and emancipation were conceived along these lines with the explicit aims of liberating women (both as individuals and as a group) from patriarchal forms of constraint and empowering them to participate on an equal footing with men in areas of social activity.

It is this connection between the individual and the feminist collective that has come to be the focus of contemporary examinations of postfeminism and its supposed apolitical agenda. Postfeminism is said to sever the link between individual women and the feminist movement by embracing a singular, self-centred form of agency that undermines the communal aspects of feminism and its distinct social and political goals. As we noted in the Introduction, some critics have taken issue with postfeminism's individualistic credo, which, they argue, is 'driven by representational concerns and commodity logic' and based on an overly optimistic formulation of 'choiceoisie' that assumes that the second wave's struggle for women's rights and equality is now redundant (Dow 213; Probyn). Underlining personal choice rather than structural necessity, postfeminism's individualism is seen to effect a decollectivisation of the feminist movement that, critics are concerned, works to obliterate feminism's political dimensions and collective self-understanding. In these readings, the postfeminist subject is at best a token achiever – who affirms female oppression while neutralising that affirmation in an individualistic rhetoric – while at worst she is a traitor to the feminist cause, guiltily standing over 'the corpse of feminism' (Hawkesworth 969). In Angela McRobbie's words, the 'ruthless female individualism' of postfeminist women – whom she labels 'TV blondes' – presents a fantasy of female omnipotence but in 'the longer term it may prove fatal', as it means 'living without feminism' ('Good Girls' 363, 370, 372).

By contrast, we want to reconceptualise the postfeminist individual by re-imagining the connections between public and private spheres and expanding the range of political actions to allow for more diverse and conflicting forms of agency that combine emancipatory objectives with individual choices. Following the social theorist Patricia Mann, we contend that it is more politically compelling to conceive of the postfeminist subject in terms of the 'multiple agency positions' – 'a confusingly varied set of motivations, obligations, and desires for recognition' – that we occupy in contemporary society and that provide 'the context for political struggle and social transformation' (171, 160). During this time of 'social confusion' in which we operate in a 'sometimes terrifying array of relationships and connections within both domestic and public arenas', a successor form of individualism – which Mann calls 'engaged individualism' – has emerged as a result of the reorganisation of everyday life brought about by the social enfranchisement of women (4, 115, 121). The 'engaged individuals' that Mann refers to – she also uses the terms 'conflicted actors' and 'micro-political agents' – respond to the contradictions of the postmodern age by experimenting with 'multiple and changing forms of individual agency' while struggling to preserve a 'shifting and always contingent sense of . . . integrity' (32).

Mann's notion of engaged individualism acknowledges that new modes of agency and identity are gradually developing and transforming forms of social and political behaviour, beyond but not necessarily in opposition to collective and activist strategies (favoured, for instance, by second wave feminism). As she writes, a contemporary feminist approach needs to adapt itself to an era in which communal forms of political action are on the wane and more complex notions of individual agency – which are capable of delineating the heightened level of personal choice and responsibility – begin to come into play (100). Analyses such as these provide alternative ways of comprehending the category of the 'postfeminist' – personified, for example, by the 'chick', the 'do-me feminist' and the 'new feminist' – not as a patriarchal token or a failed feminist but as a complex subject position of multiply engaged individuals.

Postfeminism attributes a central position to the individual, and in this sense it can also be read in conjunction with current sociological examinations of self-identity. This line of thought is associated with the work of Anthony Giddens, who formulates a theory of the self as reflexively made by the individual. Giddens suggests that with the decline of traditions – what he designates 'the post-traditional order of modernity' – identities in general have become more diverse and malleable and, today more than ever, individuals can construct a narrative of the self (*Modernity and Self-Identity* 5). This is the reflexive 'project of the self' which takes place 'in the context of multiple choice' and allows individuals to negotiate a range of diverse lifestyle options in forming a self-identity (5). In this account, self-identity is not a set of traits or characteristics but a person's own reflexive understanding of their biography. The more society is modernised, the more subjects acquire the ability to reflect upon their social conditions and change them (Budgeon, 'Emergent Feminist (?) Identities'; Beck). There is a shift from a socially prescribed life story – constraining in particular for women who historically have been disadvantaged by the fact that they are female – to a biography that is self-produced. This construction is not optional but is an ongoing project that demands the active participation of the subject (Beck 135). As Shelley Budgeon points out, this is especially relevant for young women in contemporary society as 'processes of individualization and detraditionalization mean that not only are a wide range of options available to them in terms of their self-definition, but that an active negotiation of positions which are potentially intersecting and contradictory is necessary' (10). Individualisation thus operates as a social process that, instead of severing the self from a collective, increases the capacity for agency while also accommodating a rethinking of the individual as an active agent.

In effect, the individual comes to be seen as 'an entrepreneur' or 'an enterprise of the self' who remains continuously engaged in a project to shape his or her life (du Gay 156). The conception of the individual as an entrepreneur has been particularly influential in some political quarters that stress the importance of personal choice and self-determination. As Nikolas Rose proposes, today's 'enterprise culture' accords 'a vital *political* value to a certain image of the self' that 'aspire[s] to autonomy . . . strive[s] for personal fulfilment . . . [and] interpret[s] its reality and destiny as matters of individual responsibility' (141–2; emphasis in original). The enterprising self is motivated by a desire to 'maximise its own powers, its own happiness, its own quality of life' through enhancing its autonomy and releasing its potential (150). The presupposition of the 'autonomous, choosing, free self as the value, ideal and objective underpinning and legitimating political activity' has imbued the political mentalities of the modern West, in particular those informed by neo-liberal rhetoric (142). Prevalent in late twentieth- and early twenty-first-century Western capitalist societies, neo-liberalism is generally understood in political economy terms as the dismantling of the welfare state and the expansion of the global free trade. Its importance for cultural analysis lies in its extension of market values and rationality to other areas of life, including its construction of the individual as an entrepreneur and consumer-citizen who should self-regulate and self-care. This resonates with postfeminism's individualist and commoditised understanding of empowerment and agency, at odds with second wave notions of collective politics and community activism.

As Rosalind Gill highlights in her examination of contemporary media and gender, there is a 'clear fit between neoliberalism and postfeminist media culture': 'At the heart of both is the notion of the "choice biography" and the contemporary injunction to render one's life knowable and meaningful through a narrative of free choice and autonomy' (*Gender and the Media* 260, 262). Gill is sceptical of this neo-liberal/postfeminist focus on the individual as an 'entirely free agent', and she criticises the postfeminist subject for her return to femininity and her 'reprivatization of issues that have only relatively recently become politicized' (259–60). By emphasising notions of personal choice and self-determination, the grammar of individualism 'turns the idea of the personal as political on its head' (259). In Gill's eyes, the shift to neo-liberal/postfeminist subjectivities illustrates a change in the way that power operates, as '[w]e are invited to become a particular kind of self, and endowed with agency' on condition that – in the case of the postfeminist feminine/sexual subject – 'it is used to construct oneself as a subject closely resembling [a] heterosexual male fantasy' (258). This, Gill is convinced, represents a 'higher or deeper form of exploitation', as it implicates women in their own subjugation and objectification, imposing (male) power not 'from above or from the outside' but from within 'our very subjectivity' (258).

Similarly, Stéphanie Genz investigates the links between postfeminism and 'Third Way' philosophy – adopted throughout the 1990s by centre-left governments in Europe and the United States as a middle course between right and left ideology – to analyse the notions of postfeminist entrepreneurship and subjectivity ('Third Way/ve'). As she notes, '[p]ostfeminism is part of a Third Way political economy, participating in the discourses of capitalism and neo-liberalism that encourage women to concentrate on their private lives and consumer capacities as the sites for self-expression and agency' (337–8). She argues that female subjects in particular are addressed by neoliberal rhetoric and 'become the "entrepreneurs" of their own image, buying into standardised femininities while also seeking to resignify their meanings' (338). Genz admits that this is certainly 'a politically "impure" practice' that does not adhere to second wave conceptions of politics and social change, but in her view, it also allows for a different understanding and construction of political agency and identity.

The notions of female individualisation and enterprise have been the focus of a number of critical investigations that debate women's role in the reflexive project of the self and the possibility of expressing a politicised agency within the conditions of late modernity (McRobbie, 'Post-Feminism'; Budgeon, 'Emergent Feminist (?) Identities'). If, as Natasha Walter proposes, contemporary young women – and, we would add, men – now have to 'mak[e] up their lives' without the security of 'markers or goalposts', then we need to interrogate further the nature of postfeminist politics that comes to the fore in a neo-liberal consumer culture (2).

POSTFEMINIST MICRO-POLITICS

In her examination of agency in a postfeminist era, Patricia Mann formulates a theory of individual agency she designates 'micro-politics', which takes into account the 'multiple agency positions of individuals today' (160). Mann recognises the fundamental transformations in late twentieth-century Western societies that have occurred as a result of the enfranchisement of women and their unmooring from patriarchal relations. 'Like it or not,' she writes, 'ours is an era that will be remembered for dramatic changes in basic social relationships, within families, workplaces, schools, and other public spheres of interaction' (1). As she explains:

> [w]e may be expected to change jobs, careers, marriages, and geographical venues with the same resignation or optimism as we switch channels. We may be described, without undue exaggeration, as operating within a tangle of motivations, responsibilities, rewards, and forms of recognition unmoored from traditional male and female, public and private identities. (115)

Mann's notion of 'gendered micro-politics' is intended to provide insight into this complicated nexus of relationships and rethink agency in the context of these changes. The key to micro-political agency is an 'engaged individualism' that allows individuals to combine 'economic and interpersonal forms of agency', and experiment with 'various identities as well as diverse familial and community relationships' (124). In these circumstances, the micro-political agent is characterised as a 'conflicted actor' who is capable of individually integrating diverse desires and obligations through creatively reconfiguring his or her practices and relationships: 'We are micro-political agents insofar as we manage to operate within various institutional discourses without ever being fully inscribed within any of the . . . frames of reference that engage us' (31). This postfeminist micro-politics differs from previous political forms in its adoption of a more 'dynamic and flexible model of political agency' that arises from 'a struggle that is not only without a unitary political subject but also without a unitary political opponent' (159). What makes micro-politics so contentious is that it is not put into practice by a political community engaged in activism, but results from individual and daily gender-based struggles. As Mann admits, the playing fields of contemporary gendered conflicts are still 'under construction' and, therefore, the rules of postfeminist micro-politics are 'not clearly defined' (186).

The practice of micro-politics has also been investigated by other critics who focus more exclusively and directly on young female identities and their connection with the feminist project. Basing her study upon interviews with a number of young women, Shelley Budgeon is keen to point out that, while her interviewees are alienated by second wave feminism, their identities are informed by feminist ideas ('Emergent Feminist (?) Identities'). She relates this contradiction to the tension between second wave feminism and postfeminism, arguing that the identities under construction allow contemporary young women to 'engage in a resistant fashion with the choices they have available at the micro-level of everyday life' (7). Budgeon maintains that it is possible to create a politicised identity at the level of the individual self and foster social change from daily interactions and practices. In their understanding of female rights and inequality, young women nowadays use 'an interpretative framework that owes much of its potency to feminism' while also being derived from a brand of postfeminism that appropriates feminist ideals and grafts them onto consumable products (20, 18). For Budgeon, this intermingling of feminism, postfeminism, individualism and consumerism is not necessarily undesirable and detrimental: in effect, the 'marketability of feminist discourse in this popularized form is what renders it so accessible and, therefore, readily available to young women within the context of their everyday lives' (18).

Drawing on the work of Anthony Giddens, Budgeon proposes a politicised interpretation of postfeminism by locating it between two political frameworks: 'emancipatory' and 'life politics' (21). Reflecting 'the characteristic orientation of modernity', emancipatory politics is organised by principles of justice, equality and participation with the explicit aim of liberating individuals and groups from conditions that limit their life chances (*Modernity and Self-Identity* 211). Life politics, in contrast, is a politics of lifestyle options that focuses on the means to self-actualisation and on self-identity as a reflexive achievement (214, 9). In Giddens' analysis, the two forms of politics are not mutually exclusive and questions that arise within one type pertain to the other as well (228). Budgeon argues that – while second wave feminism is fundamentally an emancipatory discourse – postfeminism should be interpreted as a transitional moment that mingles two political strands:

> The first is the theme characteristic of a feminism with its roots in modernity and identification with the universal subject 'woman'. The second is about differences emerging within that category under postmodern conditions and the resulting shift of emphasis onto individual choices as universals dissolve. (22)

In this sense, postfeminism combines emancipatory themes of second wave feminism and a 'life politics' style of feminism that is more concerned with individual choices and self-actualisation. Budgeon suggests that postfeminism's blend of emancipatory and life politics is apparent in the lives of the young women she interviewed and in the ways in which 'gender inequality is defined as a collective problem but with an individual solution' (21). For her, the 'pitting of "old" feminism and "new" feminism' that characterises many discussions of postfeminism and 'the debates about which form of politics is a more accurate representation of young women' do not seem particularly relevant in the context of young women's negotiation of identities that are 'inherently contradictory' (24). Rather, it is more likely that postfeminist micro-politics calls into play aspects of both emancipatory and life politics, highlighting in this way the conflicting forms of agency that women take up in contemporary society. The possibilities and contradictions of a postfeminist micro-politics are especially intriguing in the case of sexualised practices and regimes of recognition that have typically been overlooked as dimensions of agency.

CASE STUDY: PERIEL ASCHENBRAND AND SEXUAL MICRO-POLITICS

In *Gender and the Media*, Rosalind Gill writes that contemporary culture is characterised by an increasing and pervasive sexualisation, which is evident in 'the extraordinary proliferation of discourses about sex and sexuality across all media forms' as well as the frequent 'erotic presentation of girls', women's and (to a lesser extent) men's bodies' (256). These depictions are part of a modernisation of femininity (and masculinity) and a shift from 'sexual objectification' to 'sexual subjectification' (258). In Gill's eyes, this process is particularly apparent in the sexualised portrayals of women who come to be seen not as victimised objects but as knowing sexual subjects: 'Where once sexualized representations of women in the media presented them as passive, mute objects of an assumed male gaze, today sexualization works somewhat differently', as '[w]omen are not straightforwardly objectified but are presented as active, desiring sexual subjects' (258). She uses the now infamous example of the little tight T-shirt bearing slogans such as '*fcuk me*' – employed by the British high-street fashion store French Connection – or 'fit chick unbelievable knockers' to illustrate this move to sexual subjecthood ('From Sexual Objectification'). As she describes the ubiquity of French Connection's generic T-shirt: 'It could be seen everywhere, emblazoned across the chests of girls and young women, and competing on the street, in the club, and on the tube with other similar T-shirts declaring their wearer a "babe" or "porn star" or "up for it", or giving instructions to "touch me" or "squeeze here"' (100).

While these everyday fashion practices have been dismissed by critics as instances of patriarchal colonisation, they also contain the seeds of a sexual micro-politics whereby women/girls use their bodies as political tools to gain empowerment within the parameters of a capitalist economy. The balancing act from high-street activity to emerging political activism has recently been achieved by controversial American designer/writer/women's rights activist Periel Aschenbrand, whose provocative T-shirt campaigns exploit sexuality to sell feminism to a new generation. Founder of the company 'body as billboard', which retails T-shirts across the United States and Europe, Aschenbrand summarises her mission statement in the following way:

> we should reject renting our bodies as billboard space for odious companies and use them instead to our advantage, to advertise for shit that matters. We should be wearing politically minded clothing, clothes that say things people aren't saying. We should use our tits to make people think about the things no one is making them think about. (*The Only Bush* 66)

As Aschenbrand reveals in an interview with the British newspaper the *Observer*, she was originally inspired by a group of female students she used to teach: 'I couldn't believe the apathy. They were not at all politicised. They'd come into class wearing idiotic T-shirts advertising garbage. "Mrs Timberlake", "Team Aniston". It was absurd. I told them: I think we should put our tits to better use' (quoted in France 3). With her range of printed T-shirts (selling for an average $44 on her website www.bodyasbillboard. com), she set out to turn women's breasts into 'advertising space' to take advantage of the fact that this particular female body part has always been 'oversexualized' (*The Only Bush* 66). As Aschenbrand suggests, her company offers 'a sweatshop-free original-artwork clothing line for women sick of companies' appropriation of their bodies for advertising' (109). Slogans include campaigns against the Bush administration, date rape, domestic violence and the erosion of American abortion legislation. Her clothing items – most (in)famously exemplified by a T-shirt bearing the words 'The Only Bush I Trust Is My Own' (which also doubles up as the title of her autobiographical polemic [2005]) – have been worn by a number of celebrities and feminist writers including Gloria Steinem, Susan Sarandon and Eve Ensler, playwright of *The Vagina Monologues*. Other T-shirt campaigns include 'What Would You Give For A Great Pair of Tits?', sold in aid of breast cancer research; 'Knockout', to raise money for victims of domestic abuse; and 'Drug Dealer', for the Keep A Child Alive organisation.

Aschenbrand's motivations can be understood in terms of a sexual micro-politics that seeks to rework the systems of sexual and economic signification.

As she succinctly puts it, '[i]f Michael Moore made being politically involved hip, I wanted to make it *sexy*': 'I am on a mission to change things – one pair of tits at a time' (67, 109; emphasis in original). Patricia Mann explains that 'sexual micro-politics seeks a redistribution of the dimensions of sexual agency such that women will have as much right to feel, express, and act upon their sexual desires as men have' (27). She argues that women have the capacity to be 'self-conscious social actors now rather than traditional passive objects of the patriarchal gaze' (87). In her view, '[w]omen have no choice but to attempt to rewrite patriarchal codes of recognition' by engaging in signifying practices and interactions that have historically played to 'the expectations of the patriarchal gaze' (87). However, Mann admits that while 'participation in such risky signifying enterprises is increasingly a part of everyday life for women', this is inevitably a 'messy process': 'The hoary old patriarchal gaze tends to be at once so ambient and so distant that the intense local discourses of feminism have difficulty connecting with it' (87–8). Sexual micro-politics is thus inherently contradictory, simultaneously playing to stereotypes of women while hoping to rewrite and resignify the patriarchal codes which deny women the subject status and quality of recognition they aspire to. Ultimately, Aschenbrand's sexualised and fashionable political stance can be said to raise as many questions as she suggests she solves, creating new fields of enquiry and interpretative ambiguities for contemporary critics to interrogate and debate.

POSTFEMINIST POLITICS

As we have seen, the notion of postfeminist politics poses a number of challenges for critics that we have only begun to examine and discuss. Popular and commoditised, emancipatory and lifestyle-oriented, postfeminist politics seeks to reconcile the seemingly irreconcilable by combining feminist concerns with female equality, neo-liberal individualism, media-friendly depictions of feminine/sexual empowerment and consumerist demands of capitalist culture. Postfeminist micro-political agents take up politically ambivalent positions by tapping into a variety of often competing discourses that highlight the multiple agency positions of individuals today. Sexual micro-politics in particular undoubtedly commoditises and objectifies female bodies; yet, at the same time, these contemporary uses of standardised sexual imagery also have the potential to 'uproot' feminine commodities and make them available for alternative meanings.

We suggest that postfeminism's critical/political stance is unavoidably compromised as the potential for innovation and change is accompanied by the threat of backlash. In fact, recuperation is ever a real possibility as postfeminist political strategies are always double-edged. This does not mean that postfeminism is disqualified from politics but rather that, as an emerging political position, it is still under construction and intrinsically paradoxical. The implications for postfeminist politics are that backlash and innovation, complicity and critique, can never fully be separated but are ambiguously entwined. As Shelley Budgeon proposes, '[t]o think productively about the capacity for postfeminism as conducive to social change is to think of it as a "politics of becoming"' ('Emergent Feminist (?) Identities' 22). A particularly contentious and, to use Mann's term, potentially 'messy' area of investigation revolves around the question of how such individualised and commodity-driven actions can be reinforced at the macro-political level. As Mann notes, 'micro-politics requires macro-political and symbolic forms of reinforcement' (196). We remain hesitant about such a prospect, yet hopeful that the old patriarchal script can be exorcised by postfeminist forms of agency that take into account the complicated entanglements that mark twenty-first-century lives. At the same time, we are aware and unwavering in our belief that the existence of postfeminist politics does not eradicate the continuing importance of other political forms and practices, nor does it undercut the basis of and need for a feminist resistance. Rather, it points to the mixed messages and conflicting demands of a neo-liberal consumer culture that holds out the possibilities of freedom and enslavement, subject and object status, for both women and men.

RECOMMENDED FURTHER READING

Budgeon, Shelley. 'Emergent Feminist (?) Identities: Young Women and the Practice of Micropolitics.' *European Journal of Women's Studies* 8.1 (2001): 7–28.

Genz, Stéphanie. 'Third Way/ve: The Politics of Postfeminism.' *Feminist Theory* 7.3 (2006): 333–53.

McRobbie, Angela. 'Good Girls, Bad Girls? Female Success and the New Meritocracy.' In *British Cultural Studies: Geography, Nationality, and Identity*. Eds David Morley and Kevin Robins. Oxford: Oxford University Press, 2001. 361–72.

Mann, Patricia S. *Micro-Politics: Agency in a Postfeminist Era*. Minneapolis and London: University of Minnesota Press, 1994.

Afterword: Postfeminist Possibilities

In this book we have investigated a number of different understandings and interpretations of postfeminism. Our analysis has allowed us to build up a comprehensive view of varied and multifarious texts, contexts and theories that contribute to and inform the postfeminist landscape. We have suggested that postfeminism's meanings arise (inter)contextually, often mingling seemingly incompatible strands of feminism, popular culture, academia and politics. We have described postfeminism as a transitional moment that addresses the complexities and changes that modernisation and detraditionalism have brought about in contemporary Western societies. Rather than adopting a unitary definition, we have sought to explore postfeminism's most prominent, controversial and productive uses and meanings, ranging from backlash to postfeminist micro-politics.

Throughout this book our guiding principle has been our conviction that an expanded and nuanced understanding of postfeminism opens up – rather than closes down – critical debates on the state of contemporary feminisms and the work of the feminist cultural critic. We have pursued avenues of investigation that have previously been neglected, proposing among other matters that postfeminism engenders a potentially rewarding political stance for the new millennium that brings into play diverse forms of individual agency. However, we have also been alert to the fact that postfeminism as a conceptual category and discursive system is still under construction and cannot escape a certain amount of confusion and contradiction. In particular, we have highlighted that postfeminism encompasses an inherently 'impure' signifying space that mingles progress and retrogression, collusion and critique, resistance and recuperation. As Patricia Mann describes the postfeminist subject/agency position: 'The old social game board is still visible beneath our feet, yet there are new players, new moves, and new rules to be negotiated. It is an old game and a new one at once' (5). Mann notes that as a consequence, there is an inevitable 'sense of lawlessness' resulting from 'having partially left behind hoary patriarchal institutions and norms, without yet having developed new sources of legitimate authority' (208). To think through the possibilities of the postfeminist phenomenon thus involves some readiness on the part of critics and readers alike to give themselves up to this postfeminist disarray and to reconsider their analytical strategies and methods of enquiry. In our eyes, postfeminism is best understood as a site of interrogation – or in Mann's words, a 'fertile site of risk' (207) – that provides an opportunity to practise conflict constructively and challenges us to broaden our interpretative frameworks and accommodate the complicated entanglements that characterise gender, culture, theory and politics in late modernity. We hope that this enquiry will lead others to cultivate the still relatively uncharted postfeminist terrain.

Bibliography

Aapola, Sinikka, Marnina Gonick and Anita Harris. *Young Femininity: Girlhood, Power and Social Change*. Basingstoke: Palgrave Macmillan, 2005.

Acker, Kathy. 'All Girls Together.' *Guardian Weekend* 3 May 1997: 12–19.

Adkins, Lisa. 'Passing on Feminism: From Consciousness to Reflexivity?' *European Journal of Women's Studies* 11.4 (2004): 427–44.

Alcoff, Linda. 'Cultural Feminism versus Post-Structuralism: The Identity Crisis in Feminist Theory.' *Signs: Journal of Women in Culture and Society* 13 (1987–8): 405–36.

Alexander, Priscilla. 'Introduction: Why This Book?' In *Sex Work: Writings by Women in the Sex Industry*. Eds Frédérique Delacoste and Priscilla Alexander. Pittsburgh: Cleis, 1987. 14–18.

Alice, Lynne. 'What is Postfeminism? Or, Having it Both Ways.' *Proceedings of the Feminism/Postmodernism/Postfeminism Conference, November 17–19, 1995: Working Papers in Women's Studies*. Albany: Massey University, 1995. 7–35.

Ang, Ien. *Living Room Wars: Rethinking Media Audiences for a Postmodern World*. London and New York: Routledge, 1996.

Aschenbrand, Periel. *The Only Bush I Trust Is My Own*. London: Corgi, 2005.

Attwood, Feona. 'Sexed Up: Theorizing the Sexualization of Culture.' *Sexualities* 9.1 (2006): 77–94.

Balsamo, Anne. *Technologies of the Gendered Body: Reading Cyborg Women*. Durham, NC, and London: Duke University Press, 1996.

Banet-Weiser, Sarah. 'What's Your Flava? Race and Postfeminism in Media Culture.' In *Interrogating Postfeminism: Gender and the Politics of Popular Culture*. Eds Yvonne Tasker and Diane Negra. Durham, NC, and London: Duke University Press, 2007. 201–26.

Barrett, Michèle. 'Feminism's "Turn to Culture."' *Woman: A Cultural Review* 1 (1990): 22–4.

Bartky, Sandra Lee. *Femininity and Domination: Studies in the Phenomenology of Oppression*. London and New York: Routledge, 1990.

Battles, Kathleen, and Wendy Hilton-Morrow. 'Gay Characters in Conventional Spaces: *Will and Grace* and the Situation Comedy Genre.' *Critical Studies in Media Communication* 19.1 (2002): 87–105.

Baudrillard, Jean. 'Game with Vestiges.' *On the Beach* 5 (1984): 19–25.

Baumgardner, Jennifer, and Amy Richards. *Manifesta: Young Women, Feminism, and the Future*. New York: Farrar, Straus and Giroux, 2000.

Bautista, Anna Marie. 'Desperation and Domesticity: Reconfiguring the "Happy Housewife" in *Desperate Housewives*.' In *Reading Desperate Housewives: Beyond the White Picket Fence*. Eds Janet McCabe and Kim Akass. London and New York: I.B. Tauris, 2006. 156–65.

Beauvoir, Simone de. *The Second Sex*. 1953. London: Vintage, 1997. Trans. of *Le Deuxième Sexe*. 1949.

Beck, Ulrich. *Risk Society*. London: Sage, 1992.

Bellafante, Ginia. 'Who Put the "Me" in Feminism?' *Time* 29 June 1998: 54–60.

Benhabib, Seyla. 'Feminism and the Question of Postmodernism.' In *The Polity Reader in Gender Studies*. Cambridge: Polity, 1994. 76–92.

Benhabib, Seyla. 'Feminism and Postmodernism: An Uneasy Alliance.' In *Feminist Contentions: A Philosophical Exchange*. Seyla Benhabib, Judith Butler, Drucilla Cornell and Nancy Fraser. New York and London: Routledge, 1995. 17–34.

Benn, Melissa. *Madonna and Child: Towards a New Politics of Motherhood*. London: Jonathan Cape, 1998.

Berlant, Lauren, and Michael Warner. 'What Does Queer Theory Teach Us about X?' *PMLA* 110.3 (1995): 343–9.

Best, Steven, and Douglas Kellner. *Postmodern Theory: Critical Interrogations*. London: Macmillan, 1991.

Beynon, John. *Masculinities and Culture*. Buckingham and Philadelphia: Open University Press, 2002.

Bly, Robert. *Iron John: A Book About Men*. Shaftesbury: Element, 1991.

Bolotin, Susan. 'Voices from the Post-feminist Generation.' *New York Times Magazine* 17 October 1982: 31.

Booth, Austin, and Mary Flanagan. *Reload: Rethinking Women + Cyberculture*. Cambridge, MA: MIT Press, 2002.

Bordo, Susan. *Unbearable Weight: Feminism, Western Culture and the Body*. Berkeley: University of California Press, 1993.

Botting, Fred. 'Flight of the Heroine.' *Postfeminist Gothic: Critical Interventions in Contemporary Culture*. Eds Benjamin A. Brabon and Stéphanie Genz. Basingstoke: Palgrave Macmillan, 2007. 170–85.

Brabon, Benjamin A. 'The Spectral Phallus: Re-Membering the Postfeminist Man.' In *Postfeminist Gothic: Critical Interventions in Contemporary Culture*. Eds Benjamin A. Brabon and Stéphanie Genz. Basingstoke: Palgrave Macmillan, 2007. 56–67.

Braidotti, Rosi. *Nomadic Subjects: Embodiment and Sexual Difference in Contemporary Feminist Theory*. New York: Columbia University Press, 1994.

Braithwaite, Ann. 'Politics and/of Backlash.' *Journal of International Women's Studies* 5.5 (2004): 18–33.

Bromley, Susan, and Pamela Hewitt. '*Fatal Attraction*: The Sinister Side of Women's Conflict about Career and Family.' *Journal of Popular Culture* 26.3 (1992): 17–23.

Brooks, Ann. *Postfeminisms: Feminism, Cultural Theory and Cultural Forms*. London and New York: Routledge, 1997.

Brunsdon, Charlotte. *Screen Tastes: Soap Opera to Satellite Dishes*. London and New York: Routledge, 1997.

Budgeon, Shelley. 'Fashion Magazine Advertising: Constructing Femininity in the "Postfeminist" Era.' In *Gender & Utopia in Advertising: A Critical Reader*. Eds Luigi Manca and Alessandra Manca. Lisle, IL: Procopian Press, 1994. 55–70.

Budgeon, Shelley. 'Emergent Feminist (?) Identities: Young Women and the Practice of Micropolitics.' *European Journal of Women's Studies* 8.1 (2001): 7–28.

Butler, Judith. *Gender Trouble: Feminism and the Subversion of Identity*. London and New York: Routledge, 1990.

Butler, Judith. 'Lana's "Imitation": Melodramatic Repetition and the Gender Performative.' *Genders* 9 (1990): 1–18.

Butler, Judith. *Bodies That Matter: On the Discursive Limits of 'Sex'*. London and New York: Routledge, 1993.

Butler, Judith. 'Imitation and Gender Insubordination.' In *The Lesbian and Gay Studies Reader*. Eds H. Abelove, M. A. Barale and D. M. Halperin. London and New York: Routledge, 1993. 307–20.

Butler, Judith. 'For a Careful Reading.' In *Feminist Contentions: A Philosophical Exchange*. Seyla Benhabib, Judith Butler, Drucilla Cornell and Nancy Fraser. New York and London: Routledge, 1995. 127–43.

Butler, Judith. *Excitable Speech: A Politics of the Performative*. London and New York: Routledge, 1997.

Butler, Judith. 'Performative Acts and Gender Constitution: An Essay in Phenomenology and Feminist Theory.' In *Writing on the Body: Female Embodiment and Feminist Theory*. Eds K. Conboy, N. Medina and S. Stanbury. New York: Columbia University Press, 1997. 401–17.

Butler, Judith. *The Psychic Life of Power: Theories in Subjection*. Stanford, CA: Stanford University Press, 1997.

Cacoullos, Ann R. 'American Feminist Theory.' *American Studies International* 39.1 (2001): 72–117.

Califia, Pat. *Sex Changes: The Politics of Transgenderism*. San Francisco: Cleis, 1997.

Cashmore, Ellis. *Beckham*. Cambridge: Polity, 2004.

Chambers, Samuel A. 'Desperately Straight: The Subversive Sexual Politics of *Desperate Housewives*.' In *Reading Desperate Housewives: Beyond the White Picket Fence*. Eds Janet McCabe and Kim Akass. London and New York: I.B. Tauris, 2006. 61–73.

Chambers, Samuel A. 'Heteronormativity and *The L Word*: From a Politics of Representation to a Politics of Norms.' In *Reading The L Word: Outing Contemporary Television*. Eds Kim Akass and Janet McCabe. London and New York: I. B. Tauris, 2006. 81–98.

Chambers, Veronica, Claudia Kalb and Julie Weingarden. 'How Would Ally Do It.' *Newsweek* 2 March 1998: 58.

Chapman, R. 'The Great Pretender: Variations on the "New Man" Theme.' In *Male Order: Unwrapping Masculinity.* Eds R. Chapman and J. Rutherford. London: Lawrence and Wishart, 1988. 225–48.

Chatterjee, Bela Bonita. 'Razorgirls and Cyberdykes: Tracing Cyberfeminism and Thoughts on Its Use in a Legal Context.' *International Journal of Sexuality and Gender Studies* 7.2 (2002): 197–213.

Chick Lit USA. 14 June 2004. www.chicklit.us/whatiscl.htm.

Clare, A. *On Men: Masculinity in Crisis.* London: Chatto & Windus, 2000.

Cloud, Dana. 'Hegemony or Concordance? The Rhetoric of Tokenism in "Oprah" Winfrey's Rags-to-Riches Biography.' *Critical Studies in Mass Communication* 13 (1996): 115–37.

Clover, Carol. *Men, Women and Chainsaws: Gender in the Modern Horror Film.* London: British Film Institute, 1992.

Cohan, S. *Masked Men, Masculinity and Movies in the Fifties.* Bloomington: Indiana University Press, 1997.

Connell, R. W. *Masculinities.* Cambridge: Polity, 1995.

Coppock, Vicki, Deena Haydon and Ingrid Richter. *The Illusions of 'Post-Feminism': New Women, Old Myths.* London: Taylor & Francis, 1995.

Cott, Nancy F. *The Grounding of Modern Feminism.* New Haven, CT, and London: Yale University Press, 1987.

Coward, Rosalind. *Sacred Cows: Is Feminism Relevant to the New Millennium?* London: HarperCollins, 1999.

Daly, Mary. *Gyn/Ecology: The Metaethics of Radical Feminism.* 1978. London: Women's Press, 1995.

Daniele, Daniela. 'Locations: Notes on (Post) Feminism and Personal Criticism.' In *Critical Studies on the Feminist Subject.* Ed. Giovanna Covi. Trento: Dipartimento di Scienze Filologiche e Storiche, 1997. 79–99.

Daughtery, Anne Millard. 'Just a Girl: Buffy as Icon.' In *Reading the Vampire Slayer.* Ed. R. Kaveney. New York: Tauris Parke, 2002. 148–65.

Davies, Liz. *Feminism after Post-Feminism: Socialist Renewal.* European Labour Forum Pamphlet No. 10. Nottingham: Russell Press, 1996.

Davis, Kathy. '"My Body is my Art": Cosmetic Surgery as Feminist Utopia?' In *Embodied Practices: Feminist Perspectives on the Body.* Ed. Kathy Davis. London: Sage, 1997. 168–81.

Deleuze, Gilles, and Claire Parnet. *Dialogues II.* Trans. Hugh Tomlinson and Barbara Habberjam. London: Continuum, 1987.

Delmar, Rosalind. 'What is Feminism?' In *What is Feminism?* Eds Juliet Mitchell and Ann Oakley. Oxford: Blackwell, 1986. 8–33.

Delombard, Jeannine. 'Femmenism.' In *To Be Real: Telling the Truth and Changing the Face of Feminism.* Ed. Rebecca Walker. London: Anchor Books, 1995. 21–33.

Denfeld, Rene. *The New Victorians: A Young Woman's Challenge to the Old Feminist Order.* New York: Warner Books, 1995.

Dentith, Simon. *Parody*. London and New York: Routledge, 2000.

Derrida, Jacques. *Limited Inc*. Evanston: Northwestern University Press, 1990.

Dicker, Rory, and Alison Piepmeier. 'Introduction.' In *Catching a Wave: Reclaiming Feminism for the 21st Century*. Boston: Northeastern University Press, 2003. 3–28.

Douglas, Susan J. *Where the Girls Are: Growing Up Female with the Mass Media*. London: Penguin, 1995.

Dow, Bonnie J. *Prime-Time Feminism: Television, Media Culture, and the Women's Movement since the 1970s*. Philadelphia: University of Pennsylvania Press, 1996.

Driscoll, Catherine. 'Girl Culture, Revenge and Global Capitalism: Cybergirls, Riot Grrls, Spice Girls.' *Australian Feminist Studies* 14.29 (1999): 173–93.

Dutton, Judy. 'Meet the New Housewife Wannabes.' *Cosmopolitan* June 2000: 164–7.

Dvorsky, George. 'Postgenderism: Beyond the Gender Binary.' 20 March 2008, accessed 28 March 2008. www.sentientdevelopments.com/2008/03/postgenderism-beyond-the-gender-binary.html.

Dworkin, Andrea. 'Against the Male Flood: Censorship, Pornography, and Equality.' In *Feminism and Pornography*. Ed. Drucilla Cornell. Oxford: Oxford University Press, 2000. 19–38.

Edwards, Tim. *Men in the Mirror: Men's Fashion, Masculinity and Consumer Society*. London: Cassell, 1997.

Edwards, Tim. *Cultures of Masculinity*. Abingdon and New York: Routledge, 2006.

Elam, Diane. 'Sisters are Doing it to Themselves.' In *Generations: Academic Feminists in Dialogue*. Eds Devoney Looser and Ann E. Kaplan. Minneapolis: University of Minnesota Press, 1997. 55–68.

Ewington, Julie. 'Past the Post: Postmodernism and Postfeminism.' In *Dissonance: Feminism and the Arts 1970–90*. Ed. C. Moore. St Leonards: Allen & Unwin, 1994. 109–21.

Faludi, Susan. *Backlash: The Undeclared War against Women*. London: Vintage, 1992.

Faludi, Susan. *Stiffed: The Betrayal of the American Man*. New York: William Morrow, 1999.

Feigenbaum, Anna. 'Remapping the Resonances of Riot Grrrl: Feminisms, Postfeminisms, and "Processes" of Punk.' In *Interrogating Postfeminism: Gender and the Politics of Popular Culture*. Eds Yvonne Tasker and Diane Negra. Durham, NC, and London: Duke University Press, 2007. 132–52.

Fekete, John. 'Introductory Notes for a Postmodern Value Agenda.' In *Life after Postmodernism*. Ed. John Fekete. New York: St Martin's Press, 1987. i–xix.

Ferrebe, A. '1945–1960 as the Origin of the Anxieties of the Modern Englishman.' *Posting the Male Conference Abstracts*. Liverpool John Moores University, August 2000.

Ferriss, Suzanne, and Mallory Young. 'Introduction.' In *Chick-Lit: The New Woman's Fiction*. Eds Suzanne Ferriss and Mallory Young. New York and London: Routledge, 2006. 1–13.

Fielding, Helen. *Bridget Jones's Diary*. London: Picador, 1996.

Fielding, Helen. *Bridget Jones: The Edge of Reason*. London: Picador, 1999.

Findlen, Barbara, ed. *Listen Up: Voices From the Next Feminist Generation*. New York: Seal Press, 1995.

Firestone, Shulamith. *The Dialectic of Sex: The Case for Feminist Revolution*. 1970. New York: Farrar, Straus and Giroux, 2003.

Fiske, John. *Understanding Popular Culture*. London and New York: Routledge, 1989.

Foucault, Michel. *Discipline and Punish: The Birth of the Prison*. 1977. London: Penguin, 1991.

France, Louise. 'Who Are You Calling a Feminist?' *Observer* 9 April 2006. http://books.guardian.co.uk.

Fraser, Nancy, and Linda J. Nicholson. 'Social Criticism without Philosophy: An Encounter between Feminism and Postmodernism.' In *Feminism/Postmodernism*. Ed. Linda J. Nicholson. London and New York: Routledge, 1990. 19–38.

Fraser, Nancy, Seyla Benhabib, Judith Butler and Drucilla Cornell. 'Pragmatism, Feminism, and the Linguistic Turn.' In *Feminist Contentions: A Philosophical Exchange*. Seyla Benhabib, Judith Butler, Drucilla Cornell and Nancy Fraser. New York and London: Routledge, 1995. 157–71.

Friedan, Betty. *The Feminine Mystique*. 1963. London: Penguin, 1992.

Fudge, Rachel. 'The Buffy Effect: A Tale of Cleavage and Marketing.' *Bitch: Feminist Response to Pop Culture* 10 (1999). 10 December 2000. http://daringivens. home. mindspring.com/buffyeffect.html.

Gamble, Sarah. 'Postfeminism.' In *The Routledge Companion to Feminism and Postfeminism*. Ed. Sarah Gamble. London: Routledge, 2001. 43–54.

Gamman, Lorraine, and Margaret Marshment, eds. *The Female Gaze: Women as Viewers of Popular Culture*. London: Women's Press, 1988.

Gauntlett, David. *Media, Gender and Identity: An Introduction*. London and New York: Routledge, 2007.

Gay, Paul du. 'Organizing Identity: Entrepreneurial Governance and Public Management.' In *Questions of Cultural Identity*. Eds Stuart Hall and Paul du Gay. London: Sage, 1996. 151–69.

Geltmaker, T. 'The Queer Nation Acts Up: Health Care, Politics, and Sexual Diversity in the County of Angels.' *Environment and Planning D: Society and Space* 10 (1992): 609–50.

Genz, Stéphanie. 'Third Way/ve: The Politics of Postfeminism.' *Feminist Theory* 7.3 (2006): 333–53.

Genz, Stéphanie. '"I Am Not a Housewife, but . . ."': Postfeminism and the Revival of Domesticity.' In *Feminism, Domesticity and Popular Culture*. Eds Stacy Gillis and Joanne Hollows. New York and London: Routledge, 2009. 49–62.

Genz, Stéphanie. *Postfemininities in Popular Culture*. Basingstoke: Palgrave Macmillan, 2009.

Gerhard, Jane. '*Sex and the City*: Carrie Bradshaw's Queer Postfeminism.' *Feminist Media Studies* 5.1 (2005): 37–49.

Giddens, Anthony. *The Third Way*. Cambridge: Polity, 1998.

Giddens, Anthony. *Modernity and Self-Identity: Self and Society in the late Modern Age.* 1991. Cambridge: Polity, 2008.

Gill, Rosalind. 'From Sexual Objectification to Sexual Subjectification: The Resexualisation of Women's Bodies in the Media.' *Feminist Media Studies* 3.1 (2003): 100–6.

Gill, Rosalind. 'Power and the Production of Subjects: A Genealogy of the New Man and the New Lad.' In *Masculinity and Men's Lifestyle Magazines.* Ed. Bethan Benwell. Oxford: Blackwell, 2003. 34–56.

Gill, Rosalind. *Gender and the Media.* Cambridge: Polity, 2007.

Gill, Rosalind, and Jane Arthurs. 'New Femininities?' *Feminist Media Studies* 6.4 (2006): 443–51.

Gill, Rosalind, and Elena Herdieckerhoff. 'Rewriting the Romance: New Femininities in Chick Lit?' *Feminist Media Studies* 6.4 (2006): 487–504.

Gillespie, Rosemary. 'Women, the Body and Brand Extension in Medicine: Cosmetic Surgery and the Paradox of Choice.' *Women and Health* 24.4 (1996): 69–85.

Gillis, Stacy. 'The (Post)Feminist Politics of Cyberpunk.' *Gothic Studies,* 9.2 (2007): 7–19.

Gillis, Stacy. 'Cyberspace, Feminism and Technology: Of Cyborgs and Women.' In *Introducing Gender and Women's Studies.* Eds Diane Richardson and Victoria Robinson. Basingstoke: Palgrave Macmillan, 2008. 205–18.

Gillis, Stacey, and Joanne Hollows. 'Introduction.' In *Feminism, Domesticity and Popular Culture.* Eds Stacey Gillis and Joanne Hollows. Abingdon and New York: Routledge, 2009. 1–14.

Gillis, Stacy, and Rebecca Munford. 'Harvesting our Strengths: Third Wave Feminism and Women's Studies.' *Journal of International Women's Studies* 4.2 (2003): 1–6.

Gillis, Stacy, and Rebecca Munford. 'Genealogies and Generations: The Politics and Praxis of Third Wave Feminism.' *Women's History Review* 13.2 (2004): 165–82.

Gillis, Stacy, Gillian Howie, and Rebecca Munford. 'Introduction.' In *Third Wave Feminism: A Critical Exploration.* Eds Stacy Gillis, Gillian Howie and Rebecca Munford. Basingstoke: Palgrave Macmillan, 2004. 1–6.

Gilman, Sander L. *Making the Body Beautiful: A Cultural History of Aesthetic Surgery.* Princeton, NJ: Princeton University Press, 1999.

Gilmore, Stephanie. 'Looking Back, Thinking Ahead: Third Wave Feminism in the United States.' *Journal of Women's History* 12.4 (2001): 215–21.

Green, Keith, and Jill LeBihan. *Critical Theory and Practice: A Coursebook.* London and New York: Routledge, 1996.

Halberstam, Judith. 'Automating Gender: Postmodern Feminism in the Age of the Intelligent Machine.' *Feminist Review* 17.3 (1991): 439–60.

Halberstam, Judith. 'F2M: The Making of Female Masculinity.' In *The Lesbian Postmodern.* Ed. Laura Doan. New York: Columbia University Press, 1994. 210–28.

Halberstam, Judith. *Female Masculinity.* Durham, NC, and London: Duke University Press, 1998.

Halberstam, Judith. *In a Queer Time and Place: Transgender Bodies, Sub-cultural Lives*. New York and London: New York University Press, 2005.

Halberstam, Judith, and Ira Livingstone. *Posthuman Bodies*. Indianapolis: Indiana University Press, 1995.

Hale, C. Jacob. 'Consuming the Living, Dis(re)membering the Dead in the Butch/FTM Borderlands.' *GLQ: A Journal of Lesbians and Gay Studies* 4.2. (1998): 311–48.

Hall, Elaine J., and Marnie Salupo Rodiguez. 'The Myth of Postfeminism.' *Gender and Society* 17.6 (2003): 878–902.

Hall, Stuart. 'On Postmodernism and Articulation: An Interview with Stuart Hall.' *Journal of Communication Inquiry* 10.2 (1986): 45–60.

Hamilton, W. L. 'The Mainstream Flirts with Pornography Chic.' *New York Times* 21 March 1999. 35–7.

Haraway, Donna J. *Simians, Cyborgs and Women: The Reinvention of Nature*. New York and London: Routledge, 1991.

Harris, Ashleigh. 'From Suffragist to Apologist: The Loss of Feminist Politics in a Politically Correct Patriarchy.' *Women's History Review* 13.2 (2004): 91–9.

Harris, Geraldine. *Staging Femininities: Performance and Performativity*. Manchester and New York: Manchester University Press, 1999.

Harts, Kate. 'Deconstructing Buffy: *Buffy the Vampire Slayer*'s Contribution to the Discourse on Gender Construction.' *Popular Culture Review* 12.1 (2001): 79–98.

Hartsock, Nancy. 'Foucault on Power: A Theory for Women?' In *Feminism/Postmodernism*. Ed. Linda J. Nicholson. London and New York: Routledge, 1990. 157–75.

Hattenstone, Simon. 'I Get Insecure Sometimes.' *Guardian* 8 July 2006: 18.

Hawkesworth, Mary. 'The Semiotics of Premature Burial: Feminism in a Post-feminist Age.' *Signs: Journal of Women in Culture and Society* 29.4 (2004): 961–85.

Hayles, Katherine N. *How We Become Posthuman: Virtual Bodies in Cybernetics, Literature and Informatics*. Chicago and London: University of Chicago Press, 1999.

Hekman, Susan. 'Reconstituting the Subject: Feminism, Modernism and Post-modernism.' *Hypatia* 6.2 (1991): 44–63.

Helford, Elyce Rae. 'Postfeminism and the Female Action-Adventure Hero: Positioning *Tank Girl*.' In *Future Females, the Next Generation: New Voices and Velocities in Feminist Science Fiction*. Ed. Marleen S. Barr. Lanham, Boulder, New York, and Oxford: Rowman & Littlefield, 2000. 291–308.

Heyes, Cressida J. 'Cosmetic Surgery and the Televisual Makeover: A Foucauldian Feminist Reading.' *Feminist Media Studies* 7.1 (2007): 17–32.

Heywood, Leslie, and Jennifer Drake. 'Introduction.' In *Third Wave Agenda: Being Feminist, Doing Feminism*. Eds Leslie Heywood and Jennifer Drake. Minneapolis and London: University of Minnesota Press, 1997. 1–20.

Heywood, Leslie, and Jennifer Drake. 'The Third Wave and Representation.' In *Third Wave Agenda: Being Feminist Doing Feminism*. Eds Leslie Heywood and Jennifer Drake. Minneapolis and London: University of Minnesota Press, 1997. 101–2.

Heywood, Leslie, and Jennifer Drake. 'We Learn America Like a Script: Activism in the Third Wave; or, Enough Phantoms of Nothing.' In *Third Wave Agenda: Being Feminist, Doing Feminism*. Eds Leslie Heywood and Jennifer Drake. Minneapolis and London: University of Minnesota Press, 1997. 40–54.

Heywood, Leslie, and Jennifer Drake. '"It's All About the Benjamins": Economic Determinants of Third Wave Feminism in the United States.' In *Third Wave Feminism: A Critical Exploration*. Eds Stacy Gillis, Gillian Howie and Rebecca Munford. Basingstoke: Palgrave Macmillan, 2004. 13–23.

Hills, Elizabeth. 'From "Figurative Males" to Action Heroines: Further Thoughts on Active Women in the Cinema.' *Screen* 40.1 (1999): 38–50.

Hinds, Hilary, and Jackie Stacey. 'Imaging Feminism, Imaging Femininity: The Bra-Burner, Diana, and the Woman Who Kills.' *Feminist Media Studies* 1.2 (2001): 153–77.

Hoggard, Liz. 'Metrosexual Man Is So Over (Sorry, Becks). So It's Uber to You George.' *Independent* 11 September 2005, accessed 11 March 2008. www.independent.co.uk/news/uk/this-britain/metrosexual-man-is-so-over-sorry-becks-so-its-uber-to-you-george-506401.html.

Hollows, Joanne. *Feminism, Femininity and Popular Culture*. Manchester and New York: Manchester University Press, 2000.

Hollows, Joanne. 'Can I Go Home Yet? Feminism, Post-Feminism and Domesticity.' In *Feminism in Popular Culture*. Eds Joanne Hollows and Rachel Moseley. Oxford: Berg, 2006. 97–118.

Hollows, Joanne, and Rachel Moseley. 'Popularity Contests: The Meanings of Popular Feminism.' In *Feminism in Popular Culture*. Eds Joanne Hollows and Rachel Moseley. Oxford: Berg, 2006. 1–22.

hooks, bell. *Outlaw Culture: Resisting Representations*. New York and London: Routledge, 1994.

hooks, bell. 'Dissident Heat: Fire with Fire.' In *'Bad Girls', 'Good Girls': Women, Sex, and Power in the Nineties*. Eds N. M. Bauer and D. Perry. New Brunswick, NJ: Rutgers University Press, 1996. 57–64.

Hutcheon, Linda. *A Poetics of Postmodernism: History, Theory, Fiction*. London and New York: Routledge, 1988.

Hutcheon, Linda. *The Politics of Postmodernism*. London and New York: Routledge, 1989.

Inness, Sherrie A. *Tough Girls: Women Warriors and Wonder Women in Popular Culture*. Philadelphia: University of Pennsylvania Press, 1999.

Jacobson, Aileen. 'Books and the Single Girl.' *NYNewsday.com*. 2004, accessed 14 June 2004. www.nynewsday.com/features/booksmags/ny-p2two.

Jameson, Fredric. 'Postmodernism and Consumer Culture.' In *The Anti-Aesthetic: Essays on Postmodern Culture*. Ed. H. Foster. Port Townsend, WA: Bay Press, 1983. 111–25.

Jameson, Fredric. 'Postmodernism, or The Cultural Logic of Late Capitalism.' In *Postmodernism: A Reader*. Ed. T. Docherty. London: Harvester Wheatsheaf, 1993. 62–92.

Johnson, Merri Lisa. 'Jane Hocus, Jane Focus: An Introduction.' In *Jane Sexes It Up: True Confessions of Feminist Desire*. Ed. Merri Lisa Johnson. New York: Four Walls Eight Windows, 2002. 1–11.

Jones, Amelia. '"Post-Feminism": A Remasculinization of Culture.' *M/E/A/N/I/N/G: An Anthology of Artists' Writing, Theory and Criticism* 7 (1990): 7–23.

Jones, Amelia. 'Postfeminism, Feminist Pleasures, and Embodied Theories of Art.' In *New Feminist Criticism: Art• Identity• Action*. Eds Joanna Frueh, Cassandra L. Langer and Arlene Raven. New York: Icon Press, 1994. 16–41.

Jong, Erica. *Fear of Flying*. 1973. London: Vintage, 1998.

Kalbfleisch, Jane. 'When Feminism Met Postfeminism: The Rhetoric of a Relationship.' In *Generations: Academic Feminists in Dialogue*. Eds Devoney Looser and Ann E. Kaplan. Minneapolis: University of Minnesota Press, 1997. 250–66.

Kaminer, Wendy. 'Feminism's Third Wave: What Do Young Women Want?' *New York Times Book Review* 4 June 1995: 22–3.

Kaplan, E. Ann. 'Madonna Politics: Perversion, Repression, or Subversion? Or Masks and/as Master-y.' In *The Madonna Connection: Representational Politics, Subcultural Identities, and Cultural Theory*. Ed. Cathy Schwichtenberg. Oxford: Westview Press, 1993. 149–65.

Kastelein, Barbara. 'Popular/Post-Feminism and Popular Literature.' Dissertation. University of Warwick, 1994.

Kavka, Misha. 'Feminism, Ethics, and History, or What is the "Post" in Postfeminism.' *Tulsa Studies in Women's Literature* 21.1 (2002): 29–44.

Kennedy, Helen W. 'Lara Croft: Feminist Icon or Cyberbimbo? On the Limits of Textual Analysis.' *Games Studies: The International Journal of Computer Game Research* 2.2 (2002). Accessed 28 July 2008. www.gamestudies.org/0202/kennedy/ ?%3Ftday=Friday.

Kim, L. S. '"Sex and the Single Girl" in Postfeminism: The *F Word* on Television.' *Television & New Media* 2.4 (2001): 319–34.

Kimmel, M. S., ed. *Changing Men: New Directions in Research on Men and Masculinity*. Newbury Park, CA: Sage, 1987.

Kingston, Anne. *The Meaning of Wife*. London: Piatkus, 2004.

Klein, Naomi. *No Logo: No Space, No Choice, No Jobs*. New York: Picador, 2002.

Kocourek, Rotislav. 'The Prefix Post- in Contemporary English Terminology: Morphology, Meaning, and Productivity of Derivations.' *Terminology: International Journal of Theoretical and Applied Issues in Specialized Communication* 3.1 (1996): 85–110.

Koenen, Anne. 'The (Black) Lady Vanishes: Postfeminism, Poststructuralism and Theorizing in Narratives by Black Women.' In *Explorations on Post-Theory: Toward a Third Space*. Ed. Fernando de Toro. Frankfurt: Vervuert; Madrid: Iberoamericana, 1999. 131–43.

Krimmer, Elisabeth, and Shilpa Raval. '"Digging the Undead": Death and Desire in *Buffy*.' In *Fighting the Forces: What's at Stake in Buffy the Vampire Slayer*. Eds Rhonda V. Wilcox and David Lavery. Lanham, Boulder, New York, and Oxford: Rowman & Littlefield, 2002. 153–64.

Kuhn, Annette. *Women's Pictures: Feminism and Cinema*. London: Routledge & Kegan Paul, 1982.

Lauretis, Teresa de. 'Upping the Anti [sic] in Feminist Theory.' In *The Cultural Studies Reader*. Ed. S. During. London and New York: Routledge, 1993. 307–19.

Lee, Janet. 'Care to Join Me in an Upwardly Mobile Tango? Postmodernism and the "New Woman."' In *The Female Gaze: Women as Viewers of Popular Culture*. Eds Lorraine Gamman and Margaret Marshment. London: Women's Press, 1988. 166–72.

Leigh, D. 'Boy Wonder.' *Sight and Sound* 10.3 (2000): 18–20.

Levy, Ariel. *Female Chauvinist Pigs: Women and the Rise of Raunch Culture*. London: Pocket Books, 2006.

Lippert, Barbara. 'Hey There, Warrior Grrrl.' *New York* 15 December 1997: 24–5.

Lockford, Lesa. *Performing Femininity: Rewriting Gender Identity*. Walnut Creek, CA: Altamira Press, 2004.

McCabe, Janet, and Kim Akass. 'Introduction: Airing the Dirty Laundry.' In *Reading Desperate Housewives: Beyond the White Picket Fence*. Eds Janet McCabe and Kim Akass. London and New York: I.B. Tauris, 2006. 1–14.

McCorquodale, Duncan, ed. *Orlan: This is My Body . . . This is My Software . . .* London: Black Dog, 1996.

Macdonald, Myra. *Representing Women: Myths of Femininity in Popular Media*. London: Edward Arnold, 1995.

McEwan, Cheryl. 'Postcolonialism, Feminism and Development: Intersections and Dilemmas.' *Progress in Development Studies* 1.2 (2001): 93–111.

McNair, Brian. *Mediated Sex: Pornography & Postmodern Culture*. London: Edward Arnold, 1996.

McNair, Brian. *Striptease Culture: Sex, Media and the Democratisation of Desire*. Abingdon: Routledge, 2002.

McRobbie, Angela. *Postmodernism and Popular Culture*. London and New York: Routledge, 1994.

McRobbie, Angela. 'More! New Sexualities in Girls' and Women's Magazines.' In *Cultural Studies and Communications*. Eds James Curran, David Morley and Valerie Walkerdine. London: Edward Arnold, 1996. 172–95.

McRobbie, Angela. 'Feminism and the Third Way.' *Feminist Review* 64 (2000): 97–112.

McRobbie, Angela. 'Good Girls, Bad Girls? Female Success and the New Meritocracy.' In *British Cultural Studies: Geography, Nationality, and Identity*. Eds David Morley and Kevin Robins. Oxford: Oxford University Press, 2001. 361–72.

McRobbie, Angela. 'Mothers and Fathers, Who Needs Them?' *Feminist Review* 75 (2003): 129–36.

McRobbie, Angela. 'Notes on Postfeminism and Popular Culture: Bridget Jones and the New Gender Regime.' In *All about the Girl: Culture, Power, and Identity*. Ed. Anita Harris. London: Routledge, 2004. 3–14.

McRobbie, Angela. 'Post-Feminism and Popular Culture.' *Feminist Media Studies* 4.3 (2004): 255–64.

Mangan, M. 'Shakespeare's First Action Heroes: Critical Masculinities in Culture both Popular and Unpopular.' Unpublished essay, 1997.

Mann, Patricia S. *Micro-Politics: Agency in a Postfeminist Era*. Minneapolis and London: University of Minnesota Press, 1994.

Mascia-Lees, Frances E., and Patricia Sharpe. *Taking a Stand in a Postfeminist World: Toward an Engaged Cultural Criticism*. Albany: State University of New York Press, 2000.

Mazza, Cris. 'Who's Laughing Now? A Short History of Chick Lit and the Perversion of a Genre.' In *Chick-Lit: The New Woman's Fiction*. Ed. Suzanne Ferriss and Mallory Young. New York and London: Routledge, 2006. 17–28.

Millett, Kate. *Sexual Politics*. 1970. London: Virago, 1989.

Modleski, Tania. *Feminism without Women: Culture and Criticism in a 'Postfeminist' Age*. London and New York: Routledge, 1991.

Moi, Toril. 'Power, Sex and Subjectivity: Feminist Reflections on Foucault.' *Paragraph* 5 (1985): 95–102.

Morgan, Kathryn Pauly. 'Women and the Knife: Cosmetic Surgery and the Colonization of Women's Bodies.' *Hypatia* 6.3 (1991): 25–53.

Mort, F. *Cultures of Consumption: Masculinities and Social Space in Late Twentieth Century Britain*. London: Routledge, 1996.

Moseley, Rachel, and Jacinda Read. '"Having it *Ally*": Popular Television (Post-) Feminism.' *Feminist Media Studies*. 2.2 (2002): 231–49.

Munford, Rebecca. '"Wake Up and Smell the Lipgloss": Gender, Generation and the (A)politics of Girl Power.' In *Third Wave Feminism: A Critical Exploration*. Eds Stacy Gillis, Gillian Howie and Rebecca Munford. Basingstoke: Palgrave Macmillan, 2004. 142–53.

Neal, Mark Anthony. 'Can Hip-Hop Be Feminist?' 14 March 2007. www.black-feminism.org/index.php/2005/04/06/can-hip-hop-be-feminist.

Negra, Diane. '"Quality Postfeminism?" *Sex and the Single Girl* on HBO.' *Genders: Presenting Innovative Work in the Arts, Humanities and Social Theories* 39 (2004): 1–15. Accessed 8 June 2004. www.genders.org/g39/g39_negra.html.

Neustatter, Angela. *Hyenas in Petticoats: A Look at Twenty Years of Feminism*. London: Harrop, 1989.

Newton, Judith. 'Feminism and Anxiety in *Alien*.' In *Alien Zone*. Ed. Annette Kuhn. London: Verso, 1990. 82–7.

Nicholson, Linda J. 'Introduction.' In *Feminism/Postmodernism*. Ed. Linda J. Nicholson. London and New York: Routledge, 1990. 1–16.

Nicholson, Linda, ed. *The Second Wave: A Reader in Feminist Theory*. New York and London: Routledge, 1997.

Nixon, Nicola. 'Cyberpunk: Preparing the Ground for Revolution or Keeping the Boys Satisfied?' In *Cybersexualities: A Reader on Feminist Theory, Cyborgs, and Cyberspace*. Ed. J. Wolmark. Edinburgh: Edinburgh University Press, 1999. 191–207.

Ouellette, Laurie. 'Victims No More: Postfeminism, Television, and *Ally McBeal*.' *Communication Review* 5 (2002): 315–37.

Owens, Craig. 'The Discourse of Others: Feminists and Postmodernism.' In *The Anti-Aesthetic*. Ed. H. Foster. Port Townsend, WA: Bay Press, 1983. 57–82.

Paasonen, Susanna, Kaarina Nikunen and Laura Saarenmaa. 'Pornification and the Education of Desire.' In *Pornification: Sex and Sexuality in Media Culture*. Eds Susanna Paasonen, Kaarina Nikunen and Laura Saarenmaa. Oxford: Berg, 2007. 1–20.

Paglia, Camille. *Sexual Personae: Art and Decadence from Nefertiti to Emily Dickinson*. Harmondsworth: Penguin, 1991.

Paglia, Camille. *Sex, Art and American Culture*. Harmondsworth: Penguin, 1992.

Palahniuk, Chuck. *Fight Club*. 1996. London: Vintage, 1997.

Pender, Patricia. '"I'm *Buffy* and You're . . . History": The Postmodern Politics of *Buffy*.' In *Fighting the Forces: What's at Stake in Buffy the Vampire Slayer*. Eds Rhonda V. Wilcox and David Lavery. Lanham, Boulder, New York, Oxford: Rowman & Littlefield, 2002. 35–44.

Pender, Patricia. '"Kicking Ass is Comfort Food": Buffy as Third Wave Feminist Icon.' In *Third Wave Feminism: A Critical Exploration*. Eds Stacy Gillis, Gillian Howie and Rebecca Munford. Basingstoke: Palgrave Macmillan, 2004. 164–74.

Plant, Sadie. 'The Future Looms: Weaving Women and Cybernetics.' In *Cyberspace, Cyberbodies, Cyberpunk: Cultures of Technological Embodiment*. Eds Mike Featherstone and Roger Burrows. London: Sage, 1995. 45–64.

Plant, Sadie. 'On the Matrix: Cyberfeminist Simulations.' In *Cultures of the Internet: Virtual Spaces, Real Histories, Living Bodies*. Ed. Rob Shield. London: Sage, 1996. 170–83.

Plant, Sadie. *Zeros + Ones: Digital Women + The New Technoculture*. London: Fourth Estate, 1997.

Probyn, Elspeth. 'New Traditionalism and Post-Feminism: TV Does the Home.' *Screen* 31.2 (1990): 147–59.

Projansky, Sarah. 'Mass Magazine Cover Girls: Some Reflections on Postfeminist Girls and Postfeminism's Daughters.' In *Interrogating Postfeminism: Gender and The Politics of Popular Culture*. Eds Yvonne Tasker and Diane Negra. Durham, NC, and London: Duke University Press, 2007. 40–72.

Quindlen, Anna. 'And Now, Babe Feminism.' In *'Bad Girls', 'Good Girls': Women, Sex, and Power in the Nineties*. Eds Nan Bauer Maglin and Donna Perry. New Brunswick, NJ: Rutgers University Press, 1996. 3–5.

Reed, Jennifer. 'Roseanne: A "Killer Bitch" for Generation X.' In *Third Wave Agenda: Being Feminist, Doing Feminism*. Eds Leslie Heywood and Jennifer Drake. Minneapolis and London: University of Minnesota Press, 1997. 122–33.

Richardson, Diane. *Rethinking Sexuality*. London: Sage, 2000.

Roiphe, Katie. *The Morning After: Sex, Fear and Feminism*. Boston: Little, Brown, 1993.

Rose, Nikolas. 'Governing the Enterprising Self.' In *The Values of the Enterprise Culture*. Eds Paul Heelas and Paul Morris. London: Routledge, 1992. 141–64.

Rosenfelt, Deborah, and Judith Stacey. 'Second Thoughts on the Second Wave.' *Feminist Studies* 13 (1987): 341–61.

Ross, J. *The Nineties*. London: Ebury, 1999.

Rubin, Gayle. 'Misguided, Dangerous and Wrong: An Analysis of Anti-Pornography Politics.' In *Gender, Race and Class in Media: A Text-Reader.* Eds G. Dines and J. M. Humez. London: Sage, 1995. 244–53.

Rutland, Barry. 'The Other of Theory.' In *Explorations on Post-Theory: Toward a Third Space.* Ed. Fernando de Toro. Frankfurt: Vervuert; Madrid: Iberoamericana, 1999. 71–83.

Sanders, Lise Shapiro. '"Feminists Love a Utopia": Collaboration, Conflict, and the Futures of Feminism.' In *Third Wave Feminism: A Critical Exploration.* Eds Stacy Gillis, Gillian Howie and Rebecca Munford. Basingstoke: Palgrave Macmillan, 2004. 49–59.

Sandison, Nikki. 'Metrosexual Man Fades as Brits Opt for Scruffy Look.' *BrandRepublic* 21 May 2008 , accessed 11 March 2008. www.brandrepublic. com/News/810615.

Sayeau, Ashley. 'Having It All: *Desperate Housewives*' Flimsy Feminism.' In *Reading Desperate Housewives: Beyond the White Picket Fence.* Eds Janet McCabe and Kim Akass. London and New York: I.B. Tauris, 2006. 42–7.

Schwichtenberg, Cathy. 'Madonna's Postmodern Feminism: Bringing the Margins to the Center.' In *The Madonna Connection: Representational Politics, Subcultural Identities, and Cultural Theory.* Ed. Cathy Schwichtenberg. Oxford: Westview Press, 1993. 129–45.

Sedgwick, Eve Kosofsky. '*The L Word*: Novelty in Normalcy.' *Chronicle of Higher Education* 16 January 2004: B10–B11.

Sedgwick, Eve Kosofsky. 'Foreword: The Letter L.' In *Reading The L Word: Outing Contemporary Television.* Eds Kim Akass and Janet McCabe. London and New York: I. B. Tauris, 2006. xix–xxiv.

Segal, Lynne. *Why Feminism? Gender, Psychology, Politics.* Cambridge: Polity, 1999.

Segal, Lynne. 'Theoretical Affiliations: Poor Rich White Folk Play the Blues.' *New Formations* 50 (2003): 142–56.

Senna, Danzy. '"To Be Real".' In *To Be Real: Telling the Truth and Changing the Face of Feminism.* Ed. Rebecca Walker. London: Anchor Books, 1995. 5–20.

Shalit, Ruth. 'Canny and Lacy: Ally, Dharma, Ronnie, and the Betrayal of Postfeminism.' *New Republic* 6 April 1998: 27–32.

Siegel, Deborah L. 'The Legacy of the Personal: Generating Theory in Feminism's Third Wave.' *Hypatia* 12.3 (1997): 46–75.

Siegel, Deborah L. 'Reading Between the Waves: Feminist Historiography in a "Postfeminist" Moment.' In *Third Wave Agenda: Being Feminist, Doing Feminism.* Eds Leslie Heywood and Jennifer Drake. Minneapolis and London: University of Minnesota Press, 1997. 55–82.

Siegel, Deborah. *Sisterhood, Interrupted: From Radical Women to Grrls Gone Wild.* Basingstoke and New York: Palgrave Macmillan, 2007.

Simpson, Mark. *Male Impersonators.* London: Cassell, 1994.

Simpson, Mark, ed. *Anti-Gay.* London: Cassell, 1996.

Simpson, Mark. 'Metrosexual? That Rings a Bell . . . ' *Marksimpson.com* 22 July 2003, accessed 11 March 2008. www.marksimpson.com/pages/journalism/metrosexual_ios. html.

Singer, Linda. 'Feminism and Postmodernism.' In *Feminists Theorize the Political*. Eds J. Butler and J. W. Scott. London and New York: Routledge, 1992. 464–75.

Smith, Joan. 'I'm a Feminist, So I Suppose I Must Be Dead.' *Independent* 6 July 2003, accessed 11 March 2008. www.independent.co.uk/opinion/comment ators/joan-smith/im-a-feminist-so-i-suppose-i-must-be-dead-585886.html.

Smith, K. 'The Inescapable Paris.' *Vanity Fair* October 2005: 280–1.

Sonnet, Esther. '"Erotic Fiction by Women for Women": The Pleasure of Postfeminist Heterosexuality.' *Sexualities* 2.2 (1999): 167–87.

The Spice Girls. *Girl Power!* London: Zone/Chameleon Books, 1997.

Stables, Kate. 'Run Lara Run.' *Sight and Sound* 11.6 (2001): 18–20.

Stacey, Judith. 'Sexism by a Subtler Name? Postindustrial Conditions and Postfeminist Consciousness in the Silicon Valley.' *Socialist Review* 96 (1987): 7–28.

Stanley, Alessandra. 'Old-Time Sexism Suffuses New Season.' *New York Times* 1 October 2004: E1, E24.

Stefano, Christine di. 'Dilemmas of Difference: Feminism, Modernity, and Postmodernism.' In *Feminism/Postmodernism*. Ed. Linda J. Nicholson. New York and London: Routledge, 1990. 63–81.

Stoller, Debbie, and Marcelle Karp. 'Editor's Letter.' *BUST: The Magazine for Women with Something to Get Off Their Chests* 4 (1992): 2.

Storey, John. *An Introduction to Cultural Theory and Popular Culture*. Harlow: Prentice Hall, 1997.

Stuart, Andrea. 'Feminism: Dead or Alive?' In *Identity: Community, Culture, Difference*. Ed. Jonathan Rutherford. London: Lawrence & Wishart, 1990. 28–42.

Sullivan, Nikki. *A Critical Introduction to Queer Theory*. Edinburgh: Edinburgh University Press, 2003.

Tasker, Yvonne. *Spectacular Bodies: Gender, Genre and the Action Cinema*. London and New York: Routledge, 1993.

Tasker, Yvonne. *Action and Adventure Cinema*. London: Routledge, 2004.

Tasker, Yvonne, and Diane Negra. 'Introduction: Feminist Politics and Postfeminist Culture.' In *Interrogating Postfeminism: Gender and The Politics of Popular Culture*. Eds Yvonne Tasker and Diane Negra. Durham, NC, and London: Duke University Press, 2007. 1–25.

Thompson, Jim. '"Just a Girl": Feminism, Postmodernism and *Buffy the Vampire Slayer*.' *Refractory: A Journal of Entertainment Media*. 2003, accessed 21 February 2004. www.refractory.unimelb.edu.au/journalissues/vol2/jimthompson.htm.

Thornham, Sue. 'Second Wave Feminism.' In *The Routledge Companion to Feminism and Postfeminism*. Ed. Sarah Gamble. London and New York: Routledge, 2001. 29–42.

Toffoletti, Kim. *Cyborgs and Barbie Dolls: Feminism, Popular Culture and the Posthuman Body*. London and New York: I. B. Tauris, 2007.

Toro, Fernando de. 'Explorations on Post-Theory: New Times.' In *Explorations on Post-Theory: Toward a Third Space*. Ed. Fernando de Toro. Frankfurt: Vervuert; Madrid: Iberoamericana, 1999. 9–23.

Vanasco, Jennifer. 'The Glamour Factor and the Fiji Effect.' In *Reading The L Word: Outing Contemporary Television*. Eds Kim Akass and Janet McCabe. London and New York: I. B. Tauris, 2006. 183–8.

Wajcman, Judy. *Feminism Confronts Technology*. Cambridge: Polity, 1991.

Walker, Rebecca. 'Becoming the Third Wave.' *Ms.* January–February 1995: 39–41.

Walker, Rebecca. 'Being Real: An Introduction.' In *To Be Real: Telling the Truth and Changing the Face of Feminism*. Ed. Rebecca Walker. London: Anchor Books, 1995. xxix–xl.

Walter, Natasha. *The New Feminism*. 1998. London: Virago, 2006.

Walters, Suzanna Danuta. 'Premature Postmortems: "Postfeminism" and Popular Culture.' *New Politics* 3.10 (1991): 103–12.

Walters, Suzanna Danuta. *Material Girls: Making Sense of Feminist Cultural Theory*. Berkeley: University of California Press, 1995.

Waugh, Patricia. *Feminine Fictions: Revisiting the Postmodern*. London and New York: Routledge, 1989.

Waugh, Patricia. 'Introduction.' In *Postmodernism: A Reader*. Ed. Patricia Waugh. London: Edward Arnold, 1992. 1–10.

Whelehan, Imelda. *Modern Feminist Thought: From the Second Wave to 'Post-Feminism'*. Edinburgh: Edinburgh University Press, 1995.

Whelehan, Imelda. *Overloaded: Popular Culture and the Future of Feminism*. London: Women's Press, 2000.

Whelehan, Imelda. *Helen Fielding's Bridget Jones's Diary: A Reader's Guide*. London and New York: Continuum, 2002.

Whelehan, Imelda. *The Feminist Bestseller: From Sex and The Single Girl to Sex and the City*. Basingstoke: Palgrave Macmillan, 2005.

Whiteley, Sheila. *Women and Popular Music: Sexuality, Identity and Subjectivity*. London: Routledge, 2000.

Whittier, Nancy. *Feminist Generations: The Persistence of the Radical Women's Movement*. Philadelphia: Temple University Press, 1995.

Wilcox, Rhonda, V., and David Lavery. 'Introduction.' In *Fighting the Forces: What's at Stake in Buffy the Vampire Slayer*. Eds Rhonda V. Wilcox and David Lavery. Lanham, Boulder, New York, Oxford: Rowman & Littlefield, 2002. xvii–xxix.

Wilkinson, Helen. 'The Thatcher Legacy: Power of Feminism and the Birth of Girl Power.' In *On the Move: Feminism for a New Generation*. Ed. Natasha Walter. London: Virago, 1999. 27–47.

Wolf, Naomi. *The Beauty Myth: How Images of Beauty Are Used Against Women*. London: Vintage, 1991.

Wolf, Naomi. *Fire with Fire: The New Female Power and How It Will Change the 21st Century*. 1993. London: Vintage, 1994.

Wollstonecraft, Mary. *A Vindication of the Rights of Woman*. 1792. Vol. 5 of *The Works of Mary Wollstonecraft*. Eds J. Todd and M. Butler. London: Pickering and Chatto, 1958.

Index